AF600415

JURISDICTION OF PASTORS IN THE EXTERNAL FORUM

THE CATHOLIC UNIVERSITY OF AMERICA
CANON LAW STUDIES
No. 378

Jurisdiction of Pastors in The External Forum

A HISTORICAL SYNOPSIS AND A COMMENTARY

A DISSERTATION

SUBMITTED TO THE FACULTY OF THE SCHOOL OF CANON LAW OF THE CATHOLIC UNIVERSITY OF AMERICA IN PARTIAL FULFILLMENT OF THE REQUIREMENTS FOR THE DEGREE OF DOCTOR OF CANON LAW

BY
BERNARD F. DEUTSCH, J.C.L.
A PRIEST OF THE ACRHDIOCESE OF ST. LOUIS

THE CATHOLIC UNIVERSITY OF AMERICA PRESS
WASHINGTON, D.C.
1957

NIHIL OBSTAT:

Clemens V. Bastnagel, S.T.L., J.U.D.
Censor Deputatus
Washingtonii, D.C., die 14 maii, 1957

IMPRIMATUR:

✠ Joseph E. Ritter, S.T.D.
Archiepiscopus Sancti Ludovici

Sancti Ludovici, die 18 maii, 1957

Printed by The Abbey Press, St. Meinrad, Indiana, U.S.A.

TO

MY MOTHER AND FATHER

FOREWORD

A good analysis of ecclesiastical jurisdiction is far from being a plentiful commodity. The historical reason is two-fold: a) the very term "jurisdiction" came into ecclesiastical parlance many centuries after the Church's foundation, as the historical conspectus attests; b) when the term did come into common usage, the exigencies of the times demanded that its treatment be more apologetical than philosophical. The modern reason is more difficult to isolate. Perhaps the concept of jurisdiction is taken for granted, as it certainly appears to be, by those who deny the fact of parochial jurisdiction in the external forum. Perhaps the term receives its appraisal through a simply lethargic reverential respect. Be that as it may, the fact remains that the moment the term is mentioned the modern mind is conditioned to activate the sign "power" and, after the fashion of an automaton, subalign the three components: legislative, judicial, coercive. Here the activity generally ceases for the reason that the mind seems duly satisfied.

It is this condition of things along with the manner in which modern authors treat parochial jurisdiction that has provoked this dissertation. Even to the man not expert in canon law there seems reason for suspecting the way in which the subject of parochial jurisdiction is handled. Many authors state that pastors have no jurisdiction in the external forum; others equate parochial power with any number of things in a seeming effort to avoid the issue; still others state in one part of their work that pastors have jurisdiction only in the internal forum and remark in another part that pastors do have some jurisdiction in the external forum.

The only constant, as it were, in the title of this treatise is the term "pastors." The notions of both jurisdiction and external forum are debated. Necessarily both must be stabilized before parochial jurisdiction in the external forum can begin to be investigated. This then is the pattern of approach, both in the historical synopsis and in the canonical commentary. If this work lends any clarity to the concept of jurisdiction or of forum, it is not in vain; if it justifies its title, it completely fulfills its purpose.

The writer takes this occasion to express his gratitude to His Excellency, Joseph E. Ritter, S.T.D., Archbishop of St. Louis, for the opportunity offered for advanced study, for the personal interest shown, and for the paternal encouragement given. He also deeply appreciates the assistance and guidance offered by the members of the Faculty of the School of Canon Law, especially that of the Rev. Clement V. Bastnagel, S.T.L., J.U.D., the director of this dissertation, and Professor Stephan Kuttner, J.U.D., S.J.D., J.C.D.

TABLE OF CONTENTS

PART II

CANONICAL COMMENTARY

PART I
HISTORICAL SYNOPSIS

INTRODUCTION

Even after the evolution of thought and the development of terminology concerning the notions of jurisdiction and forum, there remains generally a veil of mystery on the subject of parochial jurisdiction in the external forum. This is due at least partially to the fact that never was there an absolute accord concerning the notions of jurisdiction and forum. Although these substantives have been defined, described, and divided, they are still used with divergent connotations.

The present heritage, in reference to such usage, has been developing for centuries. The possession of jurisdiction, for instance, has been predicated for many persons, running the gamut from the Holy Father to laymen. All the while there was a cautious class of people who used the term most sparingly or who abstracted from it completely by employing another. Both classes were represented in our present codification of Canon Law, both classes were found legislating at the Council of Trent, both classes labored simultaneously commenting on the Decretals, both classes sat at the feet of Master Gratian, and, even before that, both classes were found clad in Roman togas.

The Code of Canon Law speaks of the pastor's *iurisdictio paroecialis* in one canon and of his *cura animarum* in another. The Council of Trent (1545-1563) indicated in one session that pastors have the "care of souls," and in another that they are to "rule." The Decretals and the *Decretum*, and most commentators on both, used the word *"iurisdictio"* and the expression *"cura animarum"* almost interchangeably. In partial exemplification of this situation of seeming inconsistency, canon 334, § 2, states concerning residential bishops: "In regimen tamen dioecesis neque... sese ingerere possunt, nisi prius eiusdem dioecesis possessionem canonice ceperint," while canon 461 declares: "Curam animarum parochus obtinet a momento captae possessionis. . ." The *cura* here certainly is at least analogous to *regimen* or jurisdiction.

The general procedure of this historical conspectus is first to demonstrate the usage and the meaning of the phrase "*cura animarum*" at the time when it was practically identified with jurisdiction, and later, once the two expressions became clearly delineated, to analyze the notion of jurisdiction itself, together with that of forum, in an effort to establish the fact of parochial jurisdiction in the external forum. As the table of contents indicates, some incidental historical questions are introduced for their value in enriching the general background.

CHAPTER I

JURISDICTION AND *CURA ANIMARUM* PRIOR TO THE COUNCIL OF TRENT

ARTICLE I. THE PERIOD BEFORE GRATIAN

Originally the concept of jurisdiction had been associated with the praetor, an official of the Roman Republic. His function, *ius dicere,* grew in scope and importance with the successive phases of the judicial procedure in Roman law. Under the rigid *legis actio* he classified a dispute according to the prevailing formulas and left the adjudication to a private judge. According to the formulary system he was competent to draw up a formula to fit the particular case or to accept an existing formula presented by the parties, but the adjudication was still referred to a private judge. When the new procedure, *cognitio extraordinaria,* replaced the formulary system, the praetor controlled the entire process without referring the case to a private judge.[1]

Evolution of the concept continued through the instrumentality of the Roman jurists, so that by the time of Emperor Justinian (527-565) jurisdiction embraced both judicial and administrative power with the general connotation of public power to rule a community.[2]

It was with this general meaning that the term found its way into ecclesiastical sources, as was indicated by its first use in a letter of Pope Gregory the Great (590-604).[3]

[1] Buckland, *A Textbook of Roman Law* (2. ed., Cambridge: University Press, 1932), pp. 607, 608; Schulz, *Classical Roman Law* (Oxford: Clarendon Press, 1951), p. 13.

[2] Kerckhove, "De Notione Jurisdictionis in Jure Romano," *Jus Pontificium* (Romae, 1921-1940), XVI (1936), 60-63.

[3] *Monumenta Germaniae Historica* (incomplete, Hannoverae, 1826—), *Registrum Epistolarum,* tom. I, *Epistolae Gregorii Papae* (ed. P. Ewald and L. M. Hartmann, Berolini, 1887-1899), I, 167 (hereafter cited *MGH*); Jaffé, *Regesta Pontificum Romanorum ab condita ecclesia ad annum post Christum natum MCXCVIII* (2. ed., by G. Wattenbach, F. Kaltenbrunner, P. Ewald, S. Loewenfeld, 2 vols., Lipsiae, 1885-1888), JE, n. 1211 (hereafter cited JK, JE, and JL).

The same pontiff, however, also used the term in its stricter and more specific sense of judicial power only.[4]

In Roman law a great variety of synonyms was employed, along with the term "jurisdiction," to express the notion of a general administration of justice and equity. Accordingly a similar list of synonyms, of which one was *"cura animarum,"* was used in ecclesiastical legislation to express the whole power of the Church.[5]

It was evident that the organs of ecclesiastical legislation had not as yet worked out a uniform notion of jurisdiction and simply chose to use a variety of terms to express the notion of power in general or particular. In the latter event it was known from the context what was specifically meant. As a plausible consequence of such a practice, the word "jurisdiction" almost disappeared from canonical nomenclature from the eighth to the twelfth century. No doubt, however, existed as to the sense of *ditio, auctoritas, curam animarum habere, potestas, sub iure habere,* and the similar terms which were found in texts of the canons of the councils. All these expressions were synonymous with jurisdiction, and to them was attributed the prevailing significance of administrative power in general.[6]

Naturally such usage would present a challenge tó the canonists of later centuries. While one may grant that such a practice was accepted and clearly understood by most in their own day, future scholars would have to hunt and choose, divide and subdivide, in an effort to analyse precisely the matter of the past and to synthesize it clearly in the light of developments up to their own time. It was only after the glossators of the classical period of Canon Law had labored over necessary distinctions, and had reestablished the word "jurisdiction" in canonical legislation, that any uniform usage could begin to be found.

[4] *MGH, Registrum Epistolarum,* II, 285; JE, n. 1812.

[5] Tirado, *De Iurisdictionis Acceptione in Iure Ecclesiastico* (Romae: Officium Libri Catholici, 1940), pp. 56-61 (hereafter cited *De Iurisdictionis Acceptione*).

[6] Kerckhove, *ibid.,* p. 65, note 2.

In considering the notion of *cura animarum* or jurisdiction as used before Gratian, one must look to the people who exercised it. There was no doubt about its having been enjoyed by those who possessed the episcopal character.[7]

Archdeacons and archpriests also exercised the *cura animarum.*[8]

Concerning the ordinary parish priest, Decretists and Decretalists later admitted that prelates had the *cura animarum,* but argued whether the pastor or parish priest was a prelate. In this period before Gratian, however, several pertinent sources did presume that the parish priest was a prelate. Certainly someone who rules has power, and in the early centuries one having such power had the *cura animarum,* the jurisdiction, or the power as described by any of the other synonyms in vogue. In a source attributed by Gratian to an unidentified Council of Rheims the parish priest was found ruling:

> Sicut in unaquaque ecclesia unus presbyter debet esse, ita ipsa, quae sponsa vel uxor eius dicitur, non potest dividi inter plures presbyteros, sed unum tantummodo habebit sacerdotem, qui eam caste et sincere regat.[9]

In the ninth century Pope Leo IV (847-855) wrote to the Bishops of Britain:

> Regenda est unaquaeque parochia sub provisione ac tuitione episcopi per sacerdotes, vel ceteros clericos, quos ipse cum Dei timore providerit, cui iure pertinere videtur, et circumire, ut sibi necessarium visum fuerit ecclesiastica utilitate cogente.[10]

[7] "Sanctis canonibus constitutum est, [ut] animarum cura et pecuniarum ecclesiasticarum dispensatio in episcopi iudicio et potestate permaneat."—Pope Calixtus II (1119-1124) in c. 4, I Council of the Lateran (1123); c. 11, C. XVI, q. 7; JL, post n. 7027.

[8] "Ut archipresbyter sciat se subesse archidiacono, et eius praeceptis sicut sui episcopi obedire et, quod specialiter ad eius pertinet ministerium, super omnes presbyteros in ordine presbyterali positos curam agere animarum."—c. 1, X, *de officio archipresbyteri,* I, 24, a pseudo-Isidorian Decretal attributed to an unidentified Council of Toledo.

[9] C. 4, C. XXI, q. 2.

[10] C. 4, C. X, q. 1; *MGH, Registrum Epistolarum,* V, 594; Mansi,

In this writing was expressed the same idea of the parish being ruled by its parish priest. In this text, however, one may discover the added notion of the possibility of other clerics in the ruling of parishes, and therefore having the *cura animarum* or jurisdiction. The third and final example, contained in a letter of Pope Urban II (1088-1099), likewise indicated that the *cura animarum* belonged to the parish priest, although he had to answer to his bishop concerning it:

> In parochialibus ecclesiis presbyteri per episcopos instituantur, qui eis respondeant de animarum cura, et his, quae ad episcopum pertinent.[11]

It may be concluded from the uniformity of the examples here cited that the parish priest was considered to possess the *cura animarum* or jurisdiction before Gratian's time. Therefore, the parish priest was accordingly presumed to possess the character of a prelate.

Article II. Gratian and the Early Decretists

In Gratian's *Decretum* the previously mentioned synonyms of jurisdiction, *cura animarum, dictio, potestas,* etc., were all found. But the word "jurisdiction" itself appeared very rarely.[12] The reason for its infrequent occurrence can be explained simply by the fact that it was similarly infrequent in the documents which Gratian gathered into his *Decretum.* When the term was used, it was in a very generic sense only.

Cura animarum and other expressions were constantly employed as meaning generally the same thing as jurisdiction. But the question now is: What did jurisdiction mean? It was at this time, in view undoubtedly of the revival of the study of Roman law at Bologna, that canonists

Sacrorum Conciliorum Nova et Amplissima Collectio (53 vols. in 60, Parisiis, 1901-1927), XIV, 883 (hereafter cited Mansi); JE, n. 2599.

[11] C. 6, C. XVI, q. 2.

[12] C. 3, D. 94 (dictum Grat.); c. 39, C. XI, q. 1; c. 6, C. XIII, q. 2 (dictum Grat.); c. 52, C. XVI, q. 1 (superscrip.); c. 34, C. XXIV, q. 1.

attempted to isolate the meaning of jurisdiction and its component parts. In the century between the Decree of Gratian and the Decretals of Gregory IX there emerged three distinct developments in three stages: 1) from Gratian (ca. 1140) to Sicardus to Cremona inclusive (ca. 1180); 2) from Huguccio (ca. 1188) to Joannes Teutonicus inclusive (ca. 1215); 3) from the IV Council of the Lateran (1215) to Bernard of Parma inclusive (ca. 1263).[13]

SECTION 1. FROM GRATIAN TO SICARDUS OF CREMONA

In the first stage canonists hardly used the word "jurisdiction," and *lex dioecesana* gave to jurisdiction the sense of administrative power in general, temporal and spiritual. The power of orders was neither clearly distinguished from the power of jurisdiction nor defined.[14] While it cannot be stated with certainty, the more probable meaning of the term "*lex dioecesana*" before the time of Huguccio († 1210) seemed to include the total power of rulership which the bishop had over his diocese.[15]

There was no indication to the contrary that *cura animarum* meant anything different than it had previously. There was an indication at that time, however, supplied by Rufinus († 1190), regarding the question whether pastors were prelates:

> Unde patet quia duo, non minus, oportet esse sacerdotes in una ecclesia. Sed aliud est unam ecclesiam plures habere dominos atque rectores, quod hic interdicitur; aliud autem unum habere praelatum et alium coadiutorem, quod ibi conceditur.[16]

And the conclusion, of course, was that the pastor of a church was a prelate.

[13] Kerckhove, "De Notione Jurisdictionis apud Decretistas et Priores Decretalistas (1140-1250)," *Jus Pontificium*, XVIII (1938), 10-14.

[14] Kerckhove, *ibid.*, p. 12.

[15] Kerckhove, *loc. cit.;* Tirado, *De Iurisdictionis Acceptione*, p. 88.

[16] *Summa Decretorum*, in c. 4, C. XXI, q. 2 (ed. Heinrich Singer, Paderborn, 1902), p. 385.

SECTION 2. FROM HUGUCCIO TO JOANNES TEUTONICUS

In this second period the use of the term "jurisdiction" was more frequent. By the introduction of the *lex iurisdictionis,* which was first found in Huguccio, administrative power over temporal goods was excluded from the comprehension of the notion of jurisdiction. He wrote in the gloss at the introduction of Cause X, question 1:

> For a better understanding, it is noted that there are two laws in which consists the whole power which the bishop has over the churches of his episcopate. They are the *lex iurisdictionis* and the *lex dioecesana.* To the *lex iurisdictionis* pertain the care of souls or its conferral, the punishment of delicts, the regulating of churches and altars, the consecration of virgins, the conferral of chrism and of all the Sacraments generally. To the *lex dioecesana* pertain the institution and investiture of clerics, the invitation to the synod and obsequies of the dead, the cathedraticum . . . and similar things.[17]

While the notion of *cura animarum* logically embraced both forums, canonists before the IV General Council of the Lateran (1215) did not use the single word "jurisdiction" for designating power of the Church in the internal forum. They spoke rather of sacerdotal power or of the power of orders.[18] Thus, there were found at the end of this second period two expressions, the *"lex iurisdictionis"* and the *"lex dioecesana,"* which together indicated the totality of ecclesiastical power. It is to be noted that the *cura animarum* belonged to the *lex iurisdictionis,* which in embracing all power except the administration of temporalities included whatever pertained to the power of orders.

Concerning the "priest-prelate" question, there was a continuation of the affirmative trend previously indicated all the way to the Decretals of Gregory IX, as seen in the

[17] *Summa,* gloss in C. X, q. 1; Latin text is recorded by Kerckhove, "De Notione Jurisdictionis apud Decretistas et Priores Decretalistas," *Jus Pontificium,* XVIII (1938), 12. The translation is the writer's.

[18] Kerchove, *ibid.,* p. 13.

remark of Joannes Teutonicus († 1245): "Sed plures possunt esse in eadem ecclesia: sed tantum erit unus praelatus."[19]

SECTION 3. FROM THE IV GENERAL COUNCIL OF THE LATERAN TO THE DECRETALS OF GREGORY IX

In this third period, which the writer treats more briefly than Kerckhove in view of the extensive consideration to be given to the notion of jurisdiction and of the *cura animarum* in the following article, the word "jurisdiction" was quite common among canonists. To the *lex iurisdictionis* they did not give the full value it had been accorded in the previous period, but clearly discerned the power of orders from the power of jurisdiction, and to the power of jurisdiction they gave the significance, after excluding the administration of temporal things, of the public power of ruling a self-contained or juridically perfected community.[20]

The significant difference, therefore, between this and the preceding period was that whatever pertained to the power of orders was excluded from the comprehension of jurisdiction. The sharp division between the powers of jurisdiction and orders was seen in the comment of St. Raymond of Peñafort that the pastoral office was divided into three parts, namely, contentious jurisdiction, voluntary jurisdiction, and the dispensation of the sacraments.[21]

Although there were frequent appearances of the phrase "*cura animarum*" both in the text of the *Decretum* and in the glosses, many are of little or no value in determining its nature.[22]

In general, one may say that, while in the period from Gratian to the Decretals the notion of jurisdiction was

[19] Gloss in c. 4, C. XXI, q. 2, s.v. *Non potest.*

[20] Kerckhove, *ibid.*, pp. 12, 13.

[21] "Officium pastorale consistit in tribus, scilicet in iurisdictione contentiosa et voluntaria et sacramentorum dispensatione."—cod. Vat. Borgh., 261, 102v (quoted from Tirado, *De Iurisdictionis Acceptione*, p. 87).

[22] E.g., c. 6, C. XXI, q. 1; c. 42, C. VII, q. 1; gloss in c. 5, C. XXI, q. 2, s.v. *conductitiis;* etc.

evolving, there was a simultaneous evolving of the notion of the *cura animarum*. Obviously, when predicated as a synonym of jurisdiction, this latter phrase meant whatever jurisdiction meant at that particular time. But on the whole, while the concept of jurisdiction was being refined, the notion of the *cura animarum* manifested a meaning somewhat broader and more general, notably in that it embraced not only both forums, but also both the power of orders and the power of jurisdiction.

ARTICLE III. FROM GREGORY IX TO THE COUNCIL OF TRENT

It was the logical move for the Decretalists in continuing the refinement of the concept of jurisdiction to concentrate simultaneously on its most frequently employed and previously academically neglected synonym "*cura animarum.*" Four related notions need to be considered before any specific treatment is accorded to the notion of the *cura animarum*: jurisdiction, archdeacon, prelates, and proper priest. This preliminary discussion will open the way to a more ready understanding of what was implied in the *cura animarum* and to a clearer determination of its nature.

SECTION 1. JURISDICTION

The distinction between the *lex dioecesana* and the *lex iurisdictionis* of the former century was no longer pursued. The two terms were at first used interchangeably, and very gradually even became outmoded.

> Lex iurisdictionis est quoddam ius ex quo episcopus habet conferre omnia sacramenta, cognoscere de causis, coercere delicta . . . hoc tamen notabis quod licet distinguam duas leges dioecesanam et iurisdictionis, frequenter una ponitur pro altera.[23]

Bernard of Parma († 1266) used the term in several senses, including the meaning of the power to excommunicate.[24]

[23] Godefroy de Trano, *Summa in Titulis Decretalium* (ed. Venise, 1564), p. 112r (quoted from Kerckhove, *La Notion de Juridiction* [Asissi: Collegio S. Lorenzo da Brindisi, 1937], p. 18, note 3).

[24] Gloss in c. 2, X, *de officio archidiaconi*, I, 23, s.v. *consuetudinis*.

Joannes Andreae (1272-1348), using the term in an all-inclusive sense, gave a somewhat more accurate picture by indicating the gradation of jurisdiction in pastors, in bishops, and in the pope. Speaking of several priests in one church exercising the *cura animarum in solidum,* he offered this solution:

> Hoc non obstat, quia semper ibi reperitur alius, qui praeest sacerdotibus, et parochianis, ut episcopus.... Item secundum Innocentium bene licet in una ecclesia esse plures praelatos secundum diversas.... Non enim est contra ius, quod in ecclesia sint plures praelati, sed unus sub altero, sicut episcopus est praelatus in omnibus ecclesiis sibi subiectis: et tamen singulae habent singulos praelatos. Est autem hoc ideo, quia una potestas est sub alia. Sed ut dixit Hostiensis, tres sunt personae, quibus omnes animae subsunt de iure immediate et in solidum, scilicet papa, episcopus, et curatus.[25]

By the middle of the fourteenth century a completely new phrase, not helping the situation any, was introduced by Baldus de Ubaldi (1319-1400). It referred to delegated jurisdiction: "Item non est inconveniens dicere quod iurisdictio iurisdictionis esse potest ut si habens iurisdictionem directam concedit alteri utilem."[26]

About twenty-five years later one commentator analysed jurisdiction thus:

> Iurisdictio est potestas legitima de publico introducta cum necessitate iurisdicendi [iuris dicendi] et aequitatis statuendae... Quomodo dividitur iurisdictio? Ecce plures divisiones dantur.
>
> Prima... quaedam voluntaria, quaedam contentiosa. Voluntaria, quae inter volentes redditur... Contentiosa, quae redditur in invitum.
>
> Secunda... alia ordinaria... Alias delegata... Sed quibusdam dominis legum non placet: quia

[25] *In VI Libros Decretalium Novella Commentaria* (6 vols., Venetiis, 1581), c. XV (*Cum non*), *de praebendis et dignitatibus,* nn. 2, 3 (hereafter cited *Novellae*).

[26] *Super Decretalibus... Commentaria* (Lugduni, 1547), c. *Uno delegatorum, de officio delegati,* n. 8 (hereafter cited *Commentaria*).

> bona divisio debet fieri penes species. Modo ordinaria et delegata species non differunt, secundum eos: quia delegata non est alia, nisi ordinaria demandata. Nam delegatus nullam propriam habet: sed solum exercitium alienae.
>
> Tertia . . . alia dicitur merum imperium, alia mistum imperium, alia iurisdictio stricte sumpta: alia modica coertio, idest quoddam modicum imperium, quod inest iurisdictioni.[27]

This third division, while dating back to the Roman jurists, was not previously mentioned because of the relatively minor position to which it was relegated by both the Decretists and the Decretalists.[28]

Fifty years later Panormitanus († 1453) distinguished as jurisdiction the lawful exercise of sacerdotal powers from the mere fact of having these powers.

> Videte, quia si consideremus curam respectu habitus, sacerdos, eo quod sacerdos, habet eam, licet non habeat populum, unde dictum fuit, 'Accipite Spiritum Sanctum et quorum remiseritis peccata etc.,' sed non habet exercitium curae. Sacerdos autem habens populum, habet habitum et exercitium curae.[29]

Thus, by the time of the Council of Trent (1545-1563), jurisdiction embraced everything which pertained to the administration of justice and equity.[30] A sharp division

[27] Aegidius de Bellamera, *In Secundam Primi Decretalium Libri Partem Praelectiones* (Lugduni, 1548, 1549), Rubrica, *de officio iudicis*, nn. 1-3.

[28] Laymann (1574-1635) noted that jurisdiction of the external forum, both ecclesiastical and civil, was divided by Bartolus († 1357) and Panormitanus († 1453) into imperium and simple jurisdiction. Imperium was the jurisdiction exercised in the noble office of judge. It was termed *merum* if it pertained to public utility; *mixtum*, if it pertained to private utility. Simple jurisdiction was exercised in the "mercenary office" of the judge, i.e., pertaining to that which was deserving of merely civil action. Cf. Laymann, *Theologia Moralis* (Venetiis, 1630), lib. I, tract. IV, cap. V, nn. 2-10.

[29] *Commentaria in Quinque Libros Decretalium* (5 vols. in 7, Venetiis, 1588), c. 4 (*Cum satis*), *de officio archidiaconi*, n. 2 (hereafter cited *Commentaria*).

[30] Tirado, *De Iurisdictionis Acceptione*, p. 155.

now existed between jurisdiction and the power of orders; but the exercise of the power of orders pertained to jurisdiction.

SECTION 2. THE ARCHDEACON

By the decree of Pope Alexander III (1159-1181) the Archdeacon was forbidden to confer the *cura animarum* without the bishop's mandate: "Mandamus ut nemini sine licentia et mandato episcopi curam praesumas committere animarum."[31] It is evident, however, that he himself exercised jurisdiction, for in reference to the archdeacon Innocent III wrote: "Archipresbyteri autem, qui a pluribus decani nuncupantur, eius iurisdictioni se noverint subiacere."[32]

Moreover, the *glossa ordinaria* stated: "Sic ergo archidiaconus habet coerctionem ex quo habet iurisdictionem. . ."[33] In the same gloss Bernard of Parma presented two opposite opinions on whether the archdeacon had his jurisdiction or the *cura animarum* by common law, and then gave his own solution by saying: "Sic retulit se ad ius commune, sic ergo iura quae loquuntur diversimode de iurisdictione archidiaconi, intelligenda sunt secundum diversas consuetudines diversorum locorum."[34] A decretal letter of Alexander III to the Bishop of Coventry and the Abbot of Chester[35] spoke of the archdeacon's duty to make a visitation of the churches of his district at least once a year, and the gloss of Bernard of Parma was again significant:

> Hoc idem pertinet ad curam animarum et sic est argumentum quod archidiaconus habet curam ani-

[31] C. 4, X, *de officio archidiaconi,* I, 23; Mansi, XXI, 1089; JL, n. 13898.

[32] C. 7, X, *de officio archidiaconi,* I, 23; Potthast, *Regesta Pontificum Romanorum inde ab anno post Christum natum MCXCVIII ad annum MCCCIV* (2 vols., Berolini, 1874, 1875), n. 5031 (hereafter cited Potthast).

[33] Gloss in c. 1, X, *de officio archidiaconi,* I, 23, s.v. *corrigat.*

[34] Gloss in c. 4, X, *de officio archidiaconi,* I, 23, s.v. *consuetudinis.*

[35] C. 6, X, *de officio archidiaconi,* I, 23; JL, 13857.

marum, et quod possit alii committere, sed intellige hic loqui de consuetudine.[36]

The final development on the matter in this period was expertly given by Innocent IV (1243-1254), who adverted to the fact that Bernard of Parma contended that the archdeacon had the *cura animarum*, but that Huguccio had denied this, and therefore felt the need of an explanation:

> Curam quia nec habet, nisi demandetur ab episcopo . . . sed Bernardus dixit quod archidiaconus habet curam animarum et respondet huic canoni quod hic erat contraria specialis consuetudo, quae maxime in iuribus archidiaconi servanda est. Melius distinguitur sic, cura animarum dicitur stricte potestas ligandi et solvendi, scilicet in foro poenitentiali, et haec in nullo praelato est, nisi sit sacerdos . . . quamvis dici posset quod archidiaconus et electi confirmati, et alii huiusmodi, quamvis non sint sacerdotes, tamen possunt dare ecclesias sacerdotibus; nec dant curam animarum, sed is, cui dant quando fuit factus sacerdos, simul cum ordine hanc potestatem ligandi et solvendi accepit, licet non in hos subditos, quos modo dat archidiaconus vel alius praelatus, potestatem haberet antequam per ipsum institueretur in ecclesia, quae curam habet; sed officium huius potestatis, quam non habebat, concedit . . . Argumentum. Large dicitur cura potestas eiiciendi et recipiendi in ecclesiam, corrigendi et puniendi excessus; sub hac cura est excommunicare, interdicere, visitare, et caetera talia, quae sunt ad correctionem morum; hanc curam possunt habere archidiaconi et inferiores praelati, ut ibi dicitur, de utraque istarum curarum intelligitur . . . ecclesiam autem vel praebendam conferre archidiaconus non potest, vel alius praelatus praeter episcopum, nisi hoc ex consuetudine, vel privilegio habeat; tunc facit tanquam vicarius.[37]

The conclusion can be drawn from these considerations that, certainly by the middle of the thirteenth century,

[36] Gloss in c. 6, X, *de officio archidiaconi*, I, 23, s.v. *visitandus*.

[37] *In V Libros Decretalium Commentaria* (Venetiis, 1570), c. 4 (*Cum satis*), *de officio archidiaconi*, nn. 1, 2 (hereafter cited *Commentaria*).

cura animarum had two different meanings: in the restricted sense, it meant the power to forgive sins; in the extended sense, it meant jurisdiction in the external forum, consisting in at least judicial and coercive power. Thus, Innocent IV distinguished between ministerial and jurisdictional powers.[38]

SECTION 3. PRELATES

This consideration is interesting because of the common doctrine that prelates had *cura* or jurisdiction in the external forum. As a natural consequence, the arguments centered around whether the parish priest or pastor was a prelate.

A decretal letter of Pope Lucius III (1181-1185) made it clear that rectors of churches had the *cura animarum.* If they were unable to serve at the altar by reason of infection with leprosy, "eis dandus est coadiutor, qui curam habeat animarum."[39]

The gloss of Bernard of Parma on this stated: "Ergo ille coadiutor videtur esse praelatus, ex quo habet curam animarum."[40] Similarly a gloss of Bartholomew of Brescia (1245) indicated that priests and others to whom ecclesiastical goods had been committed were prelates: "In prima parte loquitur de rebus quas praelati emunt."[41] The archdeacon Guido de Baysio explicitly taught that parish priests were prelates with jurisdiction: "Praelati habent iurisdictionem et presbyter parochialis praelatus est."[42] He add-

[38] "...Innocent IV clarified the concept of an ecclesiastical office by incisively distinguishing between the ministerial and jurisdictional powers possessed by certain officials."—Heintschel, *The Mediaeval Concept of an Ecclesiastical Office*, The Catholic University of America Canon Law Studies, n. 363 (Washington, D.C.: The Catholic University of America Press, 1956), p. 86.

[39] C. 3, X, *de clerico aegrotante*, III, 6; JL, n. 14965.

[40] Gloss in c. 3, X, *de clerico aegrotante*, III, 6, s.v. *curam animarum.*

[41] Gloss in c. 1, C. XII, q. 4, s.v. *sacerdotes.*

[42] *Rosarium seu in Decretorum Volumen Commentaria* (Venetiis, 1577), c. 11 (*Non minus*), C. II, q. 1 (hereafter cited *Rosarium*).

ed that they could excommunicate, for they had jurisdiction, and that jurisdiction was nothing if unaccompanied with the power of coercion.

It seems a safe conclusion from the weight of all this testimony that pastors were to be considered as prelates and therefore as having the *cura animarum* or some jurisdiction in the external forum. The doctrine that prelates held jurisdiction was maintained, and the view that pastors were prelates was acknowledged in the fifteenth century by Panormitanus.[43]

SECTION 4. THE PROPER PRIEST

Although this term had a special application in the question of the sacrament of penance, its consideration also contributes to a fuller understanding of the *cura animarum.* The proper priest was the parish priest having the *cura animarum.* St. Raymond of Peñafort indicated toward the beginning of the thirteenth century that a person could have several proper priests: his parish priest and others who held the ordinary *cura animarum,* such as the bishop, a papal legate, or the pope.

> Proprium Sacerdotem quoad hoc intelligo illum Sacerdotem, qui habet curam animae eius ordinariam, sicut Papa, Legatus Papae, Episcopus proprius: unde aliquis potest plures habere proprios Sacerdotes. Credo tamen, quod nisi subsit rationabilis causa, propter quam Parochianus nolit confiteri proprio Sacerdoti Parochiali, debet eis confiteri, vel alii de licentia eius generali, vel speciali.[44]

Hostiensis († 1271) presented his definition of the proper priest thus:

> Proprius sacerdos dicitur ille cui cura parochialis ecclesiae est commissa, sive persona, sive vicarius, que tenetur residentiam facere . . .[45]

[43] *Commentaria,* c. 3, X, *de officio iudicis ordinarii,* I, 31.

[44] *Summa* (Veronae, 1744), c. 4 (*De confessione*), *de poenitentiis et remissionibus,* lib. III, tit. XXXIV, p. 424.

[45] *Commentaria in Quinque Libros Decretalium* (2 vols., Venetiis,

Later, in the middle of the fourteenth century, Boich presented the culmination of thought on the subject up to his day thus:

> Unde proprius sacerdos dicitur cui cura parochialis ecclesiae est commissa, sit rector vel vicarius secundum Hostiensem et Joannem Andreae hic qui describunt curam hic dicentes quod cura est vigil, onerosa, et solicita custodia animarum, commissa alicui ut curet ne pereant, sed salventur, quae competit ex lege vel commissione canonica, aut consuetudine vel praescriptione per sedem apostolicam non improbata . . . Unde parochialis sacerdos, item Papa et Episcopus sunt proprii et immediati.[46]

SECTION 5. *Cura Animarum*

Shortly prior to the Decretals of Gregory IX *cura animarum* meant jurisdiction or at least some part of it. Lawrence of Spain stated: "Habent curam animarum . . . sed non possunt anathematizare . . ego contra . . . quia hoc non est ordinis sed iurisdictionis."[47] And since *cura animarum* was jurisdiction, if one was chosen for an office with the *cura animarum,* one was first to be ordained to the sacerdotal order.[48]

A letter of Innocent IV which dated from this time and was later incorporated in the *Liber Sextus Decretalium* also indicated that the *cura animarum* denoted jurisdiction, which the cleric received from the bishop.[49] Hostiensis set

1581), c. 12 (*Omnis*), *de poenitentiis et remissionibus,* n. 12 (hereafter cited *Commentaria*).

[46] *In Quinque Decretalium Libros Commentaria* (Venetiis, 1576), c. 12 · (*Omnis*), *de poenitentiis et remissionibus,* nn. 26, 27.

[47] *Apparatus glossorum,* Comp. I, lib. I, tit. XX, c. 1 (quoted from Kerckhove, *La Notion de Juridiction,* p. 5, note 3).

[48] "Qui ad curam animarum eligitur, debet primo promoveri ad ordinem sacerdotii, alias sit ea ipso iure privatus."—Gloss in c. 10, X, *ne clerici vel monachi saecularibus negotiis se immisceant,* III, 50, s.v. *presbyteros.*

[49] C. 1, *de verborum significatione,* Tit. XII, in VI°: ". . . ut ab eis curam recipiant animarum, cum plebes episcopis sint subiectae. . ."; Potthast, n. 15127; Mansi, XXIII, 674.

forth his idea of it thus: "Curam animarum ... ex quo iurisdictionem et subditos habent, inter quos possunt cognoscere, et diffinire circa spiritualia. Nam iurisdictio sine modica coercitione nulla est."[50] He continued saying that someone who had the *cura* of a parish but had not as yet been ordained to the priesthood could not excommunicate, nor could he absolve with the power of the keys, for this power he did not have.[51]

This last statement may seem confusing in the light of the statement of one of his contemporaries, Bernard of Parma, to the effect that the priesthood was necessary for the exercise of the *cura animarum.* But Bernard also contemplated in his statement the possibility of one who was not a priest holding a benefice and the *cura,* while a vicar exercised the *cura animarum,* as is evident from the decretal to which his gloss referred.[52]

Hostiensis cleared up this precise point. He definitely held that the *cura* partook of jurisdiction and was related to the judicial or external forum as compared with the penitential forum.

> Cura vero iurisdictionis est, non ordinis, et hanc recipit praelatus in confirmatione vel institutione. Unde et quando talis praelatus ordinatur, non datur ei cura, quam iam receperat, sed potestas ligandi atque solvendi animas sibi commissas, quam sine ordine non habebat, quamvis posset alii (sacerdoti tamen) committere, ut easdem in foro poenitentiali audiret et absolveret: quia hoc iurisdictionis est, quam ratione curae habet ... sed nec absolvere potest quis ab excommunicatione, nisi sit sacerdos; quia haec absolutio mixta est, partim fori poenitentialis et partim iudicialis, unde nec absolvitur nisi poenitens et contritus.[53]

In a way similar to that of Innocent IV but in a slightly more forceful manner, however, Hostiensis made an ex-

[50] *Summa Aurea* (Venetiis, 1570), *de sententia excommunicationis,* lib. V, n. 5 (*Nedum autem ius*).

[51] Hostiensis, *loc. cit.*

[52] C. 30, X, *de praebendis et dignitatibus,* III, 5.

[53] *Commentaria,* c. 4 (*Cum satis*), *de officio archidiaconi,* n. 7.

plicit distinction, so that when he used the term "*cura*" he did not mean *cura animarum.*

> Hic distinguendum est inter curam, et curam animarum, quandoque enim cura animarum dicitur potestas ligandi et solvendi in foro poenitentiali, et haec in nullo praelato cadit nisi sacerdos... Large etiam datur cura potestas eiiciendi et recipiendi in ecclesia, corrigendi et puniendi excessus ... sub hac cura est excommunicare, interdicere, visitare, et coetera similia, quae sunt ad correctionem morum, et hanc possunt habere archidiaconi et inferiores praelati.[54]

Up to this time *cura* and *cura animarum* were used with little distinction for the powers of both forums, internal and external. Any problem, therefore, precipitated by the remark of Bernard of Parma was solved. He contended, in the light of the distinction of Innocent IV and of Hostiensis, that one who was chosen for an office which had *cura* or jurisdiction attached to it was first to be ordained a priest, so that he might exercise the *cura animarum* or the power of orders. None the less Hostiensis, in effect, said nothing other than that archdeacons and inferior prelates had *cura* or jurisdiction, and that priests had the *cura animarum* or the power of orders, even though they might not have *cura.* In no way did he contradict the previous notion that an inferior prelate, such as a parish priest, could have jurisdiction in the external forum; he simply would have said that for such a man there existed both the *cura* and the *cura animarum.*

Later, by no more than thirty years, Guido de Baysio defined *cura,* indicated why it was so called, and explained how it was conceded, in the following manner:

> Commissis animabus, et ideo ipsarum animarum habet curam... Cura est vigil et onerosa ac solicita custodia animarum commissa alicui, ut curet ne pereant sed salventur: quae competit ex lege vel commissione canonica, vel consuetudine seu

[54] *Commentaria,* c. 4 (*Cum satis*), *de officio archidiaconi,* n. 5.

praescriptione per sedem apostolicam non improbata.[55]

It should be noted that Guido de Baysio, while formulating his definition of *cura,* which to Hostiensis meant jurisdiction only, appeared to be totally apathetic towards the latter's distinction, for he used the terms "*cura*" and "*cura animarum*" synonymously.

The opinions of a representative group of commentators of the next three centuries (14th, 15th, and early 16th) are now considered in an effort to trace the development of *cura* and *cura animarum* up to the time of the Council of Trent.

Joannes Andreae seemed to draw no such distinction as Hostiensis had done. Like Innocent III before him,[56] he too said that the *cura animarum* was called an art,[57] and he thus referred to *cura* etymologically: "Quasi cor urat. . . ." He likewise called the parish priest a pastor: "Parochialis sacerdos est pastor . . . sic et plebanus . . . et dicuntur ministri."[58] Similarly Boich at least implicitly dropped any distinction between *cura* and *cura animarum* by appropriating the very term "*cura*"[59] for that which Innocent IV had referred to as *cura animarum.*[60]

Zabarella (before 1391) proved of little if any help. He simply repeated the much used definition of *cura* attributed to Hostiensis, and said that the archdeacon had the *cura*

[55] *Rosarium,* c. 21 (*Cognovimus*), C. XVIII, q. 2.

[56] "Cum sit ars artium regimen animarum . . ."—c. 14, X, *de aetate et qualitate et ordine praeficiendorum,* I, 14.

[57] *Novellae,* c. 1 (*Clerici*), *de vita et honestate clericorum,* III, 1, in VI°, n. 1.

[58] *Novellae,* c. 14 (*Licet canon*), *de electione et electi potestate,* I, 6, in VI°, nn. 2, 3.

[59] "Cura vero iurisdictionis est non ordinis, et hanc recepit praelatus in confirmatione . . . Nam potestas clavium non est cura, sed illud per quod et mediante quo cura exercetur. Quantum tamen ad illud de quo erat questio, scilicet utrum Archidiaconus habeat curam vel non, credo distinctionem Innocentii fore veram."—*Commentaria,* c. *Cum satis, de officio archidiaconi,* n. 4.

[60] "Archidiaconus habet curam animarum, sed non principaliter . . . potest tamen excommunicare."—*Commentaria,* c. 7 (*Cum in cunctis*), *de electione et electi potestate,* I, 6, n. 6.

fori poenitentiosi.[61] But he was necessarily referring to jurisdiction in the external forum, since an archdeacon, in not having the priestly character, lacked the power to forgive sins. Also, in comparing *cura* or jurisdiction in the external and internal forums, he said that the former was the nobler of the two.[62]

Peter of Ancharano (1330-1416), in his work written shortly before the close of the fourteenth century, stressed the distinction between having the *cura* and exercising it, without making any distinction between *cura* and *cura animarum.*[63] The same distinction was made by William of Montlauzon († 1343).[64]

By the time of Panormitanus jurisdiction in the judicial external forum was considered as belonging to the *cura animarum,* which the priest possessed if he had charge of a parish.[65] And the trend at that time, as seen in authors at this century's close, was to reverse the latest notion of *cura animarum* by re-establishing it with the significance of jurisdiction only, to the exclusion of the power of orders. Thus, Bertachinus (1481) said: "Cura animarum dicitur cura iurisdictionis et differt a potestate. Sed qualiter acci-

[61] *Commentarii in Clementinarum Volumen* (Venetiis, 1504), c. un. (*Quae de ecclesiis*), *de officio vicarii,* I, 7, q. XX.

[62] "Quero quo est dignior et maior cura: an ea quae exercetur in foro contentioso: an ea in foro animae: videtur quod prima."—Zabarella, *op. cit.,* in prin. (*Si dignitatem*), *praebendis et dignitatibus,* III, 5, q. VII.

[63] "Licet tamen talibus sit commissa administratio ut exercitium curae, non tamen ipsa cura, quod fieri non potest."—*Consilia sive Iuris Responsa* (Venetiis, 1574), LIX, n. 3.

[64] *Repetitionum in Universas fere Iuris Canonici partes materiasque sane frequentiores Volumina Sex* (6 vols., Venetiis, 1587; Vol. VII, *Index Repetitionum,* Venetiis, 1587), c. *Quae de ecclesiis, de officio vicarii,* I, 7, in Clem. (hereafter cited *Repetitiones*).

[65] "Appellatione curae animarum, venit cura, nedum in foro poenitentiali, sed et in foro contentioso, ratione beneficii ecclesiastici tenetur esse sacerdos, sive habeat illam, ut rector, sive, ut perpetuus vicarius." —*Commentaria,* super I Clem., c. *Quae de ecclesiis, de officio vicarii,* I, 7, n. 1.

piatur . . . Baldus in Margarita verbo Cura."[66] This was his reference to Baldus: "Cura animarum dicitur cura iurisdictionis non ordinis, et ideo aliud est potestas, aliud est cura animarum."[67] Furthermore, Felinus Sandaeus (1444-1503) stated that inferior prelates such as pastors could exercise this jurisdiction to the exclusion of the bishop.[68]

This reversal of the fifteenth century was short lived, for the beginning of the sixteenth century found divisions of cura not as formerly between *cura* and *cura animarum,* but divisions of the term *"cura animarum"* itself, as it was understood in the narrow sense of pertaining to the internal forum or in the wide sense of pertaining to the external forum. Sylvester Prierias (1456-1523) in his writings thus stated: "Cura animarum dupliciter dicitur."[69] This division, originally that of Innocent IV, was likewise shown to be in vogue by the gloss of Joannes Chappuis (1520) on a phrase found in the *Extravagantes Communes.*[70]

In summary, it is evident that *cura animarum* suffered rapidly successive interpretations, now meaning jurisdiction even in the external forum, now meaning only the power of orders. The over-all usage generally attributed to the *cura animarum* an extended meaning, including jurisdiction in both forums and the power of orders. But, as the Council of Trent approached, this latter member tended to be supplanted by the lawful exercise of the power of orders.

[66] *Repertorium* (Venetiis, 1570), s.v. *Cura animarum,* p. 536.

[67] *Margarita Baldi de Ubaldi* . . . ad Innocentii IV Pont. Max. in V Libros Decretalium Commentarios *repertorii loco addita* (Venetiis, 1570), s.v. *Cura.*

[68] "Communis opinio est . . . praelatus inferior potest exercere curam animarum in aliqua ecclesia sibi subiecta episcopo excluso . . . contrarium tenuit Hostiensis, Joannes, et Antonius de Butrio."—*Repertorium seu Index Locupletissimus in Felini Sandei Commentarios ad quinque Libros Decretalium* (Venetiis, 1570), s.v. *curam animarum,* p. 142.

[69] *Summa Summarum* (Venetiis, 1601), s.v. *cura animarum,* p. 170.

[70] "Quod exponit Innocentius dicens, tale, scilicet curam habens in foro animae . . . sive large, scilicet si habet in foro contentioso." —Gloss in c. 3, Extrav., *de praebendis,* III, s.v. *quae alios absque.*

In view of the numerous changes in meaning, the remark of Joannes Quintinus (1500-1561) was not at all surprising: "Animarum cura multifariam intelligitur iure canonico."[71]

Neither was it surprising that with such usage the notion of the *cura animarum* gradually developed to the point of comprehending the power, the rights, and the obligations, which were the pastor's by reason of his office.

[71] *Repetitiones,* in c. *de multa, de praebendis,* n. 76.

CHAPTER II

PAROCHIAL JURISDICTION AFTER THE COUNCIL OF TRENT

During the period of the Decretists and the Decretalists up to the time of the Council of Trent (1545-1563) there was in evidence a trend consisting in a change from practically non-usage of the term "jurisdiction" to high degrees of refinement of that same term. Wherefore, towards the beginning of this later period, the notion and the import of jurisdiction were principally considered as they had been comprehended under an earlier synonym, the *cura animarum.*

Although between the Council of Trent and the codification of Canon Law the terms "jurisdiction" and "*cura animarum*" were clearly distinguished, the term "jurisdiction" continued to be used in both a strict sense either of a full legislative, judicial, and coercive power, or merely of a judicial power, as well as in a broad sense embracing a multiplicity of powers and acts even to the inclusion of purely administrative functions.

Previous to the Council both law and custom had reserved many rights and functions to pastors. By way of example, the decree on the administration of the Paschal Communion as prescribed by the IV General Council of the Lateran remained in force.[1] Similarly the right of pastors to conduct the funerals of their parishioners, or the right to the funeral portion when the parishioner chose to be buried elsewhere, existed almost from the beginning of the parochial system.[2] By the time of the Council of Trent these

[1] C. 12, X, *de poenitentiis et remissionibus*, V, 38; S.C.C., *Ferrarien.*, 15 dec. 1703, 12 ian. 1704—*Codicis Iuris Canonici Fontes* (cura Emi Petri Card. Gasparri editi, 9 vols., Romae [postea Civitate Vaticana]: Typis Polyglottis Vaticanis, 1923-1939 [Vols. VII-IX, ed. cura et studio Emi Iustiniani Card. Serédi]), n. 3011 (hereafter cited *Fontes*); Mediolanen., 22 iun., 24 aug. 1715—*Fontes*, n. 3147.

[2] Hale, *The Pastor of Burial*, The Catholic University of America

rights and functions had been fairly well stabilized, and they suffered little change in the succeeding centuries, save for a little extension.[3]

The question of parochial jurisdiction resolved itself into this: one author attributed jurisdiction in the external forum to pastors, while another denied that such jurisdiction existed, each depending upon his particular concept of jurisdiction. There was no difficulty whether a pastor had the power to do this or that, for all agreed that as a matter of fact pastors performed certain acts, but some authors termed them acts of jurisdiction, and characterized them as such even in the external forum, while others did not.

It is, therefore, obviously necessary to present a summary of the very notion of jurisdiction during this period. Since no universal legislation or authoritative definition pertinent to parochial jurisdiction in the external forum emanated during this time, it will best serve the present purpose to determine the individual authors' notions of jurisdiction and its existence in reference to pastors.

Naturally, whatever useful Tridentine or post-Tridentine authentic source material can be found will be incorporated at its appropriate place. For the sake of convenience, no distinction is made between pastors properly so called and the various types of vicars who exercised the full parochial *cura animarum.* Likewise, since in a work of this proportion many facets of a problem are not treated fully inasmuch as they are deemed less important than others, the question whether the pastor's capacity of delegating his penitential jurisdiction argued for him the possession of jurisdiction in the external forum may be dismissed with the following conclusion:

> Prior to the Council of Trent pastors freely delegated their penitential jurisdiction, and after-

Canon Law Studies, n. 234 (Washington, D.C.: The Catholic University of America Press, 1949), p. 4.

[3] Kelly, *The Functions Reserved to Pastors,* The Catholic Universtiy of America Canon Law Studies, n. 250 (Washington, D.C.: The Catholic University of America Press, 1947), p. 31.

> ward retained the radical capacity for delegating it but through disuse and because of the blending of the concepts of approbation and delegation before the Code this power lost all practical significance.[4]

But let it be noted that long before the advent of the Code this particular pastoral act of delegation was considered as a mere approbation entirely distinct from the exercise of any power of jurisdiction.[5]

Article I. The Legislation of the Council of Trent

Section 1. *Cura Animarum*

The expression *"cura animarum"* was by no means abandoned, as was evidenced in canonical works up to and including the Code of Canon Law. In the Council of Trent alone the phrase appeared in at least eighteen places.[6] But only a brief consideration of the term seems warranted here, since already at that time it began to imply not only the power but also the rights and obligations belonging to a bishop or a pastor by reason of his office.[7]

One session with a chapter entitled "When assistants are to be employed in the 'care of souls' " omitted any further mention of the *cura animarum* in its text, but twice referred to the administration of the sacraments and the

[4] Acerra, *The Extent and Character of Parochial Jurisdiction*, Typewritten licentiate dissertation (Washington, D.C.: The Catholic University of America, 1953), p. 174; cf. also pp. 147-153.

[5] Cf. Reiffenstuel, *Theologia Moralis*, (7. ed., 2 vols., Mutinae, 1745), tom. 2, tract. XIV, dist. VIII, n. 14, p. 220.

[6] Conc. Trident., sess. V, *de ref.*, c. 2; sess VI, *de ref.*, c. 2; sess. VII, *de ref.*, c. 3, 5, 7, 8; sess. XIV, *de ref.*, *introd.*, c. 7; sess. XXI, *de ref.*, c. 4; sess. XXII, *de sac. Missae*, c. 8; *de ref.*, c. 3; sess. XXIII, *de ref.*, c. 1, 14; sess. XXIV, *de ref.*, c. 12, 18; sess. XXV, *de venerat. sanct.*; *de reg. et mon.*, c. 11; *de ref.*, c. 16.

[7] "...bajo la cura de las almas se comprende la potestad y las obligaciones que al párroco le competen por razón de su oficio."—Alonso, "Los Párrochos en el Concilio de Trento y en el Código de Derecho Canónico", *Revista Española de Derecho Canónico* (Salamanca, 1946—), II (1947), 950.

celebration of the divine offices.[8] Furthermore, the expression *"cura animarum"* became objectively linked with similar terms which pointed to the reception of the sacraments and attendance at divine offices.[9]

The Council ultimately offered a descriptive definition of the *cura animarum* in these words:

> ... to know one's sheep, to offer sacrifice for for them, and to feed them by preaching the divine word, the administration of the sacraments, the example of all good works, to exercise a fatherly care in behalf of the poor and other distressed persons and to apply oneself to all other pastoral duties.[10]

Two sessions and six months after this definition, however, there appeared a construction which possibly might be construed as a distinction between the *cura animarum* and the office of teaching, which distinction may even have aided later canonists in their classification of the *magisterium* as an element of ecclesiastical power distinct from jurisdiction.[11]

It may prove helpful to note, in conclusion, that the term "jurisdiction" appeared in the text of the Council approximately as frequently as did the expression *"cura animarum"*. For each time, however, that the term "jurisdiction" was used in the restricted sense of *ius dicere* or of

[8] "... ecclesiasticis sacramentis ministrandis et cultu divino peragendo ... ad sacramenta exhibenda et cultum divinum celebrandum." —Sess. XXI, *de ref.*, c. 4. Quotations from the text of the Council of Trent are taken from Schroeder, *Canons and Decrees of the Council of Trent* (St. Louis: B. Herder Book Co., 1941), English text pp. 1-278, Latin text pp. 281-578.

[9] "... ad percipienda sacramenta et divina officia audienda."—Sess. XXI, *de ref.*, c. 4.

[10] "... oves suas agnoscere, pro his sacrificium offerre, verbique divini praedicatione, sacramentorum administratione ac bonorum omnium operum exemplo pascere, pauperum aliarumque miserabilium personarum curam paternam gerere, et in cetera munia pastoralia incumbere ..."—Sess. XXIII, *de ref.*, c. 1.

[11] "Mandat sancta synodus omnibus episcopis et ceteris docendi munus curamque sustinentibus ..."—Sess. XXV, *de invocatione, veneratione et reliquiis sanctorum, et sacris imaginibus.*

judicial power,[12] it was five times employed in the extended sense of authority or of power in general.[13]

SECTION 2. PRELATES AND DIGNITIES

As a bridge between the Council's usage of the phrase "*cura animarum*" and its consideration of pastors and parishes, its legislation on two questions previously considered may here be appropriately inserted.

In reference to the "Pastor-Prelate" question[14] the Council spoke in several sessions of prelates, and enumerated thereafter Cardinals, Patriarchs, Primates, Metropolitans, Bishops, Archdeacons, Deans, Abbots, and Visitators, but no mention was made of pastors as such.[15] The argument in earlier centuries was that only prelates had jurisdiction in the external forum, and consequently many of the Decretalists, being convinced that such jurisdiction belonged to parish priests, were compelled to call them prelates. The fact, however, that the Council of Trent omitted pastors from its listing of prelates cannot be made a basis for maintaining that pastors had no jurisdiction in the external forum, for never did the Council make the supplementary statements either that its listing was all-inclusive or that prelates alone had jurisdiction in the external forum. Such statements would indeed have been necessary in warrant of such a restrictive conclusion. Nevertheless, while the Council cannot be cited in valid refutation of a partial parochial jurisdiction in the external forum, it seems clear that the Council wished to exclude pastors from the ranks of the prelacy.

[12] Sess. XIV, *de poenitentia*, can. 7; *de ref.*, c. 5; sess. XXIV, *de ref.*, c. 20.

[13] Sess. V, *de ref.*, c. 2; sess. XIII, *de ref.*, c. 1; sess. XIV, *de ref.*, c. 4; sess. XXII, *de ref.*, c. 3; sess. XXIII, *de ref.*, c. 10; sess. XXIV, *de ref.*, c. 11, 16; sess. XXV, *de regularibus et monialibus*, c. 11, 20; *de ref.*, c. 6, 11, 20.

[14] Cf. *supra*, pp. 13, 14.

[15] Sess. XXIII, *de ref.*, c. 10; sess. XXIV, *de ref.*, c. 3; sess. XXV, *de ref.*, c. 1.

The Council twice implied under the genus of "other inferiors" that some parish priests had been exercising judicial power in the external forum. It declared that thenceforth matrimonial and criminal causes should not be left to the judgment of a dean, archdeacon, or other inferiors, but were to be left to the sole examination and jurisdiction of the bishop, even though there should at the time have been a dispute, in whatever stage of prosecution, between the bishop and the dean or archdeacon or other inferiors regarding the examination of those causes.[16] It further exempted from the cognizance of archdeacons, deans, and other inferiors all causes of clerics living with concubines.[17] The implication of pastors under the expression is certainly logical, since pastors had in times past also excommunicated certain delinquent subjects and had been included under the heading of inferior prelates. Also, in the light of the question directed to the Sacred Congregation for the Propagation of the Faith in the year 1654 and its corresponding answer that pastors had no power to impose censures, one may well imagine that some pastors had been leveling excommunications on their subjects even after the legislation of the Council of Trent had abrogated such a practice.[18]

In relation to the previously considered problem concerning the reception of dignities,[19] the Fathers of the Council

[16] "Ad haec causae matrimoniales et criminales non decani, archidiaconi aut aliorum inferiorum iudicio, etiam visitando, sed episcopi tantum examini et iurisdictioni relinquantur, etiamsi in praesenti inter episcopum et decanum seu archidiaconum, aut alios inferiores super causarum istarum cognitione lis aliqua in quacumque instantia pendeat..."—Sess. XXIV, *de ref.*, c. 20.

[17] "...supradictorumque omnium cognitio non ad archidiaconos, nec decanos, aut alios inferiores, sed ad episcopos ipsos pertineat..." —Sess. XXV, *de ref.*, c. 14.

[18] *Collectanea S. Congregationis de Propaganda Fide* (2 vols., Romae: Typographia Polyglotta S. C. de Propaganda Fide, 1907), I, 120; *Fontes*, n. 4460.

[19] Cf. *supra*, pp. 15-17; cf Heintschel, *The Mediaeval Concept of an Ecclesiastical Office*, p. 87.

made it quite clear that one could still receive a dignity without being in sacred orders provided he was of such an age as the dignity required for qualification of its reception within the time prescribed by law and the Council of Trent, which time was one year.[20] In other words, in order to receive a dignity, such as a canonry in the cathedral church, a man had to be either already constituted in the sacred order which the dignity, prebend, or portion required, or of such an age as would qualify him for the reception of that order within the time prescribed.[21]

Moreover, to receive a dignity to which was annexed the *cura animarum,* a man had to be twenty-four years of age, experienced in the clerical order, and have the necessary learning and integrity of morals.[22]

SECTION 3. PASTORS AND PARISHES

Although pastors were to have distinct parishes according to a decretal letter issued December 19, 1204, by Innocent III[23] and three hundred and fifty years before the Council of Trent, it is the Council that is remembered as having efficaciously established that each parish should have definite boundaries. Referring to the letter of Innocent III, the Council said that it was by a very good law that dioceses and parishes had been made distinct, and to each flock had been assigned its proper pastor and to in-

[20] "Facultates de non promovendo, praeterquam in casibus a iure expressis concessae, ad annum tantum suffragentur..."—Sess. VII, *de ref.,* c. 12.

[21] "Neminem etiam deinceps ad dignitatem, canonicatum aut portionem recipiant, nisi qui eo ordine sacro aut sit initiatus, quem illa dignitas, praebenda aut portio requirit, aut in tali aetate, ut infra tempus a iure et ab hac sancta synodo statutum initiari valeat." —Sess. XXIV, *de ref.,* c. 12.

[22] "Nemo igitur deinceps ad dignitates quascumque, quibus animarum cura subest, promoveatur, nisi qui saltem vigesimum quintum suae aetatis annum attigerit et, in clericali ordine versatus, doctrina ad suum munus exsequendum necessaria ac morum integritate commendetur..."—Sess. XXIV, *de ref.,* c. 12.

[23] C. 9, X, *de his quae fiunt a praelatis,* III, 10; Potthast, n. 2350.

ferior churches their rectors, each to take care of his own sheep so that the ecclesiastical order would not be disturbed.[24]

Later, under the summary title *Parochiae certis finibus distinguendae,* the Council declared that in those cities and localities where the parochial churches had no definite boundaries, and their rectors had not their own people whom they might rule but administered the sacraments indiscriminately to all who desired them, the bishops were obliged to divide the people into definite and distinct parishes and assign to each its own and permanent parish priest, who could know his people.[25]

The general establishment of the term "pastor," as meaning the parish priest, is attributed to the Council of Trent.[26] Previously the parish priest was usually referred to as the proper priest or the rector, while the bishop was the pastor. But, beginning with the Council's twenty-first session (July 16, 1562), the parish priest was known as a *parochus* or pastor as the term is used today. [27] The terms "rector" and "pas-

[24] "Et quia iure optimo distinctae fuerunt dioeceses et parochiae, ac unicuique gregi proprii attributi pastores et inferiorum ecclesiarum rectores, qui suarum quisque ovium curam habeant, ut ordo ecclesiasticus non confundatur . . ."—Sess. XIV, *de ref.*, c. 9.

[25] "In iis quoque civitatibus ac locis, ubi parochiales ecclesiae certos non habent fines, nec earum rectores proprium populum, quem regant, sed promiscue petentibus sacramenta administrantur, mandat sancta synodus episcopis pro tutiori animarum eis commissarum salute, ut distincto populo in certas propriasque parochias unicuique suum perpetuum peculiaremque parochum assignent, qui eas cognoscere valeat, et a quo solo licite sacramenta suscipiant, aut alio utiliori modo, prout loci qualitas exegerit, provideant."—Sess. XXIV, *de ref.*, c. 13.

[26] The term "*parochus,*" however, probably had its origin in the fifteenth century. Cf. Schüller, "Die Pfarrvikarie in der Diözese Trier," *Archiv für katholisches Kirchenrecht* (Innsbruck, 1857-1861; Mainz, 1862—), LXXXIX (1909), 38.

[27] The text of Sess. XXI, *de ref.*, c. 6 reads: "Quia illiterati et imperiti parochialium ecclesiarum rectores . . . ", thereby equating the term *rector* with that of *parochus* as found in the title of this chapter: "Imperitis parochis vicarii assignata parte fructuum deputentur."

tor" were used interchangeably in the chapter speaking of bishops, inferior curates, and others possessing an ecclesiastical benefice with the *cura animarum,* and at its end referring to all of them as pastors.[28] Shortly thereafter can be found an express identification of *parochus* and *pastor.*[29]

While the term *"parochus"* appeared many times in the various chapters of the Council's final sessions, nothing was mentioned explicitly concerning the nature of the pastor's jurisdiction.[30]

This treatment of the pertinent legislation of the Council of Trent is concluded by way of a summary statement regarding four further notions contained therein: 1) the pastor's duty to preach;[31] 2) the pastor's obligation of residence;[32] 3) the pastor's duty to record properly and keep safely the parish registers of baptisms and marriages;[33] 4) the need for marriages to take place *coram parocho* as a condition affecting the validity of the contract.[34]

ARTICLE II. THE DOCTRINAL CONCEPT OF JURISDICTION IN GENERAL

SECTION 1. THE NOTION OF JURISDICTION

The Council of Trent used the term "jurisdiction" in both

[28] "Postremo . . . quae adeo ex pastorum munere animarumque salute sunt frequenter omnium auribus mentibusque infligi . . ."—Sess. XXIII, *de ref.,* c. 1.

[29] "Hortatur dehinc omnes et singulos pro Christiana caritate debitoque erga pastores suos munere, ut de bonis sibi a Deo collatis episcopis et parochis . . ."—Sess. XXV, *de ref.,* c. 12.

[30] Sess. XXI, *de ref.,* c. 6; sess. XXIII, *de ref.,* c. 5; sess. XXIV, *de ref. matr.,* c. 1, 2, 7; sess. XXIV, *de ref.,* c. 4, 7, 13, 18; sess. XXV, *de ref.,* c. 12, 20.

[31] Sess. V, *de ref.,* c. 2; sess. XXIV, *de ref.,* c. 4, 7.

[32] Sess. VI, *de ref.,* c. 2; sess. VII, *de ref.,* c. 3; sess. XXIII, *de ref.,* c. 1.

[33] Sess. XXIV, *de ref. matr.,* c. 1, 2.

[34] Sess. XXIV, *de ref. matr.,* c. 1. The question whether the act of assisting at marriage was an act of jurisdiction will be treated at a later point. Cf. *infra,* pp. 60-64.

an extended and a restricted sense. The term was used in designation of the universal power of rulership[35] as well as in the restricted sense or concept of the *ius dicere.*[36] At times it was also employed in such a manner that it remained dubious whether universal power was meant.[37]

A. From the Council of Trent through the Eighteenth Century

Of great significance was the doctrine of De Molina (1535-1600) on jurisdiction, because it formed and expressed the notion of jurisdiction which came into general use, and because the majority of the later canonists retained his doctrine and clarified it. By subscribing to a rather new etymology for jurisdiction, suggesting *iuris dictio* in place of *iuris ditio,* he held that jurisdiction, or *ius dicere,* meant not only to pronounce sentence and define what the law and equity embraced, but also to govern by laws and precepts, to administer justice, and to do many more things.[38] He accordingly rejected the definition handed down from the *glossa,* contending that it was neither precise nor adequate for the comprehending of all of jurisdiction.[39] His definition of jurisdiction was: "... facultas seu ius faciendi unumquemque circa ea, quae sibi tamquam

[35] Sess. XXV, *de regularibus et monialibus,* c. 20.

[36] Sess. XIV, *de reservatione casuum,* c. 7; *de ref.,* c. 5.; sess. XXIV, *de ref.,* c. 20.

[37] Sess. V, *de ref.,* c. 2; sess. XIII, *de ref.,* c. 1; sess. XXIII, *de ref.,* c. 10; sess. XXIV, *de ref.,* c. 9; sess. XXV, *de regularibus et monialibus,* c. 11, *de ref.,* c. 2.

[38] "Alii vero rectius dicunt, iurisdictionem dici a dictione iuris: dicere vero ius, esse non solum sententiam pronuntiare et definire quid ius aequitasque contineant, sed etiam legibus ac praeceptis gubernare, iustitiam administrare, atque universim personam publicam in alios, ut in sibi subditos potestatem habentem, facere circa illos quidquid pro potestate qua sibi subduntur, efficere potest."—*De Iustitia et Iure* (5 vols., Coloniae Allobrogum, 1759), Tom. V, tract. V, disp. II, n. 1.

[39] "Sane definitio iurisdictionis a glossa tradita, et a iurisperitis communiter recepta, nec apta nec cauta mihi videtur, nec omnem iurisdictionem videtur comprehendere."—*Ibid.,* n. 5.

superiori subduntur, ea omnia, ad quae munus suum superioris se extendit."[40]

Toschi (1535-1620) similarly attributed the broadest significance to jurisdiction.

> Tribus modis consideratur iurisdictio . . . circumscriptive, seu terminaliter, quia finibus certis terminatur . . . subiective, seu materialiter, ut quando certum territorium iurisdictioni subiicitur, seu iurisdictio imprimitur . . . concessive, seu realiter, ut quando privilegium alicui conceditur, quod habet iurisdictionem cum re et commoditatibus . . . Et aliquando sumitur etiam ita large, ut iurisdictio quandoque importet administrationem tutelae, et bonorum."[41]

Towards the beginning of the seventeenth century, Laymann followed the opinion of De Molina by subscribing to his definition of jurisdiction.[42] At the same time Barbosa (1589-1649), speaking of episcopal power, made the usual division of the power of orders and the power of jurisdiction. Under the power of orders he included everything which would be included by modern canonists, such as the powers to ordain, consecrate, and confirm. Under jurisdiction he included every power not belonging to the power of orders.[43]

Fagnani (1598-1678) observed that the division of power into the *lex dioecesana* and the *lex iurisdictionis* was not doctrinal and that, since it lacked scientific foundation, it should be abandoned. He then proceeded to divide general episcopal jurisdiction into three parts: "Quaedam . . . ratione ordinis, quaedam ratione iurisdictionis, et quaedam sunt simplicis dignitatis seu potestatis."[44] Therefore he used

[40] *Loc. cit.*

[41] *Practicae Conclusiones Iuris in Omni Foro Frequentiores* (3. ed., 8 vols., Lugduni, 1634), Tom. IV, concl. 541, n. 7, concl. 543, n. 23.

[42] *Theologia Moralis*, Lib. I, tract. IV, cap. V, n. 1.

[43] *De Officio et Potestate Episcopi* (Lugduni, 1628), tit. I, cap. I, nn. 9, 11, 12.

[44] *Commentaria in primum* [*-quintum*] *librum Decretalium* (5 vols.

jurisdiction in two senses, and in the stricter sense excluded the power of orders and whatever belonged to the bishop in view of his dignity.

Passerini (1595-1677), a contemporary of Fagnani, taught that jurisdiction included legislative, judicial, and coercive or executive power.

> Jurisdictio est potestas de publico introducta, concessa ei, qui juri dicendo praeest per quam potest dicere jus statuendo, sententiando, et obligando subditos ad habendum id, quod dicitur pro justo . . .[45]

In another work he identified jurisdiction with *dominium altum*, noting that it pertained only to persons, not to things.

> Cum vero dominium distinguitur in bassum, quod res corporeas respicit, et in dominium altum, quod respicit personas, earumque gubernium . . . De hoc alto dominio hic est sermo, quod est illud, quod coincidit cum jurisdictione.[46]

Pirhing (1606-1679), retaining the distinction between the powers of orders and jurisdiction, followed De Molina's definition of jurisdiction: ". . . potestas alicujus auctoritatem circa aliorum regimen seu gubernationem, prout definit Molina."[47]

The beginning of the eighteenth century found some canonists insisting on a minute qualification of terminology in respect to jurisdiction and the power of jurisdiction. Reiffenstuel (1642-1703), for example, held that when speaking of jurisdiction as the faculty for exercising jurisdiction one should term it the power of jurisdiction.[48] Reif-

in 4, Venetiis, 1709), Lib. I, *de officio ordinarii*, cap. XVIII, n. 4 (hereafter cited *Commentaria*).

[45] *De Hominum Statibus et Officiis* (3 vols., Lucae, 1732), Tom. III, q. 189, n. 644.

[46] *Commentaria in Sextum Librum Decretalium* (2 vols., Venetiis, 1698), Lib. I, *de officio et potestate iudicis delegati*, cap. XV, n. 24.

[47] *Jus Canonicum in V Libros Decretalium Distributum* (5 vols. in 4, Delingae, 1722), Lib. I, tit. XXXI, sect. I, § 1, n. 1.

[48] 'Sumitur enim hic jurisdictio, non pro actu, seu exercitio jurisdictionis; sed pro facultate, ac potentia eam exercendi . . ."—*Jus Canonicum Universum* (5 vols. in 7, Parisiis, 1864-1870), Lib. I, tit.

fenstuel gave both a general definition of jurisdiction, following De Molina's notion, and a restricted one: "Jurisdictio est potestas publica circa aliorum regimen seu gubernationem . . . Jurisdictio est potestas publica juris dicendi . . ." and in relation to the public nature of this power he said: ". . . universim omnis ille actus jurisdictionis esse censetur, qui a superiore ex publico munere ac potestate in subditos, sive quatenus persona publica est, exercetur."[49]

Schmalzgrueber (1663-1735) retained the traditional division between the power of orders and the power of jurisdiction. He also mentioned the distinction between the *lex dioecesana* and the *lex iurisdictionis*. If anything unusual could be detected from his writings, it would be that he tended to consider jurisdiction primarily as a judicial competency, and of the power of jurisdiction he stated: ". . . per quam episcopus constituitur judex et pastor ecclesiae suae."[50] While he did not establish a trend in this regard, the same tendency nevertheless was evidenced in the works of Pichler (1670-1736), F. Schmier (1680-1728), and Böckhn (1690-1752).[51]

Berardi (1719-1768) was somewhat original. After expressing the significance which jurisdiction had among the Romans, he spoke of ecclesiastical jurisdiction as embracing every faculty belonging to the Church's competence: ". . . cunctas ambitu suo complectitur quae Ecclesiae com-

XXIX, n. 5; cf. also Verano, *Juris Canonici Universi Commentarius Paratitlaris* (3 vols., Monachii, 1703-1705), Lib. I, tit. XXIX, § VII, n. 1.

49 *Ibid.*, nn. 3, 6

50 *Jus Ecclesiasticum Universum* (5 vols. in 12, Romae, 1843-1845), Lib. I, tit. XXXI, nn. 25, 27.

51 Pichler, *Ius Canonicum secundum Quinque Decretalium Titulos Explicatum* (2 vols., Ravennae, 1741), Tom. I, lib. I, tit. XXIX, n. 5 (hereafter cited *Ius Canonicum*); F. Schmier, *Jurisprudentia Canonico-Civilis* (2 vols., Venetiis, 1754), Tom. I, lib. I, tract. V, cap. I, n. 40 (hereafter cited *Jurisprudentia*); Bökhn, *Commentarius in Jus Canonicum* (3 vols., Salisburgi, et invenitur Parisiis, 1776), Tom. I, lib. I, tit. XXIX, § 1 (hereafter cited *Commentarius*).

petunt facultates."[52] At the same time, however, he held that there were some offices and ministries pertaining not to jurisdiction in either forum but rather to public worship and external care.[53]

Finally it should be noted, especially because of a startling development at the beginning of the nineteenth century, that in the last years of the eighteenth century the division of ecclesiastical power in common acceptance was still the division that looked to the power of orders and the power of jurisdiction, as Ferrante (1754-1803) testified.[54]

B. From the Nineteenth Century up to the Code

It was the nineteenth century which heralded the tripartition of ecclesiastical power. Although Devoti (1744-1820) hinted at a threefold division of episcopal power into that of orders, jurisdiction, and the *lex dioecesana,*[55] he did divide the whole power of the Church into the power of jurisdiction, which concerned the rule and administration of the Church, and the power of orders, which pertained to the sacred ministry.[56] He also used jurisdiction in the sense of *ius dicere,* under which he included the *imperium mixtum,* that is, a modicum of coercive power, so that, if a judge took cognizance of a case, defined it, but lacked the imperium for the execution of the sentence, it was properly to be considered not in the sense of *ius dicere* but simply in the sense of *iudicare,* or, in other words, the judge in that case was equipped with *notio* but not with jurisdiction.[57]

The traditional doctrine, therefore, up to the nineteenth century was that all ecclesiastical power was divided into

[52] *Commentarium in Jus Ecclesiasticum Universum* (2 vols. in 1, Mediolani, 1846), Vol I, dissert. I, cap. I, pp. 37, 38.

[53] *Ibid.,* dissert. VI, cap. IV, p. 201.

[54] *Elementa Juris Canonici* (Romae, 1854), p. 35.

[55] *Jus Canonicum Universum Publicum et Privatum* (3 vols., Romae, 1837), II, 282.

[56] *Ibid.,* I, 196.

[57] *Ibid.,* III, 14.

that of orders and that of jurisdiction, and that all power, excluding that of orders, fell under the name of jurisdiction. The canonist who incisively broke from this tradition was Phillips (1804-1872), who adopted the threefold division of orders, of jurisdiction, and of the *magisterium* or teaching power.[58]

Soglia (1779-1855) berated Phillip's doctrine and held for the traditional division, which he regarded as better suited in explanation of the nature of the Church's power. He defined jurisdiction as the *potestas iuris dicendi,* but added that the term was used broadly in signification of all that power of imperium by which the Church is ruled and governed, to which imperium pertained the making of laws, the imposing of commands, the issuing of prohibitions, the felling of judgments, and the coercing with penalties.[59]

Similarly Tarquini (1810-1874) rejected the power of the *magisterium* as a diverse division of ecclesiastical power, and held for the twofold division of orders and jurisdiction, defining jurisdiction as "... quae ad fidelium cooperationem dirigendam, et quantum fieri potest, efficaciter urgendam instituta est."[60] He also maintained that the faculty of using the power of orders depended on jurisdiction and, therefore, that one who administered the sacraments of his order without having jurisdiction acted unlawfully but validly. He made an exception for the sacrament of penance, which has the condition of jurisdiction intrinsical-

[58] "Disons d'abord que la division de la puissance ecclésiastique en ces deux éléments: *potestas ordinis* et *jurisdictionis,* n'est pas exacte, par cela seul qu'elle exclut l'enseignement ... Pareillement, tout évêque a reçu par son ordination, dans la plénitude du sacerdoce, les pouvoirs de la prêtrise, de l'enseignement et de la juridiction ..." —*Du Droit Ecclésiastique dans ses Principes Généraux* (2. ed., 3 vols., Paris, 1855), II, 99, 103; for others following this threefold division, cf. Hinschius, *System des katholischen Kirchenrechts mit besonderer Rücksicht auf Deutschland* (4 vols., Berlin, 1869-1888), I, 170.

[59] *Institutiones Juris Publici et Privati Ecclesiastici* (12. ed., 2 vols. in 1, Boscoduci, 1857), I, 138-140.

[60] *Juris Ecclesiastici Publici Institutiones* (4. ed., Romae, 1875), p. 2.

ly and essentially connected with it, so that if it were administered by one not having jurisdiction it would be not only unlawful but invalid also.[61]

Bouix (1808-1871), like others before him, rejected the division of the *lex dioecesana* and the *lex iurisdictionis*.[62] After noting that the term "jurisdiction" was used in a relatively restricted sense in Roman law, he proceeded to give his own rather lengthy descriptive definition of the ecclesiastical usage of the term.

> Aliter sonat in jure ecclesiastico jurisdictionis nomen, et ad multo plura extenditur. Ad jurisdictionem quippe refertur potestas, tum dogmata definiendi et obligandi fideles ut definitis articulis firmiter credant; tum leges ferendi de disciplina et moribus; tum causas ecclesiasticas cognoscendi, tum inferiores corripiendi, praeceptis subjiciendi et ad recte implendum munus suum adigendi; tum beneficia regendi, atque in eis beneficiatos instituendi; necnon de bonis ecclesiasticis alienatione vel variis contractibus disponendi.[63]

He continued to say that *some* authors generally included under jurisdiction everything not of the power of orders, i.e., as attached to the character received by sacred orders from divine institution.[64] It seems, however, that in his general manner and style of writing as well as through an express statement Bouix dissociated himself from those authors, and personally preferred the tripartition.[65]

Craisson († 1881) reproved Bouix not for his tripartition but for excluding from jurisdiction the power of lawfully

[61] *Ibid.*, p. 83.

[62] *De Principiis Juris Canonici* (3. ed., Parisiis, 1882), pp. 563, 564.

[63] *Ibid.*, p. 545.

[64] "Imo, aliqui auctores sub jurisdictione comprehendunt generatim omnem ecclesiasticam potestatem quae non est potestas ordinis, id est, characteri per sacram ordinationem recepto ex divina institutione alligata. In quo sensu magisterium etiam, seu docendi potestatem includit".—*Loc. cit.*

[65] "Episcopos instituit Christus ut Ecclesiam regerent per triplicem potestatem: docendi nempe seu magisterii, sanctificandi seu sacerdotii, et gubernandi seu jurisdictionis."—*Ibid.*, p. 521.

confecting and conferring the sacraments and sacramentals. He defined jurisdiction thus: "... potestas ea omnia gerendi atque gubernandi quae ad bonum Ecclesiae conservandum et promovendum pertinent," and immediately added that jurisdiction comprehended many other things: "... facultas docendi, varias benedictiones et sacramenta permittendi, bona Ecclesiarum administrandi; uno verbo, faciendo quidquid conducere valet ad bonum Ecclesiae regimen."[66]

Vecchiotti († 1870) listed five principal parts as pertaining to jurisdiction: commanding, judging, correcting, dispensing, and administering.[67] His notion of true jurisdiction included imperium.[68]

It is interesting to note the manner in which many authors phrased their various definitions of jurisdiction, either in acceptance or rejection of previous developments. Icard (1805-1893), for example, indicated his rejection of the tripartition of power by giving first place to the power of teaching in his definition of jurisdiction.[69] De Angelis (1824-1881) simply adopted the three centuries old definition of De Molina.[70] Santi († 1885) defined jurisdiction in the broad sense as "... auctoritas praeeminens in aliquos ad eorum regimen et gubernationem."[71] His definition was

[66] *Manuale Totius Juris Canonici* (5. ed., 4 vols., Pictavii, 1877), I, nn. 258-260.

[67] "... partes praecipuae sunt quinque: hoc est iubendi, iudicandi, corrigendi, dispensandi et administrandi."—*Institutiones Canonicae* (19. ed., 3 vols., Augustae Taurinorum, 1886), I, 270

[68] "... illa potestate, quae in spirituali alicuius dioecesis regimine et administratione versatur, et potestas vera iurisdictionis vocatur, quandoquidem cum imperio coniuncta est."—*Loc. cit.*

[69] "Potestas jurisdictionis est potestas publica docendi, dispensandi bona spiritualia, et regendi, in ordine ad cultum Dei et animarum salutem."—*Praelectiones Juris Canonici* (6. ed., 3 vols., Parisiis, 1886), I, 494.

[70] "... potestas publica circa aliorum regimen seu gubernationem." —*Praelectiones Juris Canonici* (5 vols. in 9, Romae-Parisiis, 1877-1891), Tom. I, par. II, p. 5.

[71] *Praelectiones Juris Canonici* (2. ed., 5 vols. in 2, Ratisbonae, Neo Eboraci et Cincinnatii, 1892), Lib. I, tit. XXIX, n. 2, p. 240.

sufficiently broad to include even dominative power under jurisdiction. Furthermore, he explicitly included the *magisterium* under the power of jurisdiction.[72] Sanguinetti (1828-1893) summed up the power of jurisdiction in two words, calling it the *potestas pascendi.*[73]

In the closing decades of the nineteenth century the tripartition of ecclesiastical power was almost universally discredited. The influence of Phillips was still strong, however, among some German authors and continued even into the present century.[74] Aichner, (1816-1911), Smith (1845-1895), and Lombardi (1858-1908) all rejected the tripartition.

Aichner made the traditional division between orders and jurisdiction, and defined the latter thus: "... ea omnia quae ad Ecclesiam recte gubernandam pertinent."[75] He also included, as a species of jurisdiction, administrative power, and maintained that the faculty to preach was referred by the doctors to jurisdiction, but to the internal forum, while the power of granting this faculty to others pertained to the external forum. Furthermore, he added that the lawful administration of the sacraments postulated the possession of jurisdiction.[76]

Smith (1845-1895) adopted the broad definition of jurisdiction, as given by Soglia, and included the *magisterium* under jurisdiction.[77] And Lombardi (1858-1908) included under jurisdiction everything not pertaining to the power of orders.[78]

[72] *Ibid.*, tit. XXXI, n. 12, p. 267.

[73] *Iuris Ecclesiastici Privati Institutiones* (Romae, 1884), p. 182.

[74] Cf. Hilling, "Die Bedeutung der *iurisdictio voluntaria* und *involuntaria* in römischen Recht und im kanonischen Recht des Mittelalters und der Neuzeit," *Archiv für katholisches Kirchenrecht,* CV, (1925), 463, 464.

[75] *Compendium Juris Canonici* (6. ed., Brixinae, 1887), pp. 66, 69.

[76] *Ibid.*, pp. 68, 69.

[77] *Elements of Ecclesiastical Law* (3 vols., Vol. I, 6. ed., New York, Cincinnati, Chicago, 1887), I, 89.

[78] "Iure vero nostro iurisdictionis nomine omnia comprehenduntur, quae ecclesia potest in ordine ad suam finem, quaeque tamen ad po-

The beginning of the present century found Wernz (1842-1914), one of the men who labored on the present codification of Canon Law, ending the speculation on the tripartition of power by including, and rightly so, the *potestas magisterii* along with the *potestas regiminis* as a species of jurisdiction. His definition of jurisdiction was one of the finest.

> Iurisdictio vero ecclesiastica est potestas publica regendi homines baptizatos directe in ordine ad sanctitatem et beatitudinem supernaturalem, a Christo vel ab Ecclesia per iniunctionem sive missionem canonicam alicui concessa.[79]

Solieri († 1928), following the idea of Berardi, formulated the following definition of jurisdiction:

> Potestas publica quae, profluens ex natura ipsa sacerdotii ex facto Christi, competit Sacerdotibus Evangelicis ad fidelium regimen et gubernationem.[80]

He subsumed *magisterium* under jurisdiction and made a further observation, somewhat similar to that of some of his predecessors: "... ubi in iure romanorum iurisdictionis vocabulum potestatis gubernatoriae partem significat; in iure ecclesiastico, dum de Ecclesiae potestate loquimur, tota gubernatoria potestas indigitatur."[81]

By way of summary for this section one may state that the term "jurisdiction" was used in two senses: in the extended and more frequent sense it meant either legislative, judicial, and coercive power, or the total ecclesiastical power of rulership, under which some authors included even the administration of goods and dominative power; in the restricted sense it meant either the *potestas iuris dicendi* or

testatem ordinis non spectant ... ius quo ecclesia pollet fideles dirigendi et moderandi sive in credendis sive in agendis, seu tum in fide tum in disciplina."—*Iuris Canonici Privati Institutiones* (2. ed., 3 vols., Romae, 1901), I, 186.

[79] *Ius Decretalium*, II (*Ius de Personis*) (3. ed., Prati, 1915), n. 3 (hereafter cited *Ius de Personis*).

[80] *Institutiones Iuris Ecclesiastici* (2. ed., Romae, 1921), p. 36.

[81] *Ibid.*, p. 37.

potestas joined with imperium. The public character of the power of jurisdiction was stressed, but the narrow definition of the *glossa* was rejected because of the element of universality attributed to the notion of jurisdiction as also because of the phrase "*de publico introducta,*" which was considered incorrect inasmuch as the Church's power, though public, comes from Christ and not from civil power.

All authors prior to the nineteenth century, when considering the entirety of ecclesiastical power, made the essential distinction between the power of orders and the power of jurisdiction. The lawful exercise of the power of orders and, in the case of the sacrament of penance, even the valid exercise thereof postulated a possession of jurisdiction.

The doctrine of the tripartition of ecclesiastical power into the power of orders, of jurisdiction, and of the *magisterium,* contrary to the classical and traditional twofold division, rose and, for all practical purposes, fell in the nineteenth century.[82] The division of episcopal power into the *lex dioecesana* and the *lex iurisdictionis,* while occasionally used, was generally rejected and seemed to fall into complete desuetude shortly before the Code.

SECTION 2. THE DIVISIONS OF JURISDICTION

Since the *lex dioecesana* and the *lex iurisdictionis* were previously dealt with in the consideration of the nature of jurisdiction, and since furthermore this particular division was generally rejected by the major commentators, there seems to be no purpose in any further treatment. In surveying the divisions which are presented, one should well keep in mind the fact that, while many authors noted that the meanings attributed to jurisdiction were certainly different in the two systems of law, Roman and ecclesiastical, the majority of them nevertheless insisted on applying the

[82] Cf. Tirado, *De Iurisdictionis Acceptione,* pp. 190-204, where he demonstrates the reduction of the magisterial power to the power of jurisdiction both from the Code itself and from the common doctrine of post-Code authors.

Roman law divisions of jurisdiction to ecclesiastical jurisdiction.

A. From the Council of Trent through the Eighteenth Century

Grégoire (1540-1617) presented three principal divisions: 1) ordinary, delegated, and conventional, the last being acquired by reason of consent; 2) ordinary or voluntary, and contentious or necessary; 3) *infima, media,* and *suprema* or *alta,* by reason of the lesser or greater power of judging that was possessed.[83]

Laymann listed four general categories of jurisdiction, which included ordinary and delegated, contentious and voluntary, ecclesiastical and civil, the imperium and simple jurisdiction. The final category reflected his subdivision of jurisdiction of the external forum, both ecclesiastical and civil, in imitation of Bartolus and Panormitanus.[84]

Pirhing, while recognizing other divisions of jurisdiction, concentrated on what he considered to be the principal division of this ecclesiastical power, namely, the division into voluntary and contentious jurisdiction. Acts such as dispensing from vows and certain oaths, legitimating, adopting, delegating, absolving from censures and sins, and administering the sacraments, were included by him under voluntary jurisdiction.[85]

Reiffenstuel adopted the four general categories presented by Laymann, namely, ecclesiastical and civil, contentious and voluntary, ordinary and delegated, simple jurisdiction and the imperium. He noted that a cleric held ordinary jurisdiction by reason of his tenure of an office, and delegated by reason of a commission received by him from another person. His distinction between simple jurisdiction and imperium was basically the same as that of his prede-

[83] *Partitiones Juris Canonici seu Pontificii in V Libros digestae* (Lugduni, 1594), Lib. V, tit. I, cap. III, n. 2.

[84] *Theologia Moralis,* Lib. I, tract. IV. cap. V, nn. 2-10.

[85] *Jus Canonicum in V Libros Decretalium Distributum,* Lib. I, tit. XXXI, sect. I, § 1, n. 2.

cessors, inasmuch as the former meant merely the power to pass a sentence, while the latter included the power to execute the sentence. Unlike many of his forerunners, however, in the division of imperium into *mixtum* and *merum*, he included in the former the execution of civil or contentious causes together with some coercive power, but to the latter he gave the significance of the power of coercion in public crimes. He added, moreover, that the Church had imperium *merum*, but not of the supreme grade which was the *ius gladii*, or capital punishment.[86]

Pontas (1638-1728) was not hindered from making valid divisions of jurisdiction by the mere fact that he was one of any number of men who were later called parochialists [*parochistae*].[87] He divided jurisdiction into ecclesiastical and civil, contentious and voluntary, and ordinary, delegated, and subdelegated.[88]

Pichler followed the four categories as adopted by Laymann and Reiffenstuel with the simple difference that he termed the power of the State secular, rather than civil, jurisdiction. Like many before him, he too subdivided ecclesiastical jurisdiction into that of the internal and that of the external forum.[89]

Böckhn was an example of the canonist who drew in-

[86] *Jus Canonicum Universum*, Lib. I, tit. XXIX, nn. 7, 8, 11, 12, 18, 19, 25.

[87] Shortly after the Council of Trent, in view of the new prominence which it accorded pastors and the parochial office, some canonists deceived themselves into believing that the parochial office was of divine institution. This erroneous doctrine continued to be taught by a few as late as the 19th century, as is indicated by the writings of Tempesti (1747-1819). In demonstration of this aberration, which was also an error of the Jansenists, Pontas is quoted: "Per verbum autem curati... intelliguntur Sacerdotes, qui curant animas, et a Christo instituti sunt tamquam septuaginta discipulorum successores."—*Dictionarium Casuum Conscientiae* (3 vols., Venetiis, 1773), III, 3.

[88] *Ibid.*, II, 401.

[89] *Jus Canonicum*, Tom. I, lib. I, tit. XXIX, nn. 5-7; the customary divisions were listed also by Schmier, *Jurisprudentia*, Tom. I, lib. I, tract. V, cap. I, nn. 41-107.

numerable fine distinctions and, as a result, made many inconsequential divisions. He presented seven principal classifications of jurisdiction: 1) *summa,* which only the Holy Father possessed, and *subalterna,* subordinate to the first and dependent on it, e.g., territorial jurisdiction had by bishops; 2) simple, which was judicial power that lacked the element of coercion, and imperium, which included coercive power; 3) proper and ordinary, and improper and extraordinary, i.e., delegated; 4) voluntary and contentious; 5) ecclesiastical and secular; 6) personal and real or patrimonial; 7) separate or private, and common or cumulative.[90]

Ferraris († 1763) listed the four usual categories of ecclesiastical and civil, voluntary and contentious, ordinary and delegated, simple jurisdiction and imperium. He divided imperium into *merum,* a jurisdiction exercised in respect to public utility, and *mixtum,* a jurisdiction exercised in respect to private utility. He also noted that one equipped with imperium was competent to proceed *ex officio* or *motu proprio,* while one having only simple jurisdiction could proceed only at the instance of the plaintiff.[91]

B. From the Nineteenth Century up to the Code

While the nineteenth century lacked, in the development of divisions of jurisdiction, the startling significance which it manifested in the consideration of the nature of jurisdiction, it produced nevertheless several new attitudes and a proposed change of terminology for one of the existing divisions.

Bouix divided ecclesiastical jurisdiction thus: that of the internal and that of the external forum, universal and particular, voluntary and contentious, and ordinary and delegated.[92] Icard differed from Bouix only by substituting

[90] *Commentarius,* Tom. I, lib. I, tit. XXIX, § 1, nn. 2-10.

[91] *Prompta Bibliotheca, Canonica, Iuridica, Moralis, Theologica, partim Ascetica, Polemica, Rubricistica, Historica* (2. ed., 8 vols., Bononiae, sed prostat Venetiis, 1752), IV, "Iurisdictio," 402, 403.

[92] *De Principiis Juris Canonici,* pp. 561-566.

immediate and mediate jurisdiction for universal and particular jurisdiction.[93]

De Angelis remained satisfied with the four major divisions of jurisdiction into ecclesiastical and civil, contentious and voluntary, ordinary and delegated, imperium and simple jurisdiction. He also made the customary distinction, when considering ecclesiastical jurisdiction, respecting the internal and the external forum.[94] A contemporary, Sanguinetti, listed the identical divisions,[95] while another contemporary, Santi, gave particular importance to only two of the divisions, namely, ordinary and delegated jurisdiction, and contentious and voluntary jurisdiction.[96]

Aichner contributed one of the more notable developments of this century after his statement that the division of jurisdiction into voluntary and contentious proved unacceptable in view of the fact that these terms had different meanings in ecclesiastical law than they had in Roman law. He proposed, therefore, that a clearer terminology for the same division would be the substitution of the words "judicial" for "contentious," and "extrajudicial" for "voluntary." He also changed the division of ordinary and delegated jurisdiction to ordinary and vicarious jurisdiction, and placed delegated along with mandated jurisdiction under the latter.[97]

Smith, in a manner reminiscent of Böckhn, made six primary divisions of jurisdiction: ecclesiastical and civil, of the internal and of the external forum, universal and particular, voluntary and contentious, ordinary and delegated, immediate and mediate. The last division applied according as the jurisdiction could be exercised at all times or merely in the case of necessity.[98]

Lombardi followed Aichner in the substitution of the

[93] *Praelectiones Juris Canonici*, I, 496.

[94] *Praelectiones Juris Canonici*, Tom. I, par. II, pp. 7-9.

[95] *Iuris Ecclesiastici Privati Institutiones*, pp. 183, 184.

[96] *Praelectiones Juris Canonici*, Lib. I, tit. XXIX, n. 2, p. 240.

[97] *Compendium Juris Canonici*, pp. 69, 70, 707 (note 6).

[98] *Elements of Ecclesiastical Law*, I, 93-96.

terms "judicial" and "extrajudicial" in place of "voluntary" and "contentious" jurisdiction. He enumerated five divisions of jurisdiction *ratione fontis, extensionis, modi residendi, finis, et modi quo exercetur,* which divisions were, respectively, jurisdiction from divine and human law, universal and particular, ordinary and delegated, of the internal and of the external forum, judicial and extrajudicial.[99]

It should be noted that during the last quarter of the last century the division of imperium and simple jurisdiction was not in vogue, and it did not regain prominence in the present century. Shortly before the Code, Solieri offered the following fourfold division of ecclesiastical jurisdiction: universal and particular, according as the jurisdiction was exercised in the whole Church or only among certain persons and within certain boundaries; contentious and voluntary, according as the exercise of the jurisdiction did or did not require a judicial process; ordinary and delegated, according as the jurisdiction was attached to an office or merely commissioned by another person; real and personal, according as the jurisdiction adhered to a dignity or to a person. He added that real jurisdiction was always ordinary and did not cease on the death of the prelate, while personal jurisdiction could never be ordinary.[100]

In recapitulation, it may be noted that in the doctrinal development regarding the divisions of jurisdiction there existed this apparent anomaly: authors noted that the acceptance of the term "jurisdiction" differed in ecclesiastical law from that in Roman law, but at the same time diligently endeavored to transpose the Roman law divisions into the realm of ecclesiastical jurisdiction. Accordingly the two divisions into ordinary and delegated jurisdiction, and voluntary and contentious jurisdiction were the most important and most common, though authors differed greatly as to the character and extent of each. Finally, more prominence than ever before was given to the division of

[99] *Iuris Canonici Privati Institutiones,* I, 190-192.

[100] *Institutiones Iuris Ecclesiastici,* pp. 39-42.

ecclesiastical jurisdiction into that of the internal and that of the external forum.

ARTICLE III. INDICATIONS OF PAROCHIAL JURISDICTION IN THE EXTERNAL FORUM

Because of the various peculiar notions of the authors, both in times past and in the present day, concerning the notion of jurisdiction in the external forum, it is altogether mandatory, in order to understand the subject, that both the concept of the external forum and the notions of jurisdiction in that forum, especially as it applied to pastors, be explored. After these fundamental considerations there is presented the often debated problem of the nature of the faculty of assisting at marriage, and finally there is offered a brief survey of the power of pastors to grant dispensations.

SECTION 1. THE EXTERNAL AND THE INTERNAL FORUM

A thorough treatment of either forum could provide adequate matter for a separate dissertation. While the present study, however, is concerned with jurisdiction in the external forum only, it would be difficult to present any idea of that forum apart from a comparison with and a definition of the internal forum.

As was previously seen, the terminology employed prior to the Council of Trent in relation to the two forums was far from being universal among the authors, the external being called judicial or contentious, the internal being called the *forum animae,* and both being called, at one time or another, penitential. Even the simple word "forum" had various meanings, the two most common of which, according to which gender was used, were the place where judgment was passed and the territory of the judge.[101]

[101] "...forus cum est masculini generis denotat locum, ubi judicium exercetur... Quando autem est generis neutri, tunc forum denotat territorium judicis..."—Panormitanus, *Commentaria,* Tom. VII, *de verborum significatione,* cap. X (*Forus*), n. 1; cf. also Sabelli, *Summa Diversorum Tractatuum* (4 vols., Venetiis, 1692), Tom. II, p. 199.

De Oliva († ca. 1650), after adverting to the usual meanings for forum, e.g., laws, territory, place of judgment, noted that under the name of forum, regardless of gender, came judgment, jurisdiction or power, and anything of a jurisdictional nature, as long as the matter under discussion left room for it.[102] He said that the concept of forum was divided principally into two parts, ecclesiastical and secular. He then subdivided the ecclesiastical forum into the external, or contentious, and the internal, or non-contentious, forum, and in turn divided the latter into the penitential or sacramental forum and the forum of conscience. Furthermore, he noted that the penitential forum could also pertain to the forum of conscience, but not *vice versa,* for there were many things that could pertain to the forum of conscience which necessarily belonged outside the penitential forum.[103]

Pirhing differed from De Oliva by restricting the penitential forum to sacramental confession. He agreed, however, in that he considered the external forum identical with the contentious forum, and stated this identification as the common doctrine of theologians and jurists. He also remarked that the external forum was customarily called the *ius fori* or *forum fori,* while the internal forum was termed the *jus poli* or *forum poli.*[104]

Van Espen (1646-1728) added little to the development of the notion of forum, although he did provide a historical note to the effect that before the eleventh or twelfth cen-

102 "Accipitur etiam hoc vocabulum (forus) seu (forum) pro judicio, jurisdictione, vel potestate... appellatione fori, si materia subjecta patitur, veniunt jurisdictionalia."—*Tractatus de Foro Ecclesiae* (Coloniae Allobrogum, 1733), par. I, q. I, n. 4.

103 *Ibid.*, nn. 5, 6, 16.

104 "... forum communiter a Theologis, et Jurisperitis distingui in forum externum sive contentiosum, et forum internum, hoc est forum poenitentiae aut conscientiae; quamvis hoc latius pateat, quam forum poenitentiae, sive Sacramentalis confessionis... Forum externum vocari solet jus fori, seu forum fori; internum jus poli, seu forum poli..."—*Jus Canonicum in V Libros Decretalium Distributum,* Lib. II, tit. II, sect. I, § 1, n. 4.

tury there seemed to be no complete separation of the internal and external forum.[105]

The eighteenth century witnessed a significant development in the concept of forum. This development is traceable, at the beginning of the century, to Pichler (1670-1736), and, toward the close of the century, to Berardi (1719-1768).

While it is true that Pichler tended to consider jurisdiction primarily as a judicial competency, he did leave room in his definition of jurisdiction for matters other than contentious ones in the external forum.[106]

F. Schmier contributed little more than the following list of the many things denotable with the term "forum":

> Forum nomen homonymum est ac... denotat locum negotiationis, contractuum, et nundinarum ... locum, in quo spectacula exhibentur ... locum, e quo spectacula videntur ... locum, in quo Jurisdictio exercetur, vel lites et negotia controversa ventilantur. In quarta et propria significatione Forum aliquando vocatur auditorium ... audientia ... jus ... jurisdictio ... tribunal competens ...[107]

Berardi withdrew from the tradition that referred jurisdiction in the external forum primarily to the judicial forum and jurisdiction in the internal forum primarily to the sacrament of penance, and maintained that the principal characteristic of each forum was the manner in which the jurisdiction exercised therein referred to the utility of the recipient. If the exercise of jurisdiction referred directly and principally to the private spiritual utility of individuals, he considered it jurisdiction in the internal forum,

[105] "Porro haec Episcoporum jurisdictio integra mansisse videtur usque ad saeculum XI aut XII quousque scilicet ipsum forum externum seu contentiosum a foro interno, et Sacramentali non fuit omnino disjunctum."—*Jus Ecclesiasticum Universum* (10 vols. in 5, Venetiis, 1769), Tom. III, par. III, tit. IV, n. 18.

[106] "Ecclesiastica alia est fori interni, quae in sacro Poenitentiae tribunali et conscientiae tantum; alia fori externi, quae extra Poenitentiae et conscientiae tribunal etiam locum habet."—*Jus Canonicum*, Tom. I, lib. I, tit. XXIX, n. 6.

[107] *Jurisprudentia*, tom. I, lib. II, tract. I, cap. III, n. 2.

even though it referred secondarily to public utility. Conversely, he held that any exercise of jurisdiction referring directly and principally to the public utility of the community was to be considered jurisdiction in the external forum.[108] As examples of jurisdiction in the internal forum he cited the following: the administering of the sacraments and sacramentals, the conducting of public prayers, the executing of documents, and the issuing of admonitions.[109] His distinction was reminiscent of that recorded by Ferraris in reference to *merum* and *mixtum* imperium.[110]

Jakob Zallinger zum Thurn (1735-1813) did not clearly indicate whether he adopted the distinction of Berardi. He simply referred jurisdiction in the external forum to laws, trials, and penalties, while he considered jurisdiction in the internal forum as being exercised over the mystical body by way of illumination of the faithful through doctrine and the perfecting of them by means of the sacraments.[111]

Bouix, on the other hand, both cited and followed Berardi's doctrine based on private or public utility.[112] De Angelis did likewise, adding that jurisdiction in the external forum pertained only to persons and their rights and not to the distribution of goods or the fulfillment of the duties of office, which were matters of administration, not jurisdiction.[113] Similarly Aichner adopted Berardi's distinction.[114]

Shortly before the Code, the state of development of this matter was succinctly given by Ojetti (1862-1932) thus:

> Forum ecclèsiasticum subdividitur in externum et internum. Forum externum respicit publicam

[108] *Commentarium in Jus Ecclesiasticum Universum,* Vol. I, dissert. I, cap. II, p. 42.

[109] *Loc. cit.*

[110] Cf. *supra,* p. 44.

[111] *Institutiones Juris Naturalis et Ecclesiastici Publici* (5 vols. in 3, Romae, 1823), III, 93.

[112] *De Principiis Juris Canonici,*. p. 561.

[113] *Praelectiones Juris Canonici,* Tom. I, par. II, pp. 7, 8.

[114] *Compendium Juris Canonici,* p. 69.

> utilitatem fidelium, seu ipsius corporis ecclesiae; internum vero ea respicit, quae ad privatam singulorum fidelium utilitatem referuntur. Internam seu conscientiae iterum vel sacramentale est... vel conscientiae simpliciter... Forum poenitentiae modo significat forum sacramentale, modo forum extra-sacramentale seu conscientiae simpliciter.[115]

Solieri noted that just as the Church took the word "jurisdiction" from Roman law and amplified its concept, so also did the Church take the word "forum" and develop its significance, and just as in Roman law the judges *passed sentence* in the forum, so also in ecclesiastical law the Church *exercised jurisdiction* or governing power in the forum.[116] He described the two forums thus:

> In interno foro iurisdictionem Ecclesia exercet quae directe et immediate et singulorum fidelium utilitatem refertur, quorum sanctificationem in individuis immediate curat, ut est facultas praedicandi Evangelium... in foro e contra externo Ecclesia iurisdictionem immediate et directe in fidelium societatem exercet, eaque mediante singulorum sanctificationem curat. Talis est facultas concedendi facultatem praedicandi.[117]

Although there were many and varied meanings of the term "forum," the common acceptance of external forum before the eighteenth century denoted the contentious or judicial forum. After the eighteenth century jurisdiction in the external forum was generally viewed as that which concerned the public utility of the faithful, while jurisdiction in the internal forum had reference to the private utility of individual members of the Church.

The current modern view is concisely stated thus:

> ... jurisdiction is divided into—jurisdiction for the external forum or that power which regulates the social actions of the faithful primarily and directly respecting the public good and having its judicial and social effects recognized *coram Eccle-*

[115] *Synopsis Rerum Moralium et Iuris Pontificii* (3. ed., 4 vols., Romae, 1909-1914), n. 2236, s.v. *Iurisdictio*.

[116] *Institutiones Iuris Ecclesiastici*, p. 37.

[117] *Ibid.*, p. 38.

sia. Jurisdiction for the internal forum is that power which regulates the moral relations of the faithful, primarily and directly respecting the private good and having its effects only *coram Deo.*
Jurisdiction for the internal forum is subdivided into—sacramental jurisdiction, if it can be exercised only within or upon the occasion of the sacrament of penance, and extra-sacramental, if it can be used outside the tribunal of penance.[118]

SECTION 2. PAROCHIAL JURISDICTION

Throughout the presentation of the opinions of prominent authors on the specific subject of parochial jurisdiction in the external forum, a point to be kept in mind is that practically every author who held a negative opinion in this regard did so because he had a strict notion either of jurisdiction or of the external forum which was totally incompatible with the idea that pastors, as pastors, could possess jurisdiction of such a nature. While these commentators almost universally spoke of parochial jurisdiction, some avoided qualifying that jurisdiction, some necessarily excluded from it any jurisdiction in the external forum as the result of their peculiar strict understanding of jurisdiction in the external forum as either complete legislative, judicial, and coercive power, or simply contentious judicial jurisdiction, and finally, some clearly stated that pastors did have some jurisdiction in the external forum. Many of the authors in denying this jurisdiction to pastors referred to canonists and theologians of times past and affirmed that that was the common opinion. If evidence to the contrary, however, could be produced in the very authors thus cited, there would be room at least for doubt whether such an opinion was really the common doctrine.

Toschi spoke of parochial jurisdiction without qualifying it:

[118] Kelly, *The Jurisdiction of the Simple Confessor,* The Catholic University of America Canon Law Studies, n. 43 (Washington, D.C.: The Catholic University of America, 1927), p. 13.

> Parochus solus habet in sua parochia iurisdictionem spiritualem . . . quia quaelibet parochia habet suum territorium separatum, et divisum, in quo non est licitum alteri parochiae aliquid facere, quia dicitur data iurisdictio distincta.[119]

It is to be noted that the spiritual jurisdiction of which he spoke did not mean jurisdiction in the internal forum, but simply ecclesiastical jurisdiction in contradistinction to civil jurisdiction.

Suarez (1548-1617) denied jurisdiction in the external forum to pastors on the basis of his understanding such jurisdiction, when he considered it in relation to pastors, as the competency to inflict censures.

> Unde sit, ut Parochi non numerentur inter eos, qui hanc potestatem ordinariam habent . . . neque etiam eorum muneri est, per se loquendo, necessaria: quia ipsi non sunt ordinarii iudices in foro exteriori."[120]

Boverio (1568-1638) was so occupied with rejecting the errors of the parochialists that he did not describe the nature of parochial jurisdiction other than to indicate its source.[121] Similarly Pignatelli († 1675) rejected the error that parochial jurisdiction came directly from God, but he professed, and rightly so, that it was instituted by God in general only, as also was episcopal jurisdiction. Furthermore, he held that parochial power was proper and ordinary, and he possibly implied, by his manner of comparing pastors with bishops, that it also extended to the external forum.[122]

119 *Practicae Conclusiones Iuris in Omni Foro Frequentiores,* Tom. VI, concl. 95, nn. 1, 7.

120 *De Censuris* (Lugduni, 1608), Disp. II, sect. II, n. 10.

121 ". . . id tamen certum est, Parochus nihil Iurisdictionis in Ecclesiae sibi commissae regimine arrogare posse, quo iure Divino immediate illis [Episcopis] collatum fuerit: sed totam eorum Iurisdictionem in specie ab Ecclesiastico iure pendere."—*Censura Paraenetica in Quatuor Libros de Republica Ecclesiastica* (Mediolani, 1621), Lib. II, cap. IX, p. 369.

122 "Addo et illud, Parochorum jurisdictionem, sicut etiam Episcoporum a Deo in genere tantum institutam esse. Quare errant quicum-

Gonzales-Tellez († after 1673) stated that pastors lacked jurisdiction in the external forum. That statement, however, taken in text and context, referred to contentious power in the external forum. While he rightly denied to pastors the power of excommunicating as well as the power of doing similar things in a judicial way, he did not thereby completely exclude all parochial power from the external forum, if this power was not in any way connected with the judicial order.[123] Another example of the same attitude was that of Reiffenstuel.[124]

Begnudelli (1644-1713) seemed to imply parochial jurisdiction in the external forum with his remark that the pastor had, in his own parish and in a certain measure, the power which the bishop had in his own diocese: "Parochus in propria Parochia habet potestatem quodammodo, quam habet Episcopus in propria Dioecesi."[125]

Petra (1662-1747), like many other authors, always spoke not only of parochial jurisdiction as being necessary for the administration of baptism, but also of the general administration of the sacraments as pertaining to the jurisdiction of the local pastor. Then, later, he said that the administration of baptism was not the exercise of jurisdiction, for otherwise, just as the absolution given by a priest lacking jurisdiction was invalid, so also would a baptism be invalid if not administered by the proper pastor.[126]

que presbyteros Parochos propriam, atque ordinariam potestatem habere negant. Sunt enim quasi parvi Episcopi, qui vere officium in suis populis presbyterorum exercent."—*Consultationes Canonicae* (11 vols. in 5, Coloniae Allobrogum, 1700), Tom. I, cons. LII, n. 2.

[123] *Commentaria in Quinque Libros Decretalium* (5 vols., Maceratae, 1756), tom. I, tit. XXXI, cap. III, n. 2.

[124] *Jus Canonicum Universum*, Lib. I, tit. XXXI, n. 29; cf. also Verano, *Juris Canonici Universi Commentarius Paratitlaris* (3 vols., Monachii, 1703-1705), Lib. I, tit. XXXI, § VIII, n. 4.

[125] *Bibliotheca Juris Canonico-Civilis Practica* (4 vols., Mutinae, 1757), III, 288 (hereafter cited *Bibliotheca*).

[126] *Commentaria ad Constitutiones Apostolicas* (5 vols., Venetiis, 1729), Tom. II, Constitutio IX Innocentii III, n. 13; *ibid.*, Tom. IV, Constitutio II Gregorii XI, n. 29; cf. De Luca, *Theatrum Veritatis*

Schmalzgrueber, at first glance, seemed to sustain the negative opinion. His words were clear that pastors lacked jurisdiction in the external forum, but the acts which he listed in exemplifying his statement manifestly indicated that he was referring to jurisdiction in a strict sense, since all the acts enumerated by him supposed not merely some jurisdiction but also a quasi-episcopal jurisdiction.[127]

F. Schmier appeared to be the first author to make the needed distinction for the upholding of the affirmative opinion. He stated that, when he denied to pastors a jurisdiction in the external forum, he precisely had in mind contentious jurisdiction, which could readily be separated from voluntary jurisdiction, and that he did not know of anyone who denied this.[128] Therefore, Schmier expressly held the affirmative view.

Before F. Schmier's death (in 1728) the trend of using jurisdiction in a broad sense in questions before the Sacred Congregation of the Council began, and it lasted for at least a century. The term "parochial jurisdiction," or its equivalent, appeared both in the questions and in the answers as referring to the administration of the sacraments and to parochial functions in general. None of these, however, aided in determining the nature of parochial jurisdiction.[129]

et Justitiae (16 vols., Coloniae Agrippinae, 1706), Lib. II, disc. XXIII, nn. 7, 15, 19.

[127] *Jus Ecclesiasticum Universum,* Lib. I, tit. XXXI, n. 40.

[128] "Et licet *in cap. 6, n. 116,* Parochis Jurisdictionem in foro externo negaverim; studiose tamen Jurisdictionis Contentiosae memini, quae quod a Voluntaria separari potest, neminem scio, qui inficietur." —*Jurisprudentia,* Tom. I, lib. I, tract. V, cap. VIII, n. 47.

[129] S.C.C. *Ulixbonen. Occidentalis,* 21 nov. 1721—*Thesaurus Resolutionum Sacrae Congregationis Concilii* (167 vols., Romae, 1718-1908), II, 105 (hereafter cited *Thes. Resol.*); *Melevitana,* 21 maii 1735—*Thes. Resol.,* VII, 57; *Mileten.,* 28 ian. 1747—*Thes. Resol.,* XIII, 5; *Bononien.,* 10 iul. 1790—*Thes. Resol.,* LIX, 128; Ravennaten., 13 iun. 1789—*Thes. Resol.,* LVIII, 130; *Bovinen.,* 27 maii 1820—*Thes. Resol.,* LXXX, 156; *Ordinis Praed.,* 24 ian. 1846—*Thes. Resol.,* CVI, 38.

Pope Benedict XIV (1740-1758), when considering the external forum in relation to pastors, had in mind the power to inflict an excommunication and he accordingly denied such jurisdiction to pastors. It seems manifest that he had no intention of excluding all jurisdiction in the external forum; rather, he seemed concerned merely with refuting a contrary thesis to the effect that pastors could excommunicate.[130]

Rechiusi († ca. 1764) made what seemed to be a rather isolated distinction. After speaking of parochial jurisdiction as necessary for the exercise of parochial functions, he stated that parishes were divided into mother and filial, or jurisdictional and non-jurisdictional, with jurisdiction in the external forum being attributed to the former and jurisdiction in the internal forum only being attributed to the latter.[131]

Giraldi (1692-1775) vehemently denied that pastors possessed jurisdiction in the external forum. Anyone, if he held the same notion of the external forum that Giraldi held, would have had to agree with him, because he identified the external with the contentious forum.[132]

Nardi (1777-1837) indeed admitted that pastors had specific rights, but he has been accused of denying them any jurisdiction whatsoever.[133] He could easily be exonerated, however, from this accusation on the basis of holding a strict notion regarding jurisdiction. Furthermore, the practice of understanding the unmodified noun "*iurisdictio*" as jurisdiction in the external forum was prevalent in his time.[134]

[130] *De Synodo Dioecesana* (3 vols., Romae, 1783), Tom. I, lib. V, cap. IV, n. 2.

[131] *Tractatus de Re Parochiali* (Romae, 1773), Par. I, tit. II, nn. 27, 28, 30.

[132] *Expositio Juris Pontificii* (2 vols., Romae, 1769), I, 105.

[133] "Il Parroco può avere ed ha dei *jus;* ma non ha, e non può avere giurisdizione. Ogni uffizio ha i suoi *jus*, benchè non abbia giurisdizione."—*Dei Parrochi, Opera di Antichità Sacra e Disciplina Ecclesiastica* (2 vols., Pesaro, 1829, 1830), I, 404.

[134] "Quando autem ponitur absolute vox jurisdictio, intelligitur ex-

Bouix asserted the negative opinion in accord with his understanding of jurisdiction in the external forum as implying legislative, judicial, and coercive power.

> Jurisdictionis fori externi vocabulo intelligi solet potestas legitima subditos praeceptis et legibus gubernandi, eosque puniendi, atque tribunal ad causas processu publico excutiendas et definiendas erigendi . . .[135]

Therefore, he considered all pastoral acts, with the exception of the act of hearing confessions, as mere administration.[136] In consequence of a similar understanding of jurisdiction in the external forum, De Angèlis stated that pastors, when participating in the pastoral jurisdiction of the bishop, had jurisdiction for the administration of sacred things, but lacked jurisdiction in the external forum.[137]

Santi recognized the existence of jurisdiction in the external forum in respect to pastors, though he stated that with reference to the common law their ordinary jurisdiction pertained properly and directly to the internal forum.[138]

Towards the end of the nineteenth century two Spanish co-authors implied that pastors had jurisdiction in the external forum by their almost poetic comparison of papal, episcopal, and parochial power. The substance of their analogy was that, like the Pope over the Church Universal, so the bishop had jurisdiction over his diocese, with all the papal rights of supremacy duly honored, and like the bish-

terni fori."—Bouix, *Tractatus de Parocho* (3. ed., Parisiis, 1880), p. 137.

[135] *Tractatus de Parocho*, p. 137. This view was held also by Berengo, *Enchiridion Parochorum seu Institutiones Theologicae Pastoralis* (2. ed., Venetiis, 1877), pp. 25, 26.

[136] *Ibid.*, pp. 218, 219.

[137] *Praelectiones Juris Canonici*, Tom. II, par. II, pp. 42, 43.

[138] "Hodierno autem jure parochiale munus revera ordinariam dicit jurisdictionem, eam nempe quae dispositione ipsa juris acquiritur et censetur adnexa ipsi officio. Haec vero jurisdictio spectato jure communi forum internum proprie et directe respicit . . . censuras aut poenas publica in forma judiciali non fert, nec ab illis absolvit, quamvis hanc potestatem ex consuetudine vel ex privilegio posset adipisci." —*Praelectiones Juris Canonici*, Lib. I, tit. XXXI, n. 195, p. 348.

op in his diocese, so the pastor had jurisdiction in his parish, with all the superior episcopal rights left intact. The remainder of the comparison follows:

> El obispo tiene territorio proprio con personas y cosas que le están sometidas en razón de su oficio y beneficio: también el párroco. El obispo tiene los dos sacramentos de su especial administración (confirmación y orden), el párroco tiene el sacramento del bautismo solemne y el del matrimonio, en el cual su intervención es de necesidad. Tiene cancelaría ó archivo parroquial... Tiene facultades especiales en materia graciosa.[139]

Aichner mentioned that the pastor had the *cura animarum,* or a jurisdiction, which was ordinary and proper but subordinated to the bishop. Thereupon he designated as common the opinion that the pastor had no jurisdiction in the external forum. In its behalf he cited both Pope Benedict XIV and Schmalzgrueber.[140]. When one adverts to the notion of the two authors just cited on this subject, however, one will recall that they both supported a very restricted interpretation with reference particularly to contentious and judicial jurisdiction. Aichner himself relegated even administration to the realm of jurisdiction, and consequently he must have admitted that pastors had jurisdiction in the external forum in a broad sense.

Wernz held that the exercise of parochial power did not pertain to the external forum, inasmuch as jurisdiction in the external forum necessarily entailed an exercise of legislative, judicial, or coercive power.

> ...potestas parochorum non est fori *externi.* Nam vera iurisdictio fori externi *proxime* et *directe* refertur ad promovendum bonum *commune* per exercitium quoddam *perfectum* iurisdictionis scl. potestatis legislativae, iudicialis, coercitivae etiam per censuras et poenas graves... parochi *ex officio externa* et *publica* possunt dare praecepta (vetitum matrimonii) aut investigare (in exa-

[139] Gómez de Salazar-de la Fuente, *Lecciones de Disciplina Eclesiástica* (3. ed., 2 vols., Madrid, 1880), I, 206-208.

[140] *Compendium Juris Canonici,* pp. 423, 424.

> mine sponsorum de impedimentis) aut moderate coercere discolos; item ex missione canonica exercent *publicum* magisterium et iurisdictionem quandam *voluntariam.* Ergo potestas parochorum licet vera perfectaque iurisdictio fori *externi* non sit, tamen est potestas quaedam *oeconomica* vel domestica in parochiam ut societatem *imperfectam,* quae praeter iurisdictionem fori poenitentialis *administrationem* quoque vere *externam* habet adnexam.[141]

Wernz referred, however, to the disagreement on the subject of parochial jurisdiction in the external forum, and wisely remarked that this controversy pertained more to terminology than to the substance of the matter.[142]

Laurentius (1861-1927) stated that the pastor did have an imperfect power of jurisdiction in the external forum.[143] He also contended that the power which is called "economic" was actually a power of jurisdiction in the external forum, but certainly an imperfect one.

> "... quaedam praecepta dare, morum disciplinam urgere, voluntariam quandam iurisdictionem assistendo matrimoniis, fidem faciendo documentis ex libris parochialibus extractis vi officii exercere parochi valent, qui actus sunt potestatis oeconomicae in parochiam et imperfectam potestatem fori externi indicant.[144]

In summary, it is to be pointed out that the contention which supports as common among the pre-Code authors the opinion which denied to pastors a jurisdiction in the external forum is simply false, unless such jurisdiction be understood in a restricted sense of judicial jurisdiction or of the full power of rulership comprehending legislative,

[141] *Ius de Personis,* n. 828.

[142] "... quare haec controversia potius videtur spectare ad *terminologiam* magis minusve aptam, quam ad substantiam rei."—*Ibid.,* note 56.

[143] "Iurisdictio parochi est fori interni et modo tantum imperfecto fori externi, quia potestas legislativa, iudiciaria, coercitiva ei non competit."—*Institutiones Iuris Ecclesiastici* (Friburgi Brisgoviae, 1903), p. 165.

[144] *Ibid.,* pp. 165, 166.

judicial, and coercive power. That no author denied to pastors an imperfect power in the external forum, which modern authors are wont to designate with a variety of names, is evident both from the lack of any express contrary evidence and from the consideration that many parochial acts would necessarily have been excluded from the pastor's power if he had not possessed some jurisdiction in the external forum.

SECTION 3. THE FACULTY OF ASSISTING AT MARRIAGE

With the decree *Tametsi* the Council of Trent enacted the first universal law of the Church requiring that marriage take place in the presence of the pastor as a condition affecting the contract's validity.[145] A later decree, issued in 1907 and known as *Ne temere,* limited the meaning of pastor to the local pastor.[146]

The function of assisting at marriage is a right or faculty of exercising the office of a qualified witness. The question, therefore, is resolved into whether such a faculty or right is a social power properly understood.

Sanchez (1550-1610) argued that it was not an act of jurisdiction, and stated that in line with the more probable opinion the act of giving to another the permission to assist was likewise not the exercise of jurisdiction.[147] He also observed that such assistance was not the exercise of the power of orders, but simply the certified testifying of a person having the necessary dignity. He did admit, however, that a contrary opinion existed, which considered the delegating of this faculty to be the exercise of jurisdiction.[148]

Laymann considered only the act of delegating the faculty to assist at marriage as being an act of jurisdiction,

[145] Sess. XXIV, *de ref. matr.*, c. 1.

[146] S.C.C., 2 aug. 1907—*Fontes*, n. 4340.

[147] *De Sancto Matrimonii Sacramento Disputationum Libri Tres* (3 vols. in 1, Venetiis, 1726), Lib. III, disp. XXI, nn. 4, 7.

[148] *Ibid.*, disp. XIX, n. 11.

not the act of assistance itself.[149] Similarly Barbosa attempted to prove that the pastor of domicile, and not the pastor of origin, was the proper pastor for marriage. In so doing he referred to the jurisdiction necessary for the administration of the sacraments. Still, in view of many decrees of the Sacred Congregation of the Council, especially those of March 12, 1593, and July 31, 1617, which declared valid the assistance at marriage given by a suspended or excommunicated pastor, he finally concluded that neither the act of assistance was of a jurisdictional character, nor the delegation thereof, adding that the latter was at least not an act of contentious jurisdiction.[150]

Spada (1597-1675) asserted the opposite opinion concerning the act of assistance, claiming that the pastor did exercise ecclesiastical jurisdiction in that act.[151]

De Oliva, on the other hand, took the negative view and proposed that the pastor assisting at marriage exercised no voluntary jurisdiction and that the assistance was required of him only as a public person.[152] Likewise Fagnani denied that the act of assistance partook of the nature of jurisdiction, and held the same for the act of delegation. He believed that the pastor's presence pertained no more to jurisdiction than the presence of the other witnesses. In reference to the act of delegation, he explained that the pastor's permission was a mere faculty, while the authority to assist came from the Council of Trent, although the pastor's permission was still necessary. He argued from the Council's terminology to the effect that a marriage could

[149] *Theologia Moralis*, Lib. V, tract. X, cap. IV, n. 5.

[150] *De Officio et Potestate Parochi* (Lugduni, 1665), Cap. XXI, nn. 36, 58, 63.

[151] "Et cum Parochus in illo actu exercet jurisdictionem spiritualem, necesse est, quod sciat se posse illam exercere, et esse remotum impedimentum..."—*Consilia* (3 vols., Parmae, 1720), Tom. II, cons. 149, n. 9.

[152] "Parochus assistens matrimonio... jurisdictionem aliquam voluntariam non exercet... sed tantum assistentiam ejus requiri tamquam persona publica..."—*Tractatus de Foro Ecclesiae*, Par. III, q. X, n. 2.

take place before another priest with the *permission* of the pastor, instead of before another priest *delegated* by the pastor.[153]

De Luca (1614-1683) clearly termed the pastor's function an act of voluntary jurisdiction.

> . . . Parochus loci . . . juridice se opponere potest, ne alter Parochus in ejus Territorio crucem erigat, aliasque jurisdictionales peragat functiones, dum sacramentum matrimonii est actus voluntariae jurisdictionis.[154]

Begnudelli also considered it an act of jurisdiction.[155]

Schmalzgrueber stated that neither was the assistance an act of jurisdiction, nor was there any transfer of jurisdiction when there was delegated the permission to assist.[156]

F. Schmier proposed the question whether such an act of assistance on the part of the pastor fell within the category of voluntary jurisdiction. His solution, as follows, was in the affirmative:

> . . . ex sententia D. Braun . . . qui verius esse, scribit, eamdem assistentiam ad Jurisdictionem Voluntariam referri posse: cum non minus illa in Matrimonio, quam praesentia Judicis in emancipatione v.g. ita requiritur, ut, si desit, Matrimonium valore destituatur. Quae ipsa ratio et me in hanc tradit sententiam; hoc unico adnotato, quod illa assistentia, non ut alii actus Jurisdictionis Simplicis, a quocumque Parocho, sed solum *a proprio* exhiberi debeat per Trid. sess. 24, cap. 1.[157]

Pope Benedict XIV invented the classic phrase that describes the nature of assistance at marriage. He said that

[153] *Commentaria,* Lib. IV, *de clandestina desponsatione,* cap. II, nn. 39-47.

[154] *Theatrum Veritatis et Justitiae,* Lib. II, Suppl. *de Parochis,* disc. XLI, n. 6.

[155] "Parochus potest assistere matrimonio suorum Parochianorum, quamvis non sit Sacerdos, quia assistentia non est actus ordinis, sed jurisdictionis."—*Bibliotheca,* III, 285.

[156] *Jus Canonicum Universum,* Lib. IV, tit. III, n. 210.

[157] *Jurisprudentia,* Tom. I, lib. I, tract. V, cap.VIII, nn. 45, 46.

the pastor assisted as the witness capable of approving the marriage in the name of the Church in these words: "... tamquam testis auctorizabilis pro ecclesia."[158]

During the period of the next one hundred years there was little discussion of the matter, and in the decades immediately preceding the Code the negative opinion, in regard both to assistance and to the delegation thereof, constituted the more acceptable doctrine.

Aichner held that assistance at marriage was not an act of jurisdiction.[159] Similarly, Wernz declared that it was an exercise neither of the power of orders nor of the power of jurisdiction.[160]

Gasparri (1852-1934) bore witness both to the legislation of the Council of Trent and to the jurisprudence of his day.

> Juxta relatum decretum Tridentinum parochus ... assistens matrimonio ... non est minister ipsius contractus et sacramenti, nec, dum assistit contractui, exercet ullam potestatem aut ordinis aut jurisdictionis; sed assistit tamquam testis qualificatus, *auctorizabilis,* ut aiunt, pro Ecclesia, seu testis, cui Ecclesia fidem habet.[161]

He held, therefore, that in assisting at marriage the officiating pastor did not exercise any power either of orders or of jurisdiction. He also declared that the act of delegating permission to assist was not an act of jurisdiction.[162]

Laurentius seemed to stand alone in holding the contrary opinion. He expressly labeled the act of assistance as jurisdiction by enumerating it among the acts in the external

[158] *De Synodo Dioecesana,* Tom. III, lib. XIII, cap. XXIII, n. 6.

[159] *Compendium Juris Canonici,* p. 641.

[160] *Ius Decretalium,* IV (*Ius Matrimoniale*) (2. ed., Prati, 1911), n. 182.

[161] *Tractatus Canonicus de Matrimonio* (3. ed., 2 vols., Parisiis, 1904), II, n. 1044.

[162] "... concessio hujus licentiae non est actus jurisdictionis ecclesiasticae parochi aut Ordinarii, sed est actus potestatis substituendi, quam testis auctoritativus habet a Concilio [Tridentino]."—*Ibid.,* n. 1124.

forum for the performance of which the pastor was competent.[163]

From the weight of the testimony presented, though somewhat divided, but even more from the very nature of the act, it should be concluded that prior to the Code the act of assistance at marriage was not regarded as an act of jurisdiction. A social power is a subjective right of efficaciously establishing or determining something and of guiding subjects to the attainment of the end of society. But the official act of a qualified witness cannot be considered an exercise of power properly so called, since the notion of any person's determinative attainment of the end of society is difficult to verify in the act of assisting at marriage.[164]

SECTION 4. THE POWER OF DISPENSING

Time and time again history reveals instances wherein the pattern of the law finally became equated with practices which had existed for years. In these cases the law simply brought canonical recognition to reasonable practices which had become customs. That is the story on the side of pastors with reference to their ultimate legal acquisition of dispensatory powers. Since, as all authorities admitted, dispensing from a law pertained to the sphere of jurisdiction just as much as did the making of the law, there can be no doubt that the exercise of the pastor's powers of dispensing reflects acts of jurisdiction, and often in the external forum. The pastor's dispensatory powers, which are attached to his office, and therefore ordinary,[165] are the following: to dispense individuals from the precepts of fast, of abstinence, and of the observance of the feast days, from marriage impediments under certain conditions, and from the interpellations required for the valid use of the Pauline privilege.[166] With the exception of the last men-

[163] *Institutiones Iuris Canonici*, p. 165.

[164] Cf. Tirado, *De Iurisdictionis Acceptione*, pp. 216-221.

[165] Can. 197, § 1.

[166] Cans. 1245, § 1; 1043-1045; 1125.

tioned power, which became an ordinary power for all pastors only with the promulgation of the Code, these powers were commonly and almost universally recognized long before 1918.

It would not serve the purpose of this dissertation to present either a historical outline of the divers obligations subjected to the possibility of a pastor's act of dispensation or to marshal for an inspection the pertinent writings of all the authors. Just a few commentators are here cited in corroboration of the above made statements.

Sanchez pointed out that pastors were able, by reason of long-standing custom, to dispense from the observance of feasts and from the fast,[167] while Barbosa specifically added that the power of dispensing from the obligation to abstain from servile work obtained on the condition that recourse to the bishop or his vicar could not be had.[168]

The fact that the earlier writers generally referred only the abstention from servile work to the observance of feasts led Pirhing to mention that assistance at Mass was also included.[169] Furthermore, a debate on another point in the earlier periods of the development of this custom induced Schmalzgrueber to add that the pastor could exercise these powers even in the presence of the bishop.[170]

Böckhn indicated that the exercise of these powers of dispensing reflected acts of jurisdiction in the external forum, although he maintained, in line with his restricted notion of such jurisdiction, that in virtue simply of their office pastors were incapable of exercising jurisdiction in the external forum properly so called.

> Demum de Parochis asserimus, solum pro foro interno quoad tribunal Poenitentiae, ac sacramenta

[167] "Item quia etsi ex consuetudine possint [parochi] dispensare in festis et in ieiuniis . . ."—*Opus Morale in Praecepta Decalogi* (2 vols., Lugduni, 1661-1669), Tom. I, lib. IV, cap. XXXIX, n. 25.

[168] *De Officio et Potestate Parochi*, Cap. XVI, n. 6.

[169] *Jus Canonicum*, Lib. I, tit. XXXI, sect. V, n. 140.

[170] *Jus Ecclesiasticum Universum*, Lib. I, tit. XXXI, n. 40; cf. also Reiffenstuel, *Theologia Moralis*, Tom. II, tract. X, dist. II, n. 77.

> administranda jurisdictionem ordinariam ipsos aliis exclusis habere . . . non vero jurisdictionem proprie dictam pro foro externo: licet ex consuetudine vel benigna interpretatione propter frequentem necessitatem Parochis omnes ferme jus tribuant dispensandi in jejunio, et quoad opera servilia diebus festis ob gravem causam.[171]

Bouix considered all the previously mentioned powers, with the possible exception of the power to dispense from the obligation of assisting at Mass, and declared as the common doctrine that pastors had these powers.[172]

The foundation for the pastor's participation in the power of granting matrimonial dispensations was laid relatively late in history by the decree of 1889 from the Sacred Congregation of the Holy Office declaring that a certain faculty given to all ordinaries the year before could be subdelegated to pastors.[173] The decree of the year before granted to all ordinaries the faculty of dispensing the sick, in danger of death and when time did not permit recourse to the Holy See, from matrimonial impediments, even public ones, except the ones arising from the order of Priesthood and from affinity in the direct line when it had its origin in lawful intercourse.[174]

All this was reconfirmed and extended, by a later decree from the Sacred Congregation of the Sacraments, to any priest assisting at the marriage of persons in danger of death when the pastor or ordinary, or their delegate, could not be reached.[175] In general, the decrees of the years following 1889 tended to widen these powers, now for pastors,

[171] *Commentarius*, Tom. I, lib. I, tit. XXXI, § 2, n. 73.

[172] *Tractatus de Parocho*, pp. 509, 510.

[173] S.C.S. Off., litt. encycl. 1 mart. 1889—*Acta Sanctae Sedis* (41 vols., Romae, 1865-1908), XXI (1888-1889), 696 (hereafter cited *ASS*); *Fontes*, n. 1113.

[174] S.C.S. Off., litt. encycl. 20 febr. 1888—*ASS*, XX (1887-1888), 543; *Fontes*, n. 1109.

[175] *Acta Apostolicae Sedis, Commentarium Officiale* (Romae, 1909-), I (1909), 468, 469 (hereafter cited *AAS*); *Fontes*, n. 2097.

now for any priest, until the Code gave the definitive determination noted above.[176]

[176] S.C.S. Off., 23 apr. 1890—*ASS*, XXVI (1893-1894), 385-387; *Fontes*, n. 1121; S.C.C., 2 aug. 1907—*ASS*, XL (1907-1908), 523-530; *Fontes*, n. 4340; S.C. de Sacramentis, *Venetiarum*, 16 aug. 1909—*AAS*, I (1909), 656; *Fontes*, n. 2099; S.C. de Sacramentis, *Romana et aliarum*, 29 iul. 1910—*AAS*, II (1910), 650; *Fontes*, n. 2102; S.C. de Sacramentis, 31 ian. 1910—*AAS*, VIII (1916), 36, 37; *Fontes*, n. 2114.

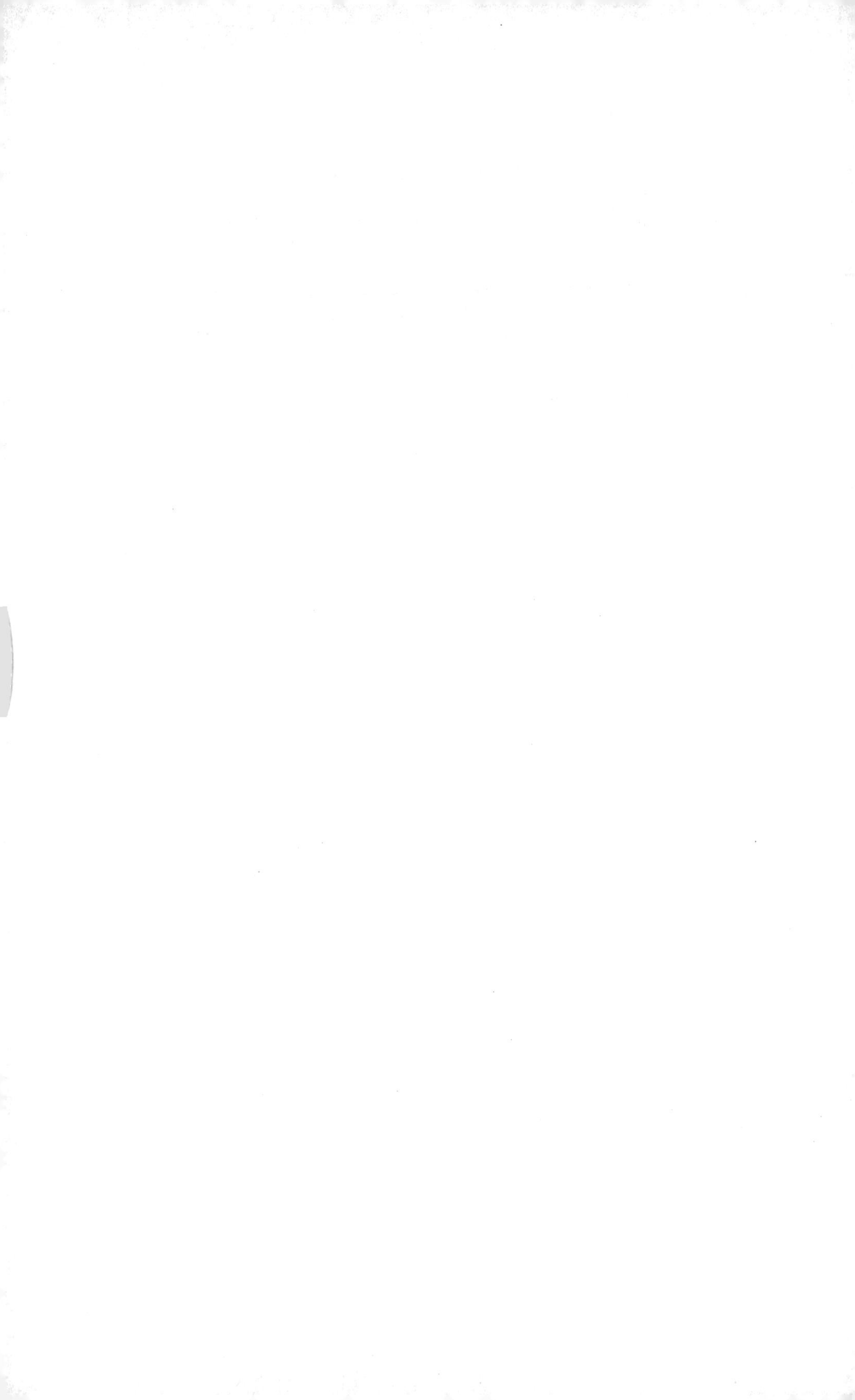

PART II
CANONICAL COMMENTARY

INTRODUCTION

It often happens that when words are understood in different meanings and thus give rise to controversies, the discord that is thought to be present concerning the matter is actually a question only of name or nomenclature. Perhaps it is thus with the term "jurisdiction." In theology the term has several meanings; in canon law it has many more.

The problem of the term's canonical usage can be simply reduced to whether the notion of jurisdiction in canon law today corresponds to that broad significance which was commonly retained before the Code. The answer seems to be in the affirmative for two reasons: a) many men labored on the codification, so that the opinions prevailing as most common among them held sway, and b) nowhere does the Code formally define jurisdiction, and much less does it give any indication that the meaning has been changed.

The bare appraisal from the principles of philosophy would give little indication of the true concept of ecclesiastical jurisdiction, whether in view of the divergent uses of the term or whether because of the particular pre-eminence of its nature when considered as the spiritual power that it is. Therefore, recourse is had to speculative theology. This is done in the first chapter. Thereupon the very concept of forum is explored as antecedent to the notion of jurisdiction and of the powers related to it in the Code. And then, after the necessary principles of jurisdiction and forum have been established, the final chapter attempts to realize the original intention of this treatise, namely, to demonstrate the propriety and validity of the expression "jurisdiction of pastors in the external forum," and to secure a firmer grasp of its concept.

Many controversies connected with the notion regarding jurisdiction but lying beyond the limits of this work's objective can be considered only incidentally. Furthermore, several reflections appearing in the historical synopsis served only as general background, are now no longer of consequence, and hence may be dismissed.

CHAPTER III

THEOLOGICAL NOTIONS OF JURISDICTION

Jurisdiction is one of the two essentially distinct hierarchical powers. The theologian alone can give the word "hierarchy" its highest meaning. He does not use it indiscriminately for any subordination of powers. The hierarchy, in its most general sense, is in his eyes a sacred principate comprising several co-ordinated degrees and endowed with power and knowledge to lead a multitude to union with and likeness to God. The hierarchy is thus defined by its essential principles (*ordo, scientia, actio*) and by its end (*ad Deum unitas et similitudo*).[1]

ARTICLE I. THE CONCEPT OF HIERARCHY

> The hierarchy is *mysterious* and, as such, an object of faith, in so far as it is a dispenser of divine grace and truth, and in so far as it is the instrumental cause of the Body of Christ which is the Church. But it is also *miraculous*, and, as such, observable, inasmuch as in the turmoil and confusion of the world it communicates a constancy, a persistence, to all that we can see of the Church—a constancy of doctrine and of practice which the laws that preside over the evolution of human societies cannot sufficiently explain.[2]

While Christ was on earth, He acted upon man both *from a distance*, by scattering His graces far and wide, and *by contact*, the more intimate way, whereby Christ communicated grace by touching man. In fact, human nature is

[1] St. Thomas Aquinas, *Opera Omnia* (34 vols., ed. L. Vivès, Parisiis, 1871-1880), Vol. VIII (1873), *Commentum in Quattuor Libros Sententiarum*, in II, dist. 9, q. 1, a. 1.

[2] Journet, *The Church of the Word Incarnate*, Vol. I, *The Apostolic Hierarchy* (translated by A. H. C. Downes, London and New York: Sheed and Ward, 1955), p. 21 (hereafter cited *The Apostolic Hierarchy*). The writer has used this excellent work extensively in this first chapter. Journet's thoughts pertaining to jurisdiction appear in condensed form with commentary added.

wounded and it needs a sensible stimulus to awaken it connaturally to the life of grace; therefore, it requires the action of Christ by sensible contact. Surely the now ascended Christ is not restricted to action from a distance. Before He left men He willed that always there would be among them certain ones given divine powers, by whom His action initiated from heaven might be sensibly conveyed to all and continue to reach men in the only way connatural to them, a direct contact. In this consist the two hierarchical powers, the essentially ministerial or transmitting powers, of orders and jurisdiction.

The divine power is certainly not confined to the use of visible instruments. And though the least beings in the universe are directly present to God, He has chosen nevertheless to rule them by a chain of created intermediaries; below the First Cause exist genuine secondary causes.

> God has chosen to endow creatures not only with being and the perfection by which they exist, but also with the causative virtue and the perfection by which they act.[3]

For this reason there is a visible hierarchy.

Christ acts on His Church in two ways. By a hidden influx from within, He mysteriously communicates the life of grace; from without, He teaches the ways of truth. From this twofold action of Christ comes the distinction of the two hierarchical powers, the power of orders and that of jurisdiction, which differ in their purpose, in their nature, and in the mode of their transmission. The power of orders, serving to bring redemptive virtue to souls, is a participation of the *priesthood* of Christ and, being physical, is normally conferred by way of a consecration. The power of jurisdiction, serving for the external preaching of the Christian truth, both speculative and practical, is a participation of the *kingship* of Christ and, being moral, is normally conferred by way of injunction or commission.

There is then but one hierarchy, with two distinct and interdependent powers.

[3] Journet, *op. cit.*, p. 18.

> There are two essentially distinct hierarchical powers: that of order conferred by consecration and consequently not able to be lost, and that of jurisdiction, conferred by designation and so capable of being lost. But these two powers do not make two hierarchies. It is merely by inadvertence that we speak of a "hierarchy of order" and a "hierarchy of jurisdiction." The power of order and the power of jurisdiction are interdependent. They are the two halves of a single hierarchy.[4]

God normally awakens supernatural life in souls by the power of orders, which corresponds to the power of jurisdiction, whereby God normally shows the souls which way to go. Both powers are necessary, the one to give sanctifying grace the fullness of its being and vigor, the other to direct and specify it.

> It [hierarchy] is there already with the first degrees of the power of order. It reaches completion in the bishops, in whom resides the plenitude of the power of order, and who possess permanent jurisdiction by ordinary and proper title. It is finally consummated in the Bishop of Rome, in whom alone resides permanent universal jurisdiction. The ministers of lower rank, and the priests, belong to the hierarchy, but their powers are incomplete and dependent; the two permanent powers of the hierarchy, those of order and of jurisdiction, are fully reunited only in the body apostolic directly constituted by the Pope and the bishops.[5]

Article II. The Concept of Jurisdiction

In the Church the priesthood of Christ is participated in only in a purely instrumental manner. The power of orders,

[4] Journet, *op. cit.*, p. 493.

[5] Journet, *op. cit.*, p. 25. The term "permanent" is used here in contradistinction to *apostolic* or *extraordinary* jurisdiction. The latter refers to the special powers given to the Apostles, the first depositaries of the transmittible or permanent jurisdiction. Extraordinary jurisdiction was necessary for the foundation of the Church, but permanent jurisdiction suffices for its conservation.

the ministers of the sacraments, and the sacraments themselves are purely external *instruments* used by Christ as mere transmitters of impulses coming from Him. However, it is somewhat different with His kingship.

> Jesus is the fountain-head of a universal kingship, and He never ceases to exercise it from heaven where He sits at the right hand of the Father. And yet, so that men might not be deprived of the help His living voice had brought them, He has in His mercy left them a visible power, continuing to speak with authority in His name—the power of jurisdiction.[6]

SECTION 1. ITS NATURE

Proposing to minds a speculative or a practical message from without is a work more connatural to men, and one in which they can have a greater share in the initiative. The interior influx of grace can be transmitted by ministers as instruments only, but the exterior government of the Church can be communicated to the ministers as *second causes*.

The efficient cause may be divided into instrumental cause and principal cause. The latter may be subdivided into first cause and second cause. With this distinction can be seen the precise difference between the operations of the powers of orders and jurisdiction. The instrumental cause and the second cause have this in common: they act only when moved by a superior agent. But the motion of the higher agent serves only to bring into action the second cause, whereby the latter then undertakes to act of itself and produces an effect of the same order as itself. The motion of the superior agent, in the case of a mere instrument, is not assimilated and elaborated, but simply transmitted, so that the effect identically conforms to the purpose of the superior agent and is always better than the instrument.

Therefore, while the powers of orders and jurisdiction

[6] Journet, *op. cit.*, p. 125.

are both ministerial causes, and while the power of orders is the more excellent, the depositaries of jurisdiction, with certain initiatives and responsibilities, act as *second causes* rather than as mere conveying instruments. The seeming disadvantage of giving men the privilege of being second causes is that their natural fallibility in proportion to the importance of their office would tend to enter the government of the Church. This contingency, however, is amply provided for with the particular providence of divine assistance: "... and behold, I am with you all days, even unto the consummation of the world."[7]

> Christ is the Head, the Ruler, the Foundation of the Church as Priest-Savior and as King. As Priest-Savior He is so to the exclusion of all others, and men are never in this respect anything but instruments, mere transmitters. As King, He is so in participation with others whom in His love He makes His associates. But in Him the title is primary, universal, permanent; in the others it is derived, restricted and temporary.[8]

A power is a potency endowed with pre-eminence and with authority to act.[9] Therefore, the power of spiritual jurisdiction, in consideration of its generic end, may be generally defined as the power of authoritatively proposing to men what is needed to bring them to eternal beatitude. More specifically, it is the active potency whereby a man authoritatively acts as a principal second cause in directing the faithful to their end.

SECTION 2. ITS DIVISIONS

Journet proposes four major divisions of the power of jurisdiction after setting aside the secondary divisions to which canonists have recourse.[10] The first is "formal,"

[7] Matt., XXVIII, 20.

[8] Journet, *The Apostolic Hierarchy*, p. 126.

[9] St. Thomas Aquinas, *Opera Omnia*, Vol. XI (1874), *Commentum in Quattuor Libros Sententiarum*, in IV, dist. 24, q. 1, a.1, quaest. 2, ad 3: "Potestas autem proprie nominat potentiam activam cum aliqua praeeminentia."

[10] *The Apostolic Hierarchy*, pp. 157-159.

concerned with the rôle or form of the jurisdictional mediation. The second is "material," concerned with the material character of the measures prescribed by the jurisdictional power. The third division considers the degrees of the jurisdictional power, or simply the proximate end. The fourth is "accidental," relating directly and essentially to the quality of the assistance promised by God to the jurisdictional authority.

In the "formal" division, the jurisdictional power, or the power to state the law, is viewed either as an indispensable condition for declaring, recalling, or explaining the higher decisions of the divine law, or as a real intermediary cause, itself promulgating the decisions of ecclesiastical law. The former is termed a declaratory power. It is ministerial as it intervenes only to give expression to decisions that are immediately divine. Its rôle is that of an indispensable condition and, therefore, not instrumental. The latter is called a canonical power, serving as the basis of a law that is immediately ecclesiastical and only mediately divine. It enacts, establishes, prescribes, and promulgates decisions immediately ecclesiastical. It subdivides into multiple divisions, the most comprehensive of which is that of legislative, judicial, and executive power.

In the "material" division, the power of jurisdiction is viewed as it prescribes measures diverse in their material character, namely, as it proclaims speculative truth to be believed or practical truth to be performed. This distinction could be supplanted by another division into: a) doctrinal or magisterial, which would include both the speculative and practical division above, as it proposes what is to be interiorly accepted for both belief and action, and b) practical or disciplinary, as it concerns the exterior performance of acts demanded by life in common.[11]

[11] These four major divisions naturally overlap, since each has as its object the entire jurisdictional power, e.g., the magisterial power and the disciplinary power effect the entire jurisdictional power, whether declaratory or canonical.

The third division considers the proximate end, and consequently the degrees, of the power of jurisdiction. By divine institution there are but two degrees: the supreme pontificate and the subordinated episcopate; by ecclesiastical institution others have been added.[12] The supreme pontificate is directed immediately to the good of the universal Church. The episcopal jurisdiction is directed to the good of a particular Church (e.g., a diocese) and the jurisdictional power of inferiors to the good of a particular Church (e.g., a diocese) or some part thereof (e.g., a parish).

The fourth and "accidental" division considers the jurisdictional power in respect to the kind of assistance promised it by God. Thus arises the threefold division into absolutely infallible, prudentially infallible, and fallible jurisdiction. In the first, the divine assistance appears in its preeminent form; in the latter two, the aid of the Holy Spirit leaves an increasing margin to human initiative. The first of the three considers the proposition of the revelation and necessitates the absolute assistance of infallibility. The second and third jurisdictional powers concern the protection of the revelation and necessitate only prudential assistance. By way of general category, the second power is related to universal decisions, such as the laws of the Church, while the third power is related to particular decisions, such as concrete measures of legislative application. Each of these species of canonical decisions has its relative or prudential assistance. For prudentially infallible jurisdiction, it divinely guarantees the prudence of each particular canonical decision of general interest. But for the fallible jurisdiction, there is in proper parlance no prudential guarantee. Therefore, the type of obedience, of faith or of piety, will depend on whether the jurisdictional intervention is simply declaratory or truly mediatory, and on the respective degrees of their infallibility.

[12] Can. 108, § 3.

ARTICLE III. PAROCHIAL JURISDICTION

If anyone states that pastors have no jurisdiction in the external forum, he must also state, in order to preserve the intelligibility, consistency, and validity of his statement, that pastors have absolutely no jurisdiction. This statement could assuredly be sustained, as has been seen in the opening words of this chapter, through an acceptance of the terms "jurisdiction" and "hierarchy" in their highest meaning. Once the admission is made, however, that pastors have any jurisdiction, even if only in the internal forum, the acceptance of the term "jurisdiction" is no longer reflected in its highest meaning. Consequently, if one predicates of pastors any jurisdiction whatsoever, one is speaking of a derived and imperfect, but nevertheless true and genuine, jurisdiction.

> The other divisions of the power of jurisdiction [other than papal and episcopal] do not arise from the divine law but from the ordinances of ecclesiastical law. Just as, in effect, the Church has extended the power of order of deacons, of the simple ministers, to several inferior functions (sub-diaconate and Minor Orders), so she has extended the power of jurisdiction to several inferior levels. The power of the sovereign pontificate, participated up to a point, has given birth to the power of the Cardinals, of the Roman Curia, of the Legates, of the Patriarchs, of the Primates, of the Metropolitans, of the Vicars and Prefects Apostolic, of the superiors of religious and so on. . . . The *episcopal* power is shared by the Vicars-General, for example, or, in a limited way, by the simple parish priests who can preach, administer the sacraments and grant certain dispensations. But the jurisdiction *proper* to the Pope is never devolved otherwise than partially—for example, on the Roman Congregations; hence, although it is ordinary, that is to say attached to their office, the jurisdiction of the Roman Congregations is not a proper but vicarious jurisdiction. So also the jurisdiction proper to the bishops is only partially devolved on the parish priests; hence, although it is ordinary, i.e., attached to their of-

> fice, their jurisdiction is not a proper but a vicarious jurisdiction.[13]

Similarly, if anyone refuses to term as jurisdiction the power of pastors, he should also, in order to be consistent, deny them the very title of pastor.

> . . . if simple parish priests are called pastors, they are known to be so only in a vicarious way (their ordinary jurisdiction derives, by a provision of ecclesiastical law, from that of the bishops), and partially (they can preach, and administer the sacraments, grant certain dispensations, but not legislate).[14]

Journet, in referring to pastors, again thus implies the same notion: ". . . the power of the priest, being imperfect, is under the power of the bishop both by its own nature and by the divine law."[15]

In practice, no one denies the title of pastor to the parish priest. Again, in practice, no one fails to speak of the pastor's "jurisdiction" in the internal forum. Accordingly no one should refuse, or even hesitate, to utter the phrase "jurisdiction of pastors in the external forum," since it can be shown, once true jurisdiction is admitted for the pastor, that this power extends also, in certain instances, to the external forum.

The final note on parochial jurisdiction, made by Journet from the field of speculative theology, is this: "Ordinary jurisdiction is called 'proper' when the office is exercised as by a second cause, and 'vicarious' when exercised as by a mere transmitter in the name of another."[16] Not to lose sight of the principle that all jurisdiction, however, even delegated, is exercised not as by an instrumental cause but rather as by a principal second cause, Journet finds it necessary to clarify his statement by drawing a further distinction from a canonical standpoint. In the light of the type of power with which the principal second cause may op-

[13] Journet, *The Apostolic Hierarchy*, p. 390.
[14] Journet, *op. cit.*, p. 393.
[15] *Op. cit.*, p. 394.
[16] *Op. cit.*, p. 395.

erate, namely with a delegated, a proper ordinary, or a vicarious ordinary jurisdiction, his further distinction is drawn from the consideration of *vicarious* jurisdiction.[17] It may be a *principal* derived jurisdiction, as, for example, that which a bishop shares with his parish priests, or an *instrumental* derived jurisdiction, such as that which a bishop shares with his vicar-general.

This distinction, while yet theological, is made from a canonical standpoint. It is introduced for showing the canonical distinction between proper and vicarious jurisdiction. Theologically, only papal and episcopal power can be considered *proper;* all other, then, is *vicarious* or derived. This theologically derived power, however, may be considered canonically as a *principal* derived jurisdiction or as an *instrumental* derived jurisdiction according as it is or is not *exercised in one's own name.* Nevertheless, both of these divisions, the principal derived jurisdiction and the instrumental derived jurisdiction, fall under the theological classification of operations of principal second causes, since both, regardless of species, belong to the genus of true jurisdiction.

It is precisely this confusion between theological and canonical notions and nomenclature which is responsible for the controversy whether the pastor's power may be termed "proper." Obviously, in the theological sense, parochial jurisdiction is not to be classed as a "proper" jurisdiction. In canonical parlance, however, wherein the term "proper" connotes an "exercise in one's own name," the parochial power may and must be termed *proper.*[18]

[17] It must be kept in mind that *vicarious* is here taken in the theological sense of *derived,* and not in the canonical sense contraposed to *proper.*

[18] "Ordinaria subdividitur in *propriam* seu adnexam officio quod nomine proprio, ut titularis, quis possidet, v.gr., parochus; et *vicariam,* inhaerentem officio quod quis nomine alieno exercet, ut vicarius oeconomus."—Regatillo, *Institutiones Iuris Canonici* (4. ed., 2 vols., Santander: Sal Terrae, 1951), I, 255, 256 (hereafter cited *Institutiones*). Cf. also cans. 197, § 2, and 451, § 1.

When the term "jurisdiction" is applied in its highest meaning, it must be theologically admitted that pastors have no such jurisdiction. Nevertheless, after abstracting from the highest meaning of jurisdiction, one may theologically maintain that pastors do have some jurisdiction and that some of their powers are exercised even in the external forum.

CHAPTER IV

THE NOTION OF FORUM

ARTICLE I. THE PHILOSOPHICO-JURIDICAL CONCEPT OF FORUM[1]

The distinction between an external forum and an internal forum is impractical for non-ecclesiastical jurists. In civil law, whether ancient or modern, this distinction is ignored, not by any deficiency of juridic science but by the nature of things. In no way can there be in civil law and in civil society an internal forum replete with the connotations realized in ecclesiastical law. Civil juridic life is concerned with only one forum, which by its nature is external or public. Whatever is referred to the forum, in the common sense of the word, pertains to that part of human life which is public. The joining of the words "internal" and "forum" constitutes an etymological and semantic contradiction in terms.

SECTION 1. THE VALIDITY OF THE ECCLESIASTICAL INTERNAL FORUM

The concept of internal forum and the juridic value of the distinction must be investigated from a philosophico-juridical aspect. Anyone who too readily accepts the distinction understands less perfectly the true sense of the distinction together with its consequences.

The fundamental question, of course, is why the internal forum is stressed in ecclesiastical law and not in civil law, or why the internal forum, as ecclesiastical society com-

[1] The concept of forum to which the writer ascribes is substantially that expounded by Louis Bender, O.P. (cf. "Forum Externum et Forum Internum," *Ephemerides Iuris Canonici* [Romae, 1945-], X [1954], 9-27). However, the writer departs from Bender's views, here presented, whenever such deviation is demanded to preserve specific points of Journet's doctrine presented in the preceding chapter.

prehends it, is an inconceivable thing in civil society. As the cause of this juridic phenomenon nothing other can be designated than the proper nature of the Church. The Church is a supernatural society, operating in the supernatural order, so that in its own way or in the way proper to the society it leads its members to some supernatural end. The supernatural order, however, is an order altogether elevated above the powers and exigencies of human nature. In the supernatural order the principal first cause, or the principal and primary agent, is God, and God alone.

This fact, however, does not have the effect that in the supernatural order man himself can do nothing, or, which means the same thing, that any human operation remains below and therefore outside the supernatural order and without any efficacy for attaining a supernatural end. These things follow only for a purely natural human operation, in which God does not so directly intervene. If God directly intervenes, it is a different matter. The true condition of things, or how things really are, depends properly on the positive will of God and on the manner in which God wills to constitute the supernatural order. In other words, this depends on the way in which God, as the efficient cause in the supernatural order, wills to lead man to the supernatural end proposed to him. God is able *absolutely* to lead man to the supernatural end in two ways: either so that He would be the only agent and man would play a merely passive rôle, or so that He would be the principal and primary agent, but not the only agent, and man would be an instrumental agent or a secondary agent. In the latter case God would move man so that he would attain the supernatural end by performing his proper natural actions, which would be the means to that end. Therefore, man can operate by nature alone, but not so as to attain a supernatural end, for God alone knows this end and disposes the adequate means toward it. God can so move the human agent, however, that he attains the supernatural end by his own operations.

It pertained to God to establish, by decree of His free will, in which of the two ways He actually wished to lead men to the supernatural end and, thereafter, to communicate His decision to men by revelation. God chose the second way; He Himself moves men, causing their operations by their own power, elevating and directing them to an end exceeding human nature itself and its powers.

Moreover, God raised not only the powers of men when acting individually, but also the powers of men when acting socially or when habitually united for the purpose of cooperating. God did this by instituting a certain supernatural society, perfect and independent of any other natural society, even one supreme and perfect in its own order. In His society men work toward their supernatural end by their own operations, but always under the motion of God as the principal cause or, in other words, under the motion of divine grace. Therefore, the following proposition is true both for the individual man and his operations and for the Church, or the supernatural society, and its operations: whatever is done in the supernatural order is done in consequence of an instrumental or a secondary cause, that is, of the instrument or the agent of God, who elevates the faculties and operations by His power and makes them operative in the supernatural order.

The order in which man operates as a *Christian,* and the Church as a supernatural society, is the divine order. The order of ecclesiastical operations, then, is the divine order. It is at the same time, however, the *social* order or the order of life itself whereby men live together and mutually communicate. As it is the divine order, its principal ruler is God, who knows not only public things but also secret things. He knows our external acts and our internal acts. Therefore, it is proper that this divine rector should rule men both in their public operations and also in their occult operations.

God is able, then, in the supernatural social order, as instituted and ruled by Him, to comprehend all the acts of the faithful both public and occult, both external and internal. In order that even occult and internal acts be really comprehended under the supernatural social order, it is indeed required but it also suffices that God should will it and, consequently, give the power even over occult and internal acts to the persons whom He constitutes in the Church as superiors with supernatural power. Furthermore, it would be necessary to make this divine disposition known to all the faithful, superiors and subjects alike. God has done this. He gave the power to the rulers of the Church to confer sacraments, to legislate, to judge and punish public transgressions of laws, to judge and absolve sins committed occultly, even if they be purely internal, such as hate, deliberate complacency, or voluntary doubt on some article of faith. What everyone knows at least practically has just been established, namely, that the power of the Church extends to the external and internal, public and occult, acts of the faithful.

The exercise of power in itself is a social act, an act towards another, an act of a superior having power over a subject subjected to that power. This is the reason why the exercise of power always and necessarily demands an external act. Men cannot communicate among themselves by way of internal acts. Even an act as extremely secret as the absolution of sins in the sacrament of penance is an external act which is perceived by two persons, the priest and the penitent. As *social,* an act of this kind is a *juridic* act or one pertaining to juridic life, to the life which is regulated also by human laws.

Certainly no man, and therefore no superior, can act toward others by reason of some act of theirs which is internal or occult unless he knows these acts. This is valid also for those acts which are performed in the supernatural order. This principle and this condition of things in the natural order, in which man is the principal agent, leads to the doctrine that a ruler or a person in exercising power rules his subjects only in regard to external acts; in other words, it brings one to the adage: *"de internis non curat praetor."* The same does not follow for the supernatural order, properly because therein the principal agent is not man but God. What follows is that only part is true of what is often repeated concerning the Church, *"de internis Ecclesia non iudicat."* If it were otherwise, any judgment in the internal forum, sacramental or non-sacramental, would have to be rejected.

God is the ruler, however, who by reason of His very nature knows all acts of men, both internal and occult acts. Therefore, God, the ruler of men, rules also that part of human operations which is occult and internal. God, actually intermingling Himself in the operations of men in order to lead them to the supernatural end, is able to proceed in two ways: by an immediate influx or by a mediate influx. By an immediate influx He actually does so in many things, e.g., when He excites men to contrition and thereafter remits venial sins, when He remits punishment due to sins already forgiven, or when He gives the help of grace upon hearing a prayer; thus, indeed, God influences directly and solitarily. By a mediate influx God deigns to use the ministry of man acting with divine, or supernatural, power. God can proceed in this latter case in two ways also: by having man exercise supernatural power in the rôle of a mere instrument, or by allowing him to exercise this power in the rôle of a principal, but secondary, cause. God has established a social and juridic order as supernatural and divine which is ministerial in relation to the supernatural end. This social and juridic order nevertheless extends to all human acts, even occult and internal, because God is the efficient cause or principal and first agent. It was necessary, for all this to be accomplished, that God make known this ordination to all members of this order, namely, by a revelation whereby men would know the statutes of God and learn what they ought to do, either as strictly obligatory or as good and useful for them, to attain their supernatural end.

An understanding of occult and internal facts and acts under this supernatural social and juridic order, or under the juridic activity of the Church, explains how such an internal forum can exist in canon law. Consequently, it explains the distinction between the external forum and the internal forum, notwithstanding that such an internal forum is practically ignored in civil law and, moreover, impracticable. This contrariety has its foundation in the nature of natural society. A purely human society is not concerned with an internal forum. The Church is certainly a society, but not one purely human. It is supernatural or divine. It follows that the Church is able, by the ordination of God, to have in its juridic life, in its juridic order, in its law, the unique internal forum proper to it and to it alone. Consequently, the distinction between the external and internal forum can be established.

SECTION 2. THE UNITY OF THE ECCLESIASTICAL FORUM

Canon law is true law or law strictly and properly so called. Nevertheless, it must be granted that canon law is a law *sui generis,* or a law having an altogether special character. This special character does not remove or diminish the juridical character but effects that in canon law there exist elements which in civil law are neither actually nor potentially present.

Canon law is in the supernatural order and, therefore, it belongs to the theological order, and not to the purely philosophical order. Many things taught in philosophy and in the philosophy of law apply also to canon law, but not everything without exception, for the Church, as a society, is more than a natural society. Therefore, restrictions concerning the extension of social power, which in the philosophy of law and social philosophy are peremptorily proved, do not necessarily apply to ecclesiastical society. A philosophical conclusion can be fully true and, at the same time, be true only in the order of natural things, namely, in the order of things of which the philosopher speaks. The philosopher does not treat properly of the

Church or of a supernatural society; this pertains to the theologian. Therefore, the adage of the philosophy of law, as prompted by juridic science, *"de internis non curat praetor,"* and the conclusion which the philosopher rightly draws from this adage, *"princeps non potest praecipere actus internos,"* are both true. But they deal with a social superior and prince in the natural order. Whether they would be true if applied to the Church, or to a supernatural society, and its juridic order is not certain *a priori,* i.e., before it has been proved that this principle is valid also for this special juridic order and society. As demonstrated above, these doctrines do not avail in an absolute manner for the Church, although a partial application to the juridic life of the Church is not excluded.

The juridic order and moral order are not distinguished as two orders altogether distinct, or as two parts into which human life is divided. They are opposed as a part to the whole. The juridic order is a part of the moral order and, indeed, a special part, containing elements, e.g., coercion, which are not found in other parts. This avails for any juridic order, even the civil, but in a special way for canon law.

In canon law it is incorrect to assert that the juridic order is an external and public order only. That juridic order cannot be simply an external and a public order, but must embrace also an internal and occult part, precisely because there is an internal forum. In canon law many internal and occult acts pertain to the juridic order, although not always in the same way and in the same degree as external and public acts.

One should not understand the difference between the internal forum and external forum as though, by this distinction, the juridical ecclesiastical life or Christian social life is divided into two parts or diverse and separate orders of acting.[2] In this world, or in the life of man, there is

[2] Cf. Bender, *Philosophia Iuris* (Romae: Officium Libri Catholici, 1947), pp. 216-233, wherein the juridic order is shown to be part of the moral order.

only one juridic order. One may distinguish many parts in it, however, and in turn subdistinguish many more. The human body serves as an adequate example: one may distinguish in it the arms, the head, the legs, the trunk; in the arms one may distinguish the forearm, the hand, etc.; in the hand one may distinguish the fingers, the nails, etc. But in man properly so called as a living being, these parts, though truly distinct, are not divided or separated from each other either as to being or, consequently, as to acting.

In the same way one may distinguish in the one juridic order the natural law and the positive law, the canon law and the civil law, international law and national law, in the last of which, for example, one may subdistinguish Germanic law, Gallic law, etc. These distinctions designate not divided juridic orders but parts, provinces, sections or spheres, of the one entire juridic order which embraces all juridic acts of all men. This is the reason why national laws are norms of law which exercise force even for non-citizens. An example may serve to indicate the meaning intended: a person with the capacity of acquiring and possessing a house and then legitimately acquiring it has a right (*ius*) in that house, regardless whether the norms of the prevailing law are the norms of some national law or the norms of canon law, provided they are true norms of law in force for the person and the act. He then has this right simply and, therefore, before all men. Either persons with public power or private persons who take away this house from the person by force violate law and the juridic order. Even though some national law is a complexus of norms other than canon law, if the juridic negotiation was performed according to the norms in force for this person here and now, the juridic effect of the negotiation constitutes a true right which, therefore, everyone must observe.

What has been said is based on the general principle of the whole juridic order: if a person has a right, no one is allowed to violate that right, or all ought to accord him that right. If a piece of land truly belongs to a person, it is his in respect to all men who are in the world, and no one is permitted to take his land away from him unless there would be a very special title, e.g., extreme necessity or legitimate expropriation on the part of the ruler of a public society.

The validity of a juridic transaction is something objective. If the act is valid, its juridic effects have force in respect of all men. It is almost superfluous to observe that a valid contract does not give one the right of demanding the same thing from all men. The rights, however, which he obtained from the contract must be observed by all. In other words, *B* must give *A* what he owes *A*, and all others are bound not to hinder *B* from doing this.

The distinction of the ecclesiastical forum into the external forum and the internal forum is a distinction whereby a part of the juridic order, which is the ecclesiastical forum, is distinguished into two parts. There is no division here, however, as there is when two orders are divided or separated from each other. Therefore, one should accept with discretion and judgment statements such as "acts which are performed in the internal forum are not valid in the external forum." One not attending to the true sense of these words may be led into error. Practically, one knows how these sayings are interpreted and to what juridic consequences they tend. It is fitting, however, that the jurist know also the philosophic doctrine which underlies the juridic doctrine.

Certainly it cannot be that one and the same act is valid and invalid at the same time. An act or juridic transaction, if it is valid, produces its proper juridic effects; if it is invalid, it does not produce them. A marriage, for instance, cannot be valid and invalid at the same time. It can happen that a person, or even an ecclesiastical authority, considers a marriage valid while another person, or another ecclesiastical authority, considers the same marriage invalid. The judgment of one or the other is false. In reality, in the infallible knowledge of God, either the parties are married or they are not. It follows that the same marriage cannot be at the same time valid in the internal forum and invalid in the external forum, at least if the terms are taken in their proper sense.

If a confessor dispenses a person in the internal sacramental forum from the factually occult impediment of consanguinity, according to the norm of canon 1045, the impediment is removed. In reality the impediment no longer exists. The consequence is that if this person contracts marriage with the other person concerned, after all other things have been observed, the marriage is valid and simply valid. If the fact of consanguinity is later made known, truly an impediment is not disclosed, for what no longer exists cannot be made known. What is made known is the basis from which the existence of the impediment is publicly but erroneously concluded, since the conclusion is not based on full truth; in other words, the fact that the dispensation was granted is not known. This erroneous conclusion is inevitable in these circumstances, but the inevitability of the error does not prevent it from being an error.

The dispensation, then, and the marriage are valid. And since the validity of the juridic act, or the true existence and efficacy of the juridic act, is something not subjective but objective, the dispensation and the marriage cannot be valid for one part of social life or for the internal forum, and invalid for the other part or for the external forum. Therefore, in the proper sense of the words, either the dispensation and the marriage are valid, and then they are valid simply and, consequently, for both forums, or they are invalid, and then they are invalid simply and, consequently, for both forums. By adverting to this one may avoid making statements which contain contradictions.

SECTION 3. THE SENSE OF CANON 202, § 1

Realizing that an act cannot be at the same time valid in the internal forum and invalid in the external forum, in the proper sense of the words, one may ask what then is the sense of the words which appear not only among canonists but also in the Code: "Acts of the power of jurisdiction ... granted for the external forum are valid also for the internal forum; *but not vice versa.*"[3]

Before the true sense can be understood, it is necessary to explain what properly is the internal forum and what properly is the external forum. In this distinction forum signifies ecclesiastical juridic life. An act is said to pertain to the forum when its effects have some bearing on the juridic condition of others. If such is not the case, one does not speak properly in terms of a forum. The recitation of the rosary, for instance, pertains strictly to no forum; it concerns only an agent. Again, one may receive Holy Communion publicly subsequent to the public commission of a grave sin and private absolution. But this is not contrary to the precept of canon 202, § 1, which states that an act of jurisdiction exercised for the internal forum is of no avail for the external forum. The explanation is simply that even the public reception of Holy Communion is commonly considered not an act of a forum, since that act ordinarily has no effects upon others. Such an action, therefore, may be perfectly lawful; such an action is primarily the responsibility of the individual. Similarly one may in public life lawfully use a dispensation from the law of the fast which was obtained in confession provided, of course, that no scandal is given. If the circumstances so warrant, the dispensed person may inform others of the dispensation which he has obtained but which he can in no way prove. In general, then, an act of the forum may be described thus: an act whereby one demands one's right, whether explicitly or implicitly, whether directly or indirectly, and imposes the juridic obligation corresponding to that right, so that another is bound to do or omit something which he would not do or omit unless constrained by said right.

[3] "Actus potestatis iurisdictionis ... collatae pro foro externo, valet quoque pro foro interno, non autem e converso."—Can. 202, § 1.

The ecclesiastical juridic or social life is distinguished into two provinces or spheres. Each province one may identify by understanding the criterion for the distinction, which is the diverse manner in which the facts and acts are performed. One thing may be done so that it can be established by way of *juridic proof,* and another thing may be done so that it cannot be thus established. Juridic proof is that which of itself is sufficient to convince a prudent man of the certainty of the fact.[4]

If the juridic act is so performed that it can be established by juridic proof, it is done in the external forum. If not, it is done in the internal forum. By way of example, a precept given with a legitimate document or before two witnesses is a precept given in the external forum.[5] A dispensation given by the confessor is an act of the internal forum. Therefore, one may distinguish acts of the external forum and acts of the internal forum according to their manner of performance, namely, as juridically public or as juridically not public, or occult. Before one can be said to act publicly in the juridic order, one must so act that the accomplished fact can be established by way of juridic proof.

The internal forum is that province or sphere of acts performed socially which is private and ruled by private knowledge, i.e., conscience. Since man, however, must regu-

[4] *Juridic* proof should not be confused with *judicial* proof; *juridic* connotes what is legal or simply pertinent to law in general, while *judicial* implies an element that pertains to courts, proceedings, etc. It may also be noted here that an act or fact may pertain to the external forum, though no one know it but the party interested, as, e.g., when a privilege was obtained, without others knowing about it, by means of a legitimate document from a superior now dead. The act is not divulged in the knowledge of men, but it is a juridically public act for the simple reason that it falls under public knowledge. Anyone may immediately know of the concession of the privilege; it suffices that he be shown the document. Cf. can. 1037 and commentaries thereon; *AAS,* XXIV (1932), 284.

[5] Cf. can. 24. The mode of an act is normally determined by its circumstances, though sometimes by the mere intention or will of the agent.

late *all* his acts by private knowledge or conscience, the internal forum comprehends every act which pertains to the ecclesiastical forum. Just as a dispensation *occultly* obtained is a dispensation given in the internal forum, so that one may use it in conscience, so also a dispensation *publicly* obtained is a dispensation for the internal forum, for one may also use this dispensation in conscience. The difference between the two dispensations is not that one is valid in the internal forum and the other in the external forum. The difference is that one is given in the internal forum *alone,* while the other is given in both forums.

Regarding those things which are done in the external forum, it is not correct to state that they are outside the internal forum or outside the part of social life to which private knowledge extends itself. All things which are done in the external forum are also done in the internal forum and pertain to it as well; but, not *vice versa.* One might graphically represent the nature of the distinction between the external forum and the internal forum by means of two concentric circles, one larger than the other. The larger circle would depict the internal forum, and the smaller, the external forum.

Properly understood, there are no acts of the ecclesiastical forum which are performed in the external forum *alone.* Properly, the acts are thus distinguished: acts performed in the internal forum only and acts performed in both forums. Everything which pertains to the ecclesiastical forum pertains to the internal forum, because everything pertains to the life which is regulated by conscience or private knowledge. Some things, however, pertain to that part of the ecclesiastical forum which has public knowledge, or knowledge based on juridic proofs, as its norm. These juridic proofs are elements which can be brought to the knowledge of all and then, consequently, can convince all prudent men of the truth of the facts.

Therefore, one would do well to consider the internal forum and external forum as whole and part. They are two spheres of acting, one of which is located within the other as a minor section which extends itself less widely than the other. Acts pertain either to the internal forum only, or to the internal and external forum simultaneously. A public convalidation, or one in the external forum, and an occult convalidation, or one in the internal forum, concur in that each act has by its very nature its own juridic effects for the internal forum of conscience. Each convalidation effects that a man in his conscience may licitly use the rights that derive from a valid matrimonial union. The difference is that the former effects also that one may publicly conduct himself as a married person, so that no one can impede this. On the contrary, an occult convalidation does not bring this about, since this convalidation is enacted not in the external forum but only in the internal forum. The difference, therefore, does not concern the effects for the *internal* forum; it concerns only the effects for the *external* forum.

Nothing can be done in the external forum *alone*, for the external forum is a part comprehended in the internal forum just as a province is a part comprehended in the whole kingdom. What is done in the province is done also in the kingdom, but not *vice versa*. This is due to the very nature of the thing. Canon 202, § 1, therefore, is nothing other than a formula expressing that which already has force without this positive norm.

It is clear that an act of the power of jurisdiction given for the external forum, or its exercise in the external forum, is valid even for the internal forum. The principle that an act cannot be at the same time valid and invalid is not opposed to this part of canon 202, § 1. There remains the second part, *non autem e converso*, i.e., an act of the power of jurisdiction granted for and exercised in the internal forum is not valid for the external forum. It has just been shown that this is impossible.

It follows that these words cannot be understood in their proper sense. They evidently have another sense in the context. That sense is simply that an act of jurisdiction exercised in the internal forum alone cannot be accepted in the external forum, or in that part of life which is regulated by public knowledge or knowledge based on juridic proof, as an act which can stand in the public forum. In other words, it cannot be considered as an act which has effects that are reckoned in the disposition of public life. If the words are thus understood, the difficulty, i.e., the seeming contradiction between the norm of the canon and the philosophical principle, disappears. Although it is true that an act cannot be valid in the internal forum and invalid in the external forum, nothing prevents an act from being valid in the internal forum and, nevertheless, not accepted or reckoned as valid in the external forum. Thus it is when the act is not known by that special knowledge whereby the external forum is regulated, namely, knowledge based on juridic proof.

Canon 202, § 1, thus understood, does not contain a negation of the principle that an act cannot be at the same time valid and invalid, valid in the internal forum and invalid in the external forum. The sense of the words is this: an act performed in the internal forum only, while simply valid, does not have the necessary quality to be admitted as a norm of acting in the public forum. It lacks the required quality which is not validity, but rather *publicity*. Something done validly, but publicly unknown, is not accepted in the external forum as a norm of acting.

The rule of canon 202, § 1, does not admit true exceptions. The apparent exception in canon 1047 is not a true exception.[6] By means of the record of the curia, though it be secret, the granted dispensation is drawn to public knowl-

[6] The canon states that the dispensation conceded for the internal non-sacramental forum from an occult impediment shall be recorded in the secret archives of the curia and *there is no need of another dispensation in the external forum, though the impediment afterwards becomes public.* The same canon states further: if the dispensation was granted for the internal sacramental forum only, a new dispensation is required when the impediment becomes public.

edge and thus to the external forum. By this record the dispensation becomes an act in the external forum, since it becomes an act which can be established by juridic proof. Although in fact it is not diffused, it can be proved juridically by means of the authentic document or record of the curia.

The dispensation in the external forum, which is required if the dispensation was granted in the sacramental forum only and later the impediment became public, has its proper character and special effects. If the dispensation from the impediment is once lawfully and validly given, the impediment no longer exists and the marriage contracted in virtue of the dispensation is valid. Therefore, the new so called dispensation is really not a true dispensation but only an apparent one. A true dispensation, in this consideration, is an act by which an impediment is removed. But what does not exist can never be removed. What then is the real effect of this act which has the external form of a dispensation? The effect is that now it is publicly known and it can juridically be established that the impediment no longer exists. This effect exists from the moment of this new act, the so called dispensation.[7]

Whether, in any concrete case, the act of power is required in the external forum or in the internal forum does not always depend only on the matter concerned, but also on the circumstances. There are many cases, if the matter alone is considered, in which there is a free choice of fo-

[7] In the case, the juridic status of the spouses is not regulated alone by the dispensation later granted for the external forum. The one who proves the granting of this dispensation proves nothing more than the grant of the dispensation *after* the marriage was celebrated *with* the impediment. Nothing is established concerning the dispensation granted at the time of the celebration. Therefore, one who proves the granting of the dispensation does not prove the validity of the marriage. To prove the validity he must also prove that the marriage was convalidated *after the impediment was removed.* Therefore, it is necessary that, besides the dispensation in the external forum, there be a public convalidation of the marriage according to the norms of law, namely, canons 1133-1141.

rum. For example, a person guilty of the occult delict of heresy contracts an *occult* excommunication thereby.[8] He may seek absolution, however, either in the internal forum or in the external forum.[9] One who is bound by a factually occult impediment, e.g., one of affinity or of a private vow, may seek a dispensation in the internal forum. But, if it does not displease him that the fact be made known to ecclesiastical superiors and noted in the register of marriage, he may seek the dispensation in the external forum also.

If one did not advert to this truth, one might contend that certain things pertain by reason of the matter to one forum and are thereby excluded from the other forum. For instance, some authors have taught that a dispensation from occult impediments pertains by reason of the matter to the confessor and, therefore, that the pastor does not have the right and duty of interrogating the parties concerning occult impediments.[10] This is not true.[11]

Occult impediments and, in general, occult matters do not necessarily pertain to the internal forum alone. An occult impediment can be dealt with in both forums. The interrogating pastor is, therefore, not restricted to one forum. He must investigate both public and occult things. If some impediment is detected by his investigation, he should decide in which forum it should be handled and possibly dispensed. If he does not proceed to the dispensation, either

[8] Can. 2314, § 1, 1°.

[9] Can. 2314, § 2.

[10] E.g., Vlaming, *Praelectiones Iuris Matrimonii* (3. ed., 2 vols., Bussum in Hollandia, 1919-1921), I, 123.

[11] Many authors held the affirmative opinion even before the Instruction of the Sacred Congregation of the Sacraments which stated: "... parochus a sponsis percontetur num aliquo detineantur impedimento tum impediente, tum praesertim dirimente, sive publico ... sive *occulto,* immo hoc potissimum, quod rarius innotescere solet (voti, criminis, etc.)."—*AAS*, XXXIII (1941), 301; Bouscaren, *The Canon Law Digest* (3 vols., Vol. I, 7. printing, 1950; Vol. II, 5. printing, 1949; Vol. III, 1954, and Supplements 1953 through 1956, 1954-1957, Milwaukee: The Bruce Publishing Co.), II, 258 (hereafter cited *Digest*).

because it is impossible or because there is no sufficient reason, the pastor must refuse his assistance, which denial is most certainly an act of the external forum.[12] If he proceeds to the dispensation, the pastor should decide, considering all things, in which forum the dispensation should be sought and granted. The conclusion may be one of three: the dispensation should be granted in the external forum; or, the dispensation should be granted in the internal forum; or, considering all things, the pastor and the parties are able to choose the forum, internal or external.

ARTICLE II. "FORUM" AND THE CODE

The canonical use of *forum* naturally embraces the fundamental notion, as indicated in the preceding article, of a sphere of activity: external, if it is juridically public; internal, if it is juridically occult. Just as in history, however, the term was employed with many connotations, so also one might expect it to be thus used in the Code. This article considers, therefore, not the actual basic concept of forum, but the mechanics of its uses in the Code together with their connotations and extensions.

The word "forum" appears in the first title and in the heading of the first chapter of the twentieth title of Book IV. It also appears in as many as fifty-six distinct canons and reoccurs several times in many of them. Three of these canons, namely, 120, § 2, 1553, § 1, 3° and 2341, may be immediately eliminated from discussion, since they concern not the external or internal forum but the clerical privilege of the forum. In the remaining canons, besides the usual

[12] This denial is not one in the sense of can. 1039, § 1, wherein the prohibition of the local ordinary is concerned. Rather, as Bouscaren-Ellis note: "Pastors have no power whatever to 'forbid marriage.' If the term is used in connection with them, it simply means that they declare to the parties that according to the law they have no right to marry."—*Canon Law, A Text and Commentary* (Milwaukee: The Bruce Publishing Co., 1946; Reprint, 1948), p. 432 (hereafter cited *Canon Law*).

adjectives "external," "internal," and "both," some of the less frequent modifiers for the substantive "forum" are the following: secular, judicial, civil, ecclesiastical, mixed, proper, necessary, competent, sacramental, extra-sacramental, non-sacramental, contentious, and exterior.[13] Several other expressions also appear, e.g., the forum of the plaintiff, of the defendant, of the ordinary, the forum of conscience. The last expression appears as a synonym for the internal forum. It is expressly equated to the internal forum in canon 196 and it appears thrice more in the Code.[14]

As there are two principal powers that govern the world, there are two principal forums: the civil or secular and the ecclesiastical.[15] Certain matters in which both the Church and the State are equally competent are said to be of the mixed forum.[16] In the ecclesiastical forum are distinguished the external forum and the internal forum, the latter of which subdivides into the sacramental and extra-sacramental forum.[17] The terms "sacramental" and "extra-sacramental" indicate that an act transpires in the process of sacramental confession or outside such confession.[18] A synonymous expression for "sacramental forum" is the phrase "in the act of sacramental confession,"[19] and in

[13] *Exterior* appears only once in the entire Code, namely, in canon 2314, § 2, where it is used as a synonym for *external.* A complete list of the appearances of the term "forum" in the Code follows: Cans. 43; 56; 79; 110; 120, § 2; 154; 196; 202, §§ 1-3; 207, § 2; 209; 239, §1, 17°; 258, § 1; 399, § 3; 501, § 1; 524, § 1; 990, § 1; 991, § 4; 1017, § 1; 1031, §2, 2°; 1037; 1044; 1046; 1047; 1122, § 2; 1301, § 1; 1542, § 2; 1553, § 1, 3°, § 2; 1554; 1556 (title); 1559; 1560; 1562; 1563; 1566, § 1; 1651, § 2; 1916, § 1; 1933, § 3; 1960 (title); 2200, § 2; 2218, § 2; 2219, § 2; 2232, § 1; 2237, § 1, 1°; 2239, § 1; 2250, § 3; 2251; 2253, 1°; 2254, § 1; 2264; 2279, §2, 1°; 2284; 2290, § 1; 2314, § 2; 2334, 2°; 2341; 2350, § 2.

[14] Cans. 79; 1031, § 2, 2°; 2314, § 2.

[15] Cf. cans. 1301, § 1; 1542, § 2; 1554; 1651, § 2.

[16] Can. 1553, § 2; cf. cans. 1554 and 1933, § 3.

[17] Can. 196.

[18] Cf. cans. 196; 202, § 2; 1047; 2250, § 3; 2253, 1°; 2254, § 1; 2290, § 1; 2314, § 2.

[19] Can. 1044.

place of "extra-sacramental" is often found "non-sacramental."[20]

In view of the initial historical usage of the term and the corresponding canonical heritage, it would be highly improbable not to find forum used specifically in reference to judicial activity.[21] Accordingly forum may signify the tribunal of the judge to whose jurisdiction a defendant or respondent is subject.[22] Similarly, it may indicate either judicial competency or the physical district of a certain judge.[23] From such usage it is evident that a forum will often be called judicial or contentious in contrast to an extra-judicial or administrative one.[24] Moreover, the contentious forum may be voluntary, where a choice of forum exists, or involuntary or necessary, where the forum is determined by law.[25] This distinction between involuntary and voluntary forum, wherein both are judicial, must not be confused with the distinction between involuntary and voluntary jurisdiction, wherein the former is judicial and the latter is non-judicial.[26]

There are no special difficulties with the mechanical use of the terms "external forum" and "internal forum" or "forum of conscience." The Code quite often speaks simultaneously of both by means of the phrase *"utrumque forum."*[27] Equally as often it expressly contrasts or compares one with the other.[28] The term "internal forum" is

[20] Cans. 258, § 1; 991, § 4; 1047; 2250, § 3.

[21] Can. 990, § 1.

[22] Cf. cans. 1542, § 2; 1554; 1562, § 2; 1563; 2237, § 1, 1°.

[23] Cf. cans. 1559, § 3; 1560; 1566, § 1; 1916, § 1.

[24] Cf. Oesterle, "De Relatione inter Forum Externum et Internum," *Apollinaris*, XIX (1946), 68.

[25] Cf. cans. 1557 ff. and 1962 ff.

[26] Can. 201, §§ 2, 3.

[27] Cf. cans. 202, § 3; 1017, § 1; 2219, § 2; 2232, § 1; 2251; 2279, § 2, 1°.

[28] Cf. cans. 79; 154; 196; 209; 501, § 1; 1047; 2239, § 1; 2251; 2264; 2284; 2334, 2°; 2350, §2.

found alone only five times in the entire Code,[29] whereas its counter-part "external forum" is met standing alone twice as often.[30] The more frequent usage of the external forum would certainly follow from the doctrine of one juridic order and one forum. The Code would necessarily be more concerned with that special part of forum and its proper quality than with the internal forum to which all acts of the ecclesiastical forum automatically pertain.

The Code uses the preposition "in" or the preposition "for" (*in* or *pro*) in connection with forum, whether external, internal, or both.[31] A German author notes that the preposition "in" denotes the mode or manner while "pro" refers to the effect.[32] Practical commentary, however, depends little on the particular construction.

While many adjectives are attached to the term "forum," one ambiguous modifier is omitted in the Code. As was indicated in the historical synopsis, many reliable commentators equated the *penitential forum* with the sacramental forum, while to many equally reliable commentators the *penitential forum* signified the forum of conscience.[33] The Code does not settle the question; in fact, it avoids the term completely. One might be doubtful, therefore, as to what interpretation one should accord the term, if one should encounter it, for example, in a rescript. In view of the two divergent probable opinions extant prior to the Code and in the light of the fact that the Code is silent on the matter, either opinion might be followed. One's opin-

[29] Cans. 43; 207, § 2; 258, § 1; 991, § 4; 1044. The interpretation of "alone" above is that nowhere in the same canon does the term "external forum" appear.

[30] Cans. 56; 110; 239, § 1, 17°; 399, § 3; 524, § 1; 1037; 1046; 1122, § 2; 2200, § 2; 2218, § 2.

[31] Cf. cans. 202, §§ 1-3; 258, § 1; 991, § 4; 1047.

[32] "Vorweg sei bemerkt, dass die Präposition 'in' auf den Modus hinweist, die Präposition 'pro' dagegen auf die Wirkung."—Triebs, *Praktisches Handbuch des geltenden kanonischen Eherechts* (Breslau, 1933), p. 157 (hereafter cited *Praktisches Handbuch*).

[33] Cf. Blat, *Commentarium Textus Codicis Iuris Canonici*, Lib. II, *De Personis* (2. ed., Romae, 1921), p. 167.

ion, however, should not be imposed to the prejudice or disadvantage of the party concerned. And since, according to canon 50, a broad interpretation of such doubtful matters can usually be made, *penitential forum* should be interpreted according to whatever is more favorable to the party concerned.

The penitential forum may best be considered a mixture of the forum of conscience and of the sacramental forum, that is, it may be considered either. A confessor with the faculty to absolve in the penitential forum may absolve outside of sacramental confession whenever the absolution concerns matter for which sacramental absolution is not absolutely required, unless the words of the concession indicate otherwise.[34]

ARTICLE III. "FORUM" AND THE AUTHORS

Since the eighteenth century and the doctrine of Berardi (1719-1768) concerning the principal characteristic of each forum, there have been relatively few significant deviations in the authors' definitions of forum. At that time the distinguishing feature between the external and the internal forum was changed from the distinction between judicial forum and the sacrament of penance to the note of public or private utility in reference to the recipient.[35] If the common good or *public* utility was primarily and directly intended, the act pertained to the external forum; if the good of an individual or *private* utility was primarily and directly intended, the act related to the internal forum. This notion, which is more than two hundred years old, has been embraced by many eminent canonists and, therefore, must be reverenced. No one can deny, however, that ecclesiastical jurisprudence is developing today and that it will continue to develop. The writer feels that such is the condi-

[34] Cf. can. 202, § 2. This particular application of the canon is also expressed by Gennaro, "Distinzione dei Fori Giurisdizionali," *Perfice Munus* (Torino, 1926-), X (1935), 505, 506.

[35] Cf. *supra*, pp. 49, 50.

tion with the present jurisprudence on the significance of forum.

What Berardi's criterion did for the jurists of his age was to give them a sharper and more practical distinction than the one or ones which they had. It did not, however, terminate the evolution of the notion of forum, which evolution had already been continued in his own day. After the fashion of Berardi's distinction, the criterion of Bender (1894-) may possibly do the same for the jurists of today. As will presently be seen, Bender was not the first to recognize the norm of juridic publicity, but he was the first to give this criterion such unique importance and extensive explanation. All the while, as the basic definition of Berardi was being adopted by author after author, more and more criteria of distinction were infiltrating into the definitions of these authors.

There is no need to quote every author's definition of forum, since a few will suffice to demonstrate its post-Code history. The authors may be conveniently divided into two groups: those who retained Berardi's criterion either as primary or as the only one, and those who abstracted from it partially, by giving it a lesser prominence, or completely, by omitting it entirely. Four out of every five modern commentators will still list Berardi's distinction either as the primary or as the sole norm.

In the first group of authors, Bargilliat (1853-1926) is exemplary of those few who listed only the criterion of public and private utility. Thus he stated:

> Jurisdictio interna, seu fori interni, est illa quae primario et directe refertur ad privatam uniuscujusque fidelis utilitatem . . . Jurisdictio externa, seu fori externi, primario et directe respicit publicam corporis fidelium utilitatem.[36]

But the far greater percentage of this group, while retaining the norm of utility as primary, added multiple other norms. Cappello (1879-), for instance, stated:

[36] *Praelectiones Juris Canonici* (37. ed., 2 vols., Parisiis, 1923, 1924), I, 49 (hereafter cited *Praelectiones*).

> Illa [iurisdictio fori externi] *primario* et *directe* ad bonum *commune* refertur, *externas* relationes sociales ordinat et cum iuridicis effectibus *publicis* exercetur; haec [fori interni] *primario* tendit in bonum *singulorum* fidelium, relationes ad Deum *directe* ordinat, ac *per se* in occulto et cum effectibus tantum coram Deo, aut iuridicis quidem sed ordinarie *occultis,* exercetur.[37]

In the second group of authors, Regatillo (1882-) is an example of those few who partially withdrew from the utility norm.

> Divisio. *Fori externi,* quae: a) subditos regit in ordine ad societatem; b) quasi in publico exercetur; c) effectum in facie Ecclesiae sortitur; d) immediate se refert ad bonum commune. Et *fori interni,* quae: a) subditos regit in ordine ad Deum; b) in secreto exercetur; c) effectum habet in conscientia; d) immediate et directe bonum privatum respicit, ut potestas absolvendi a peccatis.[38]

But again the far greater percentage of the group withdrew from this norm completely by proposing others in its stead. Blat (1870-1943) proposed as the single measure of distinction the fact that the exercise of jurisdiction was *coram Ecclesia* or *solummodo coram Deo.*[39] Another author expressed his sole criterion thus:

[37] *Summa Iuris Canonici* (4. ed., 3 vols., Romae: Aedes Universitatis Gregorianae, 1945-1955), I, 224, 225. Cf. also Badii, *Institutiones Iuris Canonici* (3. ed., 2 vols., Florentiae, 1921, 1922), I, 129 (hereafter cited *Institutiones*); Maroto, *Institutiones Iuris Canonici ad normam novi Codicis* (2 vols., Vol. I, 3. ed., Romae, 1921), I, 857-859 (hereafter cited *Institutiones*); Cocchi, *Commentarium in Codicem iuris canonici ad usum scholarum* (4. ed., 8 vols., Taurinorum Augustae: Marietti, 1931-1946), II (1937), 228 (hereafter cited *Commentarium*); Berutti, *Institutiones Iuris Canonici* (6 vols., Taurini: Marietti, 1936-), Vol. II, Pars I (1943), p. 307 (hereafter cited *Institutiones*); Sipos, *Enchiridion iuris canonici, ad usum scholarum et privatorum* (6. ed., recognovit Ladislaus Gálos, Romae: Orbis Catholicus-Herder, 1954), p. 137 (herafter cited *Enchiridion*).

[38] *Institutiones,* I, 255.

[39] *Opusculum de Potestate Superiorum in Religionibus* (Romae: Pontificium Institutum Angelicum, 1935), p. 11. The particular prominence which Blat attributed the contrasting expressions "before the

> *Jurisdiction of the external forum* is exercised publicly; it pertains to the public regime of the Church . . . *Jurisdiction of the internal forum* is exercised secretly, in the forum of conscience; it regulates the relations of the soul with God.[40]

Another emphasized the publicity norm in practically the same words:

> Forum externum idem est ac locus publicus, qui admittat testes; forum internum idem ac locus secretus, qui non admittat testes. Forum internum vocatur etiam forum conscientiae, quia non admittitur nisi testimonium conscientiae illius de quo agitur.[41]

Finally, of course, there was Bender's development, which expressly expounded juridic publicity as the sole criterion.

The division of authors and the development of forum just presented is principally a logical one. Chronologically, and by way of terminology, the development from the single norm of utility to the single norm of juridic proof is also evident. Within the maze of definitions and norms in the authors cited, one may still identify the following development: Bargilliat used the norm of utility alone; Maroto (1875-1937) added the notion of public or private exercise of power; Blat discarded the norm of utility and retained only the norm of public or private exercise; Crnica expressed the relation of publicity and juridic proof; and, finally, Bender expressed juridic publicity as the sole criterion of distinction.[42]

Church" and "only before God" may be interpreted as a paraphrase of the terms "juridically public" and "juridically occult."

[40] Champoux, *The Juridical Position of the Laity in the Church* (Romae: Typis Pontificiae Universitatis Gregorianae, 1939), p.49.

[41] Crnica, *Commentarium Theoretico-Practicum Codicis Iuris Canonici* (2 vols., Šibenik: Typis Typographiae "Kačic," 1940, 1941), I, 196. Cf. also Oesterle, "De Relatione inter Forum Externum et Internum," *Apollinaris*, XIX (1946), 69. Another norm, which appears occasionally, is the circumstance whether jurisdiction is exercised *inter praesentes* or *inter absentes*.

[42] Each particular author here serves merely as an example or specimen and no further implications are intended.

With the previous criterion of public utility, it could be argued that the State, though it did concern its members as individuals, exercised its jurisdiction in one forum only, and that external, since in the treatment of its members as individuals it always acted primarily and directly for the common good. Now, with the new distinction of juridic proof, it can be more precisely demonstrated that the State is concerned with, and functions practically in, one forum only, and that external. In civil society there is one power, which concerns its subjects' acts which appear extrinsically and can be proved, so that whatever cannot be proved is inexorably considered as non-existent. In matters of fraud, perjury, good faith, and the like, which appear to be acts proper to the internal forum, the State takes cognizance not by reason of the internal act but by reason of the externalization of the act and its subsequent capability of juridic proof.

Be that as it may, one may reasonably draw the conclusion from the arguments proposed in this chapter that most of the modern authors are merely propagating as their criterion of distinction a superficial norm which does not reach the heart of the matter. One may conclude further that those authors who insist on the norm of public utility for distinguishing the forum would greatly reduce the conceivable sphere of parochial jurisdiction in the external forum. Nevertheless, even in the application of the criterion of public utility as the solitary norm, parochial jurisdiction in the external forum is not thereby eliminated.[43]

[43] Cf., e.g., cans. 1043-1045.

CHAPTER V

"JURISDICTION" AND THE CODE

The antiquated debate whether there is a dichotomy or trichotomy of ecclesiastical power is well-nigh terminated.[1] The intrinsic arguments from the Code are sound and almost conclusive in favor of the dichotomy.[2] The extrinsic arguments, as found among the commentators, are practically unanimous.[3] Everything indicates the dichotomy of ecclesiastical power, that is, the twofold division of power into that of orders and that of jurisdiction.[4]

Nevertheless, there appears in the Code a mention of three powers which are mutually irreducible, namely, the power of orders, the power of jurisdiction, and dominative power.[5] It is commonly known and accepted that the first of these powers relates to the confection and administration of the sacred rites, while the latter two refer to rule or government. Most of the authors indicate all the characteristics in which these powers coincide and in which

[1] Two mutual adversaries are Sotillo, cf. *Compendium Iuris Publici Ecclesiastici* (2. ed., Santander: Editorial Sal Terrae, 1951), pp. 91-99, who upholds the dichotomy, and Salaverri, cf. "La Triple Potestad de la Iglesia," *Miscelanea Comillas* (Santander, 1942-), XIV (1950), 7-84, who supports the trichotomy.

[2] Cf. Tirado, *De Iurisdictionis Acceptione*, pp. 191-196.

[3] Cf. Badii, *Institutiones*, I, 127; Bargilliat, *Praelectiones*, I, 31; Berutti, *Institutiones*, Vol. II, Par. I, p. 75; Maroto, *Institutiones*, I, 567; Sipos, *Enchiridion*, p. 137; Tirado, *De Iurisdictionis Acceptione*, pp. 194-204; Jone, *Commentarium in Codicem Iuris Canonici* (3 vols., Paderborn: Officina Libraria F. Schöningh, 1950-1955), I, 125 (hereafter cited *Commentarium*); Raus, *Institutiones Canonicae* (2. ed., Lugduni-Parisiis: Typis Emmanuelis Vitte, 1931), p. 14.

[4] Can. 108, § 3.

[5] Cf. Saucedo, "Exercitium Jurisdictionis et Superiores Laici ex Ordine Hospitalario S. Joannis de Deo," *Commentarium pro Religiosis* (Romae, 1920-1934; *Commentarium pro Religiosis et Missionariis*, Romae, 1935-), XIII (1932), 60, 61; Tirado, *De Iurisdictionis Acceptione*, p. 159. Dominative power is accorded separate treatment, cf. *infra*, pp. 133-137.

they differ. The matter at hand concerns only one of these powers, namely, jurisdiction.

The examination of the sense in which jurisdiction is used by the Code may be made in two ways: intrinsically, i.e., based on arguments from the Code, and extrinsically, i.e., based on facts and opinions outside the Code.

ARTICLE I. THE NOTION OF JURISDICTION

It is only logical that most of the legal notions that existed before the Code should be found in it, since the Code, for the most part, retains the discipline in force prior to it.[6] The notion of jurisdiction shortly prior to the Code, as gathered from the authors, was accorded a very broad signification. Neither prior to the Code, however, nor after it has the Church proposed a formal definition of jurisdiction. Therefore, if one wishes to determine what changes, if any, in the notion of jurisdiction were made in the Code, one must seek out and analyse those canons which contribute notions on the use of jurisdiction. The fundamental canons of this nature are canons 218, 196, 197, 201 and 335.

Up to this point the term "jurisdiction" has often been used in conjunction with the phrases "in the strict sense" and "in the broad sense." For the most part, the former phrase signified the complete, perfect, substantial jurisdiction which includes legislative, judicial, and executive power; the latter phrase indicated the incomplete, imperfect, partial jurisdiction which is some part of the former. A new distinction should be made at this juncture in the interests of clarity. This distinction, while it is not a real division of jurisdiction, is drawn between true jurisdiction and apparent jurisdiction. *True* jurisdiction may be *complete* or *incomplete,* as above, and is then known respectively as jurisdiction *in the strict sense* or jurisdiction *in the broad sense; apparent* jurisdiction is referred to as jurisdiction *in the broadest sense.*

[6] Can. 6.

SECTION 1. THE SENSE OF JURISDICTION IN CANON 218

In the Code of Canon Law every ecclesiastical power not belonging to the power of orders falls reducibly under the name of jurisdiction.[7] In other words, though the term "jurisdiction" is used in the strict sense, it is employed also in the broad sense, and sometimes in the broadest sense, which embraces powers which are said to pertain only reducibly to jurisdiction.

The Code contains not only disciplinary laws but also some principles both of the natural and the revealed divine law on which ecclesiastical legislation is based. Canon 218, for example, restates the doctrine of primacy defined in the fourth session of the Vatican Council (1869, 1870).[8] Canon 218, therefore, is entirely dogmatic:

> § 1. Romanus Pontifex, Beati Petri in primatu Successor, habet non solum primatum honoris, sed supremam et plenam potestatem iurisdictionis in universam Ecclesiam tum in rebus quae ad fidem et mores, tum in iis quae ad disciplinam et regimen Ecclesiae per totum orbem diffusae pertinent.
> § 2. Haec potestas est vere episcopalis, ordinaria et immediata tum in omnes et singulas ecclesias, tum in omnes et singulos pastores et fideles, a quavis humana auctoritate independens.

The general principle on the subject of ecclesiastical power is here presented, so that one may infer that the power of ruling the Church, in which subjects inferior to the pope participate, is derived from him as from the supreme and only font of universal ecclesiastical power. This canon speaks so absolutely that it would be difficult to find any power for ruling the Church not included in the words of the canon.

[7] "In Codice vox *iurisdictio* quamcumque, tum fori externi tum fori interni, potestatem, quae ordinem non spectat, designat."—Chelodi, *Ius Canonicum de Personis* (3. ed., recognita et aucta a Pio Ciprotti, Vincenza: Società Anonima Tipografica, Trento: A. Ardesi, 1942), n. 125, p. 205.

[8] Cf. McNabb, *The Decrees of the Vatican Council* (New York, Cincinnati, Chicago, 1907), p. 44.

The object of the jurisdiction in canon 218, generically considered, is both a power in relation to faith and morals and also a power in relation to discipline and rulership.

The papal power relating to faith and morals comprehends the following: infallibility;[9] supremacy relative to an Oecumenical Council;[10] protection of doctrine through the instrumentality of the Sacred Congregation of the Holy Office;[11] prohibition of books by general law;[12] benefit of recourse to the Holy See against decrees of particular councils or local ordinaries;[13] protection of doctrine by means of laws regulating and promoting preaching.[14] Furthermore, the Holy Father reserves the right of instituting universities and faculties giving degrees in the sacred sciences and the right of conferring those degrees.[15] Moreover, the pope has charge of mission territories; he promotes and safeguards Christian morals in the beatification and canonization of the servants of God; he approves religious orders and other institutes, etc., etc. Therefore, the pope has the universal and supreme power relating to faith and morals, which he exercises through the works listed. These works doubtlessly come under the name of jurisdiction in canon 218.

The papal power relating to discipline and rule may be summed up thus: the pope makes laws, authentically interprets them, and makes dispositions whereby their execution is urged, all by reason of his supreme legislative power;[16] he judges their fulfillment by reason of his supreme judicial power;[17] he coerces delinquents with just penal-

[9] Vat. Council, IV Sess.

[10] Can. 222, § 2.

[11] Can. 247, §§ 1, 2.

[12] Can. 1395.

[13] Can. 1375, § 2.

[14] Cans. 1327-1355.

[15] Cans. 1376, § 1; 1377.

[16] Cans. 218, in connection with 335, § 1; 80, in connection with 81; 17, § 1; 22; 25; 3; etc.

[17] Cans. 1557; 1569; 1962; etc.

ties by reason of his supreme penal power;[18] and by his supreme administrative power he has the free disposition of whatever else is necessary for the attainment of the Church's proper end.[19] All these things pertain to jurisdiction in this canon and, therefore, the term "jurisdiction" must be viewed here as jurisdiction in the strict sense and as jurisdiction in its greatest possible scope.

SECTION 2. THE SENSE OF JURISDICTION IN CANON 196

One may conclude from canon 196 that the power of jurisdiction is the power of rulership which is in the Church by divine institution. The canon states:

> Potestas iurisdictionis seu regiminis quae ex divina institutione est in Ecclesia, alia est fori externi, alia fori interni, seu conscientiae, sive sacramentalis sive extra-sacramentalis.

The sacred nature of jurisdiction is reconfirmed by that part of the definition of simony that violates the divine law which mentions the completely voluntary exchange of an intrinsically spiritual thing, and offers jurisdiction as one of the examples.[20] Therefore, jurisdiction is a sacred or spiritual power.

The clause of canon 196, "*quae ex divina institutione est in Ecclesia,*" which modifies the power of jurisdiction, refers to all ecclesiastical jurisdiction. Not every grade or degree of the hierarchy of jurisdiction is of divine institution, but the power in which each grade or degree participates is a spiritual power by reason of divine institution. This would imply that even the power of the Church over her temporal goods is a formally spiritual power.[21] There is no discrepancy when the Code speaks

[18] Cans. 2320; 2343, § 1; 2367; 2369, § 1; 2295; etc.

[19] Cans. 215, § 1; 329, § 2; 350, § 1; 312; 239, § 1; 320; 499; 1499; 1532; 1145; 1244; 246-257; etc.

[20] "Studiosa voluntas emendi vel vendendi pro pretio temporali rem intrinsece spiritualem, ex. gr., Sacramenta, ecclesiasticam iurisdictionem . . . est simonia iuris divini."—Can. 727, § 1.

[21] Cf. Journet, *The Apostolic Hierarchy*, p. 262.

of jurisdiction over spiritual things and jurisdiction over temporal things.[22] One should interpret the phrase "jurisdiction over the spiritual and over the temporal" as the *spiritual power* both over things spiritual in themselves and over things temporal in themselves.[23]

Moreover, *"regimen"* or rulership is found as a synonym of the jurisdiction which is in the Church by divine institution. This power of rulership excludes all other powers of rulership which are not of divine institution, e.g., mere dominative power. The term is used in many canons to signify the total power of rulership in the particular work to which it refers.[24] Therefore, no power of jurisdiction is excluded from the ambit of the word "rulership" when it is used in this fashion. Under an etymological aspect, rulership signifies the *action* of directing people toward the end contemplated for them.[25]

SECTION 3. OTHER NAMES AND USES OF "JURISDICTION"

The term "hierarchy" may be considered objectively and subjectively: objectively, it is the sacred power shared by divers subjects in different degrees; subjectively, it is the series of persons, usually subordinate to others, who participate in ecclesiastical power in different degrees. The objective hierarchy is the cause of the subjective hierarchy, inasmuch as persons are constituted in the various degrees according to the divers degrees of powers which are bestowed upon them.

The term "hierarchy" in canon 108, § 3, may be taken in both of the above senses: subjectively, inasmuch as the canon speaks of a series of persons, some subordinate to others, which series is twofold, i.e., by reason of orders and by reason of jurisdiction;[26] objectively, inasmuch as

[22] E.g., cans. 368, § 1; 435, §1.

[23] Cf. *infra*, pp. 149-152.

[24] Cf. cans. 296, § 1; 312; 322; 334, § 2; 340, § 3; 363; 366; 381, § 1, 1°; 429; 431, § 1; 472, 1°, 3°.

[25] Cf. Tirado, *De Iurisdictionis Acceptione*, p. 179.

[26] Can. 108, §§ 2, 3.

the canon assigns the cause of the twofold subjective hierarchy, namely, the hierarchy by reason of orders, or as the power of orders in divers subjects is shared in different degrees, and the hierarchy by reason of jurisdiction, or as the power of jurisdiction in different degrees is capable of a sharing on the part of various subjects. Therefore, the Code indicates that there is a duplex subjective hierarchy and a duplex objective hierarchy, or, in other words, that there is a twofold series of persons, some subordinate to others, and a twofold power shared in different degrees, namely, the powers of orders and of jurisdiction.

The power of orders and the power of jurisdiction pertain to clerics alone.[27] Laymen are not absolutely incapacitated for the reception of ecclesiastical jurisdiction, as one can readily infer from canon 219 in the at least possible event of the election of a layman to the papacy; laymen are, however, excluded from the possession of jurisdiction by the general law. The clergy, therefore, constitute the hierarchy of jurisdiction consisting of various degrees, some of which, namely, the supreme pontificate and the subordinated episcopate, are of divine institution, while the rest are of ecclesiastical institution.[28] The Code does not enumerate those clerics who belong to the hierarchy of jurisdiction instituted by ecclesiastical law, but it does affirm that those who possess ordinary jurisdiction in the external forum are properly designated by the name of prelate.[29]

This ordinary power of jurisdiction as mentioned in canon 110 should be interpreted in the light of canon 198, § 1, so as to signify episcopal or quasi-episcopal power, i.e., complete and perfect jurisdiction, or jurisdiction in the strict sense. It is from such an interpretation that arises the modern view on the subject of prelacy, namely, that only those who possess *complete* jurisdiction in the external forum can be considered as prelates. Therefore, a pastor or an official of the curia, though he possess some jurisdic-

[27] Can. 118.

[28] Can. 108, §§ 1-3.

[29] Can. 110.

tion in the external forum, is not a prelate in the proper sense.[30]

The variable use of the term "jurisdiction" in the Code is quite obvious. This use is expressed by the application of the term to numerous notions. This use is intimated in the representation of the powers of jurisdiction by various names in divers places. Some of the terms in the Code synonymous with jurisdiction are *ius, potestas, auctoritas, facultas, regimen, administratio, gubernatio,* and *cura animarum.* It must be noted, of course, that not all of these terms are used synonymously with jurisdiction each time they appear. One must go to the individual occurrence in order to determine whether these terms equate jurisdiction therein. An investigation of the terms individually, however, is entirely unnecessary to substantiate the generic use of jurisdiction in the Code, which has already been adequately demonstrated. Nevertheless, several of these terms and notions are noted.

"Auctoritas," or authority, is identified with jurisdiction in many places in the Code.[31] *"Cura animarum,"* or the care of souls, may indicate a ministry in both forums[32] and may even signify complete jurisdiction.[33] This term, however, is usually employed for the designation of jurisdiction in the broad sense.[34] Jurisdiction is the name attributed to the entire power of ruling a diocese.[35] And again, jurisdiction is the title given to the relation of superior to inferior.[36]

[30] Cf. Ojetti, "Praelatus in Codice Iuris Canonici quisnam sit," *Periodica de Re Morali, Canonica, Liturgica* (*Periodica de Religiosis et Missionariis,* Brugis, 1905-1919; *Periodica de Re Canonica et Morali, utilia praesertim Religiosis et Missionariis,* Brugis, 1920-1927; *Periodica de Re Morali, Canonica, Liturgica,* Brugis, 1927-1936, Romae, 1937-), XVII (1928), 229*-231*.

[31] E.g., cans. 218, § 2; 364, § 2, 2°; 1160.

[32] E.g., cans. 154; 2350, § 2.

[33] E.g., can. 1405, § 2.

[34] E.g., cans. 461; 464, §§ 1, 2.

[35] E.g., cans. 958, § 1; 1304, 4°; 1519, § 1.

[36] E.g., cans. 690, § 1; 1491, § 2.

By way of a scholium, it is noted that the lawful exercise of the power of orders reposes within the realm of the power of jurisdiction. The Church, by reason of its power of jurisdiction and positive legislation, regulates the entire exercise of the power of orders. That power must be exercised in accordance with ecclesiastical law in order to be considered as lawful. Therefore, by general or particular law, or even in individual cases, the subjects are assigned over whom the minister may exercise acts of the power of orders; this effects that sacraments and sacramentals may be administered to determinate persons only and in determinate places only. Thus it is that the prescriptions of the Church can affect either the validity of the sacraments or their lawfulness only.[37]

Furthermore, the use of the term "jurisdiction" is preserved in the Code in the classical sense of taking cognizance and defining, or simply in the sense of *ius dicere.* This is true not only in relation to the external forum,[38] but also in respect of the internal forum.[39]

Article II. The Divisions of Jurisdiction

Section 1. The Comprehensive Divisions Expressed in the Code

There are three principal divisions of jurisdiction evident in the Code. Each of these comprehends all of jurisdiction, but each of these, when subdivided, separates the totality of ecclesiastical jurisdiction into two mutually exclusive parts. The three principal divisions are made by reason of the object, by reason of the cause, and by reason of the mode of exercise of the jurisdiction. Thus it is that the Code speaks of jurisdiction of the external or of the internal forum, of ordinary or of delegated juris-

[37] Cf. Chelodi, *Ius Canonicum de Personis*, pp. 292, 293.

[38] Cf. cans. 1561, § 2; 1569, § 2; 1637; 1725, 3°.

[39] Cf. *infra*, p. 175; also cans. 239, § 1, 2°; 399, § 3; 872-881.

diction, and of judicial and involuntary or of non-judicial and voluntary jurisdiction.[40]

In view of the fact that an entire chapter is devoted to the external and the internal forum, there seems to be little need for any discussion here, beyond noting the common divisions of each forum. Jurisdiction in the external forum may be complete or incomplete.[41] Beyond that, jurisdiction in the internal forum may relate to the sacramental forum or the non-sacramental forum.[42]

The second principal division concerns jurisdiction either as it is attached by law to an ecclesiastical office, in which case it is known as ordinary jurisdiction, or as it is committed to a person, in which case it is known as delegated jurisdiction.[43] If the incumbent exercises in his own name the power inherent by law in his office, the jurisdiction is ordinary and proper; if in the name of another, the jurisdiction is vicarious, though also it still is ordinary in view of being attached by law to the office.[44] Any opinion that would demand that if the power is to be ordinary it must be connaturally attached to the office seems to be unfounded. Canon 197, § 1, does not demand such attachment. Canon 873, § 1, concerns the ordinary jurisdiction of cardinals for the hearing of the confessions of anyone, but this power could not be connatural to the cardinalship, to which men who were not even priests could be promoted prior to the Code. One commentary gives this appraisal of the situation:

> Ordinary power of jurisdiction is that which the law itself attaches to an office; delegated power of jurisdiction, that which is not attached to an office but is committed to a person.
>
> This division is exhaustive and the power of

[40] Cans. 196; 197; 201, §§ 2, 3.
[41] E.g., cans. 335, § 1; 1573.
[42] E.g., cans. 872; 1047.
[43] Cans. 197, § 1; 145.
[44] Can. 197, §§ 1, 2.

> jurisdiction, no matter by whom possessed, must belong to one of these two categories.[45]

It is clear, then, that when the law attaches power to an office the power is ordinary, and when the law commits power to a person the power is delegated.

Delegated power may derive either from man or from the law. Power delegated by man is that which one person commits to another; power delegated by law is that which the law itself, in some special cases, commits to a person who lacks an ecclesiastical office. The following is a condensed version of one author's evaluation of the delegation by law after the promulgation of the Code: Some men absolutely deny its existence (Hilling, Stutz, Roberti, Claeys Boúúaert, Simenon, Blat, Badii); others vigorously defend its existence and fall into error by extending the small number of cases wherein it appears in the Code (Ojetti, Fuster); others take the middle path by recognizing its existence and limiting the number of its applications (Vermeersch, Creusen, Sipos, Maroto, Coronata, Cocchi).[46]

The question of power delegated by law does not essentially concern this dissertation, inasmuch as the jurisdiction of pastors is a true jurisdiction whether it be ordinary or delegated by law. From the few principles already presented, however, a firm position may be maintained. The delegated power mentioned in the Code may be either delegated by man or delegated by law.[47] But once a power delegated by law is attached to an office, it no longer preserves the character of a delegation, but is absorbed into the ordi-

[45] Abbo-Hannan, *The Sacred Canons* (2 vols., St. Louis: B. Herder Book Co., 1952), I, 253.

[46] Crisci, "De Delegatione a Iure in Iure Canonico Vigenti," *Apollinaris*, X (1937), pp. 518-527. The conclusion of this article, as drawn by its author, is that delegation by law can exist juridically for those only who lack an office. All faculties which prior to the Code were powers delegated by law no longer preserve this character, for they have passed into ordinary power.—*Ibid.*, p. 535.

[47] As examples of a *delegatio a iure*, cf. cans. 882; 883; 1044; 2252; 2254.

nary power of that office.[48] Therefore, delegation by law can exist in the Code only in those cases wherein the power is by law conferred on one who lacks an office, and wherein, therefore, no attachment of power to an office is involved.[49]

The third principal division of the Code concerns the power of jurisdiction as it is exercised either within or outside an ecclesiastical tribunal, and which is known, therefore, as judicial and involuntary, or as non-judicial and voluntary jurisdiction.[50] Two divisions of minor importance are: universal jurisdiction, which is exercised by the supreme pontiff alone, and particular jurisdiction, which is exercised by all those who are subordinate to the pope; and territorial jurisdiction, which indicates the geographical realm of the superior's power, and personal jurisdiction, which refers to the subjects over whom the power is exercised.

[48] Can. 197, § 1.

[49] For further arguments, cf. Cabreros de Anta, "Concepto de Potestad Ordinaria y Delegada," *Revista Española de Derecho Canónico*, VIII (1953), 703-744; De Meester, "Notio Jurisdictionis Ordinariae et Delegatae," *Collationes Brugenses*, XXI (1921), 238-243; Hilling, "Begriff und Umfang der *potestas iurisdictionis ordinaria* und *delegata* nach geltendem Kirchenrecht," *Archiv für katholisches Kirchenrecht*, CIV (1924), 181-204. The question whether ordinary power is demanded or whether delegated power suffices for the constituting of an office is also debated; cf. Sipos, "Quaestiones Selectae," *Jus Pontificium*, XVI (1936), 67, 68; XIX (1939), 96, 97. Sipos upholds the latter opinion (against Hilling, Toso, etc.), by virtue of an argument based simply on canons 197, § 1, and 145, § 1; the former opinion, however, appears preferable in view of arguments both from the very concept of an office and from the principles of delegation.

[50] Can. 201, §§ 2, 3; cf. Hilling, "Die Bedeutung der *iurisdictio voluntaria* und *involuntaria* im römischen Recht und im kanonischen Recht des Mittelalters und der Neuzeit," *Archiv für katholisches Kirchenrecht*, CV (1925), 449-473; Monin, "La Notion de la Juridiction 'Volontaire'—en Droit Canonique," *Ephemerides Theologicae Lovanienses*, VIII (1931), 630-637; Johnson, "De Distinctione inter Potestatem Iudicialem et Potestatem Administrativam in Iure Canonico," *Apollinaris*, IX (1936), 258-269.

SECTION 2. THE COMPREHENSIVE DIVISION SUGGESTED BY THE CODE

There remains still another division of jurisdiction in the Code, namely, the division into legislative, judicial, and coercive power.[51] A division of a genus into the species which fully constitute that genus is surely a true and comprehensive division. This particular division, however, was not accorded consideration in the treatment of the principal divisions of jurisdiction in the Code because it is not, in the opinion of the writer, a comprehensive division of *ecclesiastical* jurisdiction. Canon 335, § 1, does not propose a definition of ecclesiastical jurisdiction; it merely describes the manner in which the jurisdiction of any perfect society is principally exercised. If one wishes to retain this description as a division of ecclesiastical jurisdiction, there is no objection. That person must, however, remember: 1) that the object of the exercise of ecclesiastical jurisdiction is greater than that of non-ecclesiastical jurisdiction, and 2) that it extends, in general, to the entire governing and teaching of the clergy and laity as well as to the administration of ecclesiastical property.[52] Furthermore, the coercive power must be viewed under a twofold aspect: that of punishment, and that of administration.[53]

The more precise and truly comprehensive division of ecclesiastical jurisdiction seems to be that which marks legislative, judicial, and *executive* power as the three species of the genus, and which subdivides executive power into coercive, governmental and administrative power. The previous treatment of canon 218 demands such a division.[54]

[51] Can. 335, § 1.

[52] Cf. Vermeersch-Creusen, *Epitome Iuris Canonici cum Commentariis ad Scholas et ad Usum Privatum* (3 vols., Vol. I, 7. ed., 1949; Vol. II, 6. ed., 1940; Vol. III, 6. ed., 1946, Mechliniae-Romae: H. Dessain), I, 351 (hereafter cited *Epitome*); Cocchi, *Commentarium,* III, 209.

[53] Cf. Abbo-Hannan, *The Sacred Canons,* I, 362.

[54] Cf. *supra,* pp. 112-114.

Many illustrious authors who are especially versed in public ecclesiastical law, and authors who have given profound thought to the notion of ecclesiastical jurisdiction, present such a division.[55] According to this division, the legislative power is the power of making the law; the judicial power is the power of judging the fulfillment of the law; the executive power is the power of realizing the fulfillment of the law, either positively, by the exercise of rulership relating to the observance of the law, or negatively, by the exercise of rulership relating to the violation of the law.

The legislative power and the judicial power of the Church are well known and require no explanation. Moreover, the coercive power, considered even as one of the three components of the executive power, is readily identifiable as the Church's native and proper right of coercing delinquent subjects with spiritual and temporal penalties. The other two components of the executive power are distinguished according as they relate to persons or to things. In general, it may be said that the rulership of persons, physical and moral, reflects the governmental power, while the rulership or the unimpeded administration of things reflects the administrative power.[56]

[55] "Attenditur triplex functio quae potestatis iurisdictionis in publico societatis regimine propria est: legifera, videlicet, iudiciaria et executiva."—Ottaviani, *Compendium Iuris Publici Ecclesiastici* (4. ed., Romae: Typis Polyglottis Vaticanis, 1954), p. 133. "Ius canonicum, nomine retento, conceptum iurisdictionis ad universam potestatem regiminis, legiferam iudicialem executivam, ampliavit."—Chelodi, *Ius Canonicum de Personis*, n. 125, p. 205. Cf. also Toso, *Ad Codicem Iuris Canonici... Commentaria Minora* (5 vols. in 2, Taurini-Romae, 1920-1927), Lib. II, Tom. I, p. 164; Montero y Gutiérrez, *Derecho Publico Eclesiástico y Normas Generales* (2. ed., Madrid: Imprenta Saez, 1948), pp. 63- 107; McManus, *The Administration of Temporal Goods in Religious Institutes*, The Catholic University of America Canon Law Studies, n. 109 (Washington, D.C.: The Catholic University of America, 1937), p. 79; Sigur, "Lay Cooperation in the Administration of Church Property," *The Jurist* (Washington, D.C., 1940-), XIII (1953), 171.

[56] Cf. Ottaviani, *op. cit.*, pp. 177-223, for the application of each of the three components of the executive power.

Many authors, of course, do not make this division of jurisdiction, and a few of them are even actively opposed to it. One author, for instance, states:

> Potestas *executiva* sensu *stricto* non est propria quaedam species potestatis socialis, sed potius ad unamquamque speciem accedit; nam *leges* (p. leg.) sententiae iudiciales (p. iud.) et *poenae* (p. coer.) sunt executioni mandandae.[57]

This argument is not entirely true. It is known from the doctrine of penal law that one entire class of penalties is incurred concomitantly with the very commission of the delict.[58] Consequently, not all penalties need execution. Penalties should rather be considered as already the execution of the law whether after an adverse judicial sentence or, as in many cases, without any judicial sentence at all.

Article III. The Definitions of Jurisdiction by the Authors

Quite naturally, the notions of the men who took part in the codification are of great value in determining the meaning of jurisdiction in the Code. They themselves used jurisdiction in a very broad sense and, therefore, the presumption is that this notion of jurisdiction passed also into the Code. Even regardless of their influence on the doctrine in the Code, the dependency of other canonists on these authors is most evident in that the former constantly transcribe the definitions of the latter and make no mention of any change of the concept or usage of jurisdiction advanced by the Code.

The vast majority of the definitions given by all the authors are good and sound, and accordingly, for the most part, repetitious. These authors recognize the broad significance of jurisdiction and, as a result, define the term by means of a proportionately generic description. The typical acceptable definition of jurisdiction follows:

[57] Badii, *Institutiones*, I, 128, note 1.

[58] Can. 2217, § 1, 2°.

> [Est] potestas publica legitimi superioris, a Christo vel ab Ecclesia per canonicam missionem concessa, regendi baptizatos in ordine ad salutem aeternam.[59]

The few authors who define ecclesiastical jurisdiction as the power of ruling the baptized and then classify that same ecclesiastical power as public or private are not precise. In fact, they err because they are only half correct. The moment that they mention the term "private" they are no longer speaking of a true ecclesiastical jurisdiction.[60] All true ecclesiastical jurisdiction is *public* power. The basic reason for this is the fact that it proceeds from a perfect society; another valid reason is the fact that it is obtained, with the exception of the case of the Holy Father alone, by means of something which is of its very nature public, namely, an injunction or a canonical mission.[61] These authors make this distinction, in the first place, in order to classify ecclesiastical dominative power as something distinct from jurisdiction.[62] In the second place, they are enabled by means of this false distinction, to discredit some parochial jurisdiction in the external forum. By no stretch of the imagination, however, could anyone deny that jurisdiction in the internal forum is, canonically considered, a true jurisdiction and *public* power, even though it is so often exercised in the utmost secrecy of sacramental confession.

It is interesting to peruse the different definitions and distinctions of jurisdiction as presented by various authors,

[59] Maroto, *Institutiones*, I, 661; Wernz-Vidal, *Ius Canonicum ad Codicis Normam Exactum* (7 vols. in 8, Vol. II, 3. ed., Romae: Apud Aedes Universitatis Gregorianae, 1943), II, 59 (hereafter cited *Ius Canonicum*); Ottaviani, *Compendium Iuris Publici Ecclesiastici*, p. 125; cf. also, Vermeersch-Creusen, *Epitome*, I, 268; Prümmer, *Manuale Iuris Cononici in usum scholarum* (5. ed., Friburgi Brisgoviae, 1927), p. 119; Bargilliat, *Praelectiones*, I, 46.

[60] Cf., e.g., Beste, *Introductio in Codicem* (3. ed., Collegeville, Minn.: St. John's Abbey Press, 1946), p. 215, who appears to support this practice in view of his examples chosen to illustrate *privata iurisdictio*.

[61] Cf. can. 109; cf. also Vermeersch-Creusen, *Epitome*, I, 214.

[62] They err even in so doing, as is demonstrated later, cf. *infra*, pp. 133-137.

because one can often detect in them some personal opinions. The moment one notices that an author departs from the traditional definitions of jurisdiction, one may suspect that he is phrasing his definition in conformity with some particular notion or notions which he may later attempt to substantiate from his very definition of jurisdiction. No particular author is accused of this.

In reference, however, to the point of accentuating distinctions in conformity with personally preferred opinions, one author is cited because he seems by so doing to err canonically.

> Potestas, quae respicit forum externum, est potestas nativa, cum Ecclesia a Christo fundata sit qua societas perfecta. Agitur ergo de potestate propria. Potestas quae respicit forum internum a Deo Ecclesiae qua societati perfectae superaddita est. Agitur de potestate vicaria.[63]

While the writer has the deepest respect for this author, in view of the fact that he is generally most profound and canonically precise in his clear and brief comments, he not only cannot agree but must actively disagree with part of the statement, at least from the canonical standpoint.

The basis for the distinction in the foregoing quotation is the point that, if the State is a perfect society and has no internal forum, the Church with its internal forum has something (some power) which is not proper but superadded and vicarious. This notion somewhat loses sight of the specific nature of the Church, which has an internal forum just as properly as the body has its soul. This same notion, at least when considered canonically, is analogous to the idea that man has his soul only vicariously or as superadded, and that it does not properly belong to the nature of man. The Church, though a perfect society with all the means for attaining its end, simply has a more excellent end than any other juridically perfect society. The Church is, in fact, a superior perfect society by that very token. The internal forum, necessitated by the very nature of the

[63] Jone, *Commentarium*, I, 408.

Church, contributes to making the Church the superior perfect society that it is.

The same author then concludes:

> Iurisdictio in sensu stricto habetur solummodo si agitur de potestate quae exercetur in bonum publicum; potestas quae exercetur in bonum animae uniuscuiusque fidelis, non est potestas iurisdictionis in sensu stricto. Inde etiam in casu in quo Ecclesia alicui conferat partem potestatis illius vicariae, hic non obtinet potestatem iurisdictionis in sensu stricto.[64]

The exercise of jurisdiction in the sacrament of penance, according to this, is not jurisdiction in the strict sense. Obviously, the author does mean something other than that which is immediately apparent from these statements, but this does not need to be pursued.

The notion of jurisdiction which the above cited authors exhibited after the Code concurs, for the most part, with the classical notion commonly retained prior to the Code. The classical definition propounded the universal power of rulership; the definition which most of the commentators offer, as best agreeing with the sense of the canons, sustains this element of the universal power of rulership. Therefore, the usage of jurisdiction which post-Code authors retain truly confirms the generic concept of jurisdiction which must be retained in the present legislation.

In recapitulation of the entire chapter, it is seen that jurisdiction has the sense of the public power of rulership in general, which by divine institution is in the Church, so that its ambit is in no way limited to any more excellent genus of the power to rule, but is extended to all the power of rulership proper to the Church by the will of God. The twofold hierarchy, orders and jurisdiction, adequately shows that the power in the Church by divine institution is twofold only, i.e., the power of orders and the power of jurisdiction, and that to the power of jurisdiction pertains everything which is not referred to orders. A further con-

[64] *Loc. cit.*

cept is exhibited by canon 196 wherein jurisdiction is called a power of rulership so that, even though in and of itself this term does not exclude any power of ruling, it is restricted by the canon to the power of rulership divinely given to the Church, and, with this restriction justly preserved, no other restriction is to be envisioned as added from the text itself. There are many texts in the Code wherein, as no one may doubt, jurisdiction enjoys the generic meaning of a power of rulership. The same can also be stated of the term *"regimen"* from its similarly generic usage whereby it appears in many texts as a synonym of a complete power of rulership. Finally, while the Code expresses three comprehensive divisions of the power of jurisdiction, it suggests still another which is more precise, namely, the division into legislative, judicial, and executive power, which executive power comprises a coercive, a governmental, and an administrative power.

All in all, it is evident that the sense of jurisdiction after the Code enjoys the same broad signification which was commonly accorded to it prior to the Code.

CHAPTER VI

THE RELATION OF OTHER POWERS IN THE CODE TO JURISDICTION

Though it is true that many authors use the term "jurisdiction" in the strict sense, in the broad sense, and in the broadest sense, there are some canonists who designate certain powers in the Code not as jurisdiction, but rather apply the norms of the Code for jurisdiction to these powers by analogy or extension, instead of by the proper signification of the words. When the Code treats of minor offices, it uses the words "right," "faculty," "power," "authority," and the like, rather than the term "jurisdiction." Obviously, this creates the difficulty of distinguishing which of these offices and their acts relate to true jurisdiction and which do not. If the principles of jurisdiction, however, which have been established thus far are sound, then the conclusions rightly deduced from them are also sound. Ecclesiastical jurisdiction, according to these principles, is the active potency, spiritual and public, given by Christ or the Church by injunction or canonical mission, whereby a man authoritatively acts as a principal second cause in directing the faithful to their supernatural end. Every power, therefore, which fulfills this concept should be designated as jurisdiction, whether it be perfect jurisdiction or imperfect jurisdiction.

The concepts of subjective right and power should be retained. A simple subjective right intimates the power or the faculty to do, omit, or demand something in one's own behalf, to which corresponds the correlative obligation in others of attributing to him what is his or of not impeding him in his right. The social subjective right, however, which is a power in a superior, contains the faculty of commanding or efficaciously impelling subjects to the end of the society, and not by mere persuasion but by imperium. It should be noted that the power whereby a society is governed for attaining its end is shared by subjects in various degrees. In one case a superior may have perfect power, such as that of a bishop, and be able to exercise legislative, judicial, and executive power.[1] In another case a superior may have imperfect power, such as that of the diocesan judge in the episcopal curia, and be able to exercise only a part of perfect power, such as judicial power only.[2] Though each participates in different degrees, each shares in the actual faculty of an efficacious directing toward the end of society.

By reason of the scope of this dissertation, the consideration of the relation of each and every faculty in the Code to the power of jurisdiction is not envisioned. Several faculties of major import, however, are surveyed in this chapter. The power of pastors in the external forum is surely of major import, but, inasmuch as this consideration is the final objective of the entire dissertation, it is appraised separately in the form of the final chapter.

If there is any general principle which could be applied as a practical guide of distinction between jurisdictional and non-jurisdictional powers, it is this: do not attend to the mere external species of an act; discern rather the power whereby the act is performed. In other words, while the notion of jurisdiction is as broad as that of law, for jurisdiction is, in a sense, the original and efficient cause of law, every act which is performed in fulfillment of or in accordance with the law is not thereby an act of jurisdiction.

Article I. The Authority of Ecclesiastical Societies

Section 1. The Power of Societies in General

Power or authority in a society is the right of obliging the members in order to attain the end of the society. The Church is a juridically perfect society and encompasses many

[1] Cf. can. 335, § 1.
[2] Cf. can. 1573, § 1.

imperfect societies. If one asks where the right of ruling in society comes from, or what is the origin of authority considered in itself, one raises a question connected with the juridic origin of the society. In view of the fact that authority is necessary for any society to remain secure and to attain its end, it follows that the juridic cause of the society is also the juridic cause of its authority or power, or, in other words, by the right whereby the society is established, by that same right is established its necessary and proportionate authority.

One may also inquire how the subject of power is constituted. The immediate subject of power has social power originally, and not by participation from other persons of the society over which he presides. If a person has authority because it was given him by the other members of his society, he is then a mediate subject of authority.

In a society altogether free, i.e., not of necessary existence, the immediate subject of authority is the group of members, because from their will emanates the power in the society; practically, however, there will be a mediate subject designated by election or acceptance. The origin of power, therefore, in even a mediate subject, is the will of the members from which proceed the necessary rights of ruling the society.

In the necessary society, the Church, the origin of power in the subject is also the same as the juridic origin of the society, because Christ Himself determined the form of ecclesiastical rulership. Therefore, all subjects of ecclesiastical power of rulership are immediate subjects of power, whether the power that they share is complete or incomplete power. Furthermore, that power is public, for it proceeds from a public and juridically perfect society.

> But how is one to know whether the authority in a society is dominative or jurisdictional? One way of solving the problem will be to examine the nature of the society which exercises the authority or jurisdiction. If it is an imperfect body, dominative power alone will be found to reside essentially in its rulers. From such an analysis

> only two societies, the Church and the State, essentially exercise jurisdiction. However, a participation in the jurisdictional power of the perfect society may be given to the rulers of those imperfect societies which are also parts of a perfect society. Thus by a positive determination of the supreme ruler of the higher body the superiors of an imperfect society may exercise jurisdiction, not essentially as rulers of the imperfect societies, but as superiors of an officially recognized part of a perfect society.[3]

In a sense, every power is dominative power, or the private power over an inferior which is proper to a superior.

> In qualibet potestate adest dominium, et hac ratione quaelibet potestas esset dominativa; sed quia dominium ethimologice a domino venit et dominus a domo, potestas privata propria domini dicitur potestas dominativa.[4]

Therefore, in every society there is private dominative power. This may be called *mere* dominative power, and in many societies this is the only power present. The Code refers to this type of power in several places.[5] This type of power in an imperfect society proceeds in no way from any juridically perfect society and, therefore, is truly private power.

> Potestas privata, quae in familia v.gr. adest, non provenit a Statu quia ipsa societas familiaris ab alio iure praevalenti sumit originem; ideo non tantum inter societatem et familiam sed inter potestatem utriusque adest aliqua contrapositio et independentia; potestas familiaris non participatur a Statu.

[3] Clancy, *The Local Religious Superior*, The Catholic University of America Canon Law Studies, n. 175 (Washington, D.C.: The Catholic University of America Press, 1943), p. 10.

[4] Fuertes, "De Potestate Dominativa in Religionibus non Exemptis," *Commentarium pro Religiosis et Missionariis*, XXXII (1953), 205.

[5] E.g., in cans. 89; 93, § 1; 1223, § 2. Cf. also cans. 501, § 1; 1312, § 1.

> Sicut in familia etiam in societatibus privatis, adest potestas quae a Statu non procedit.[6]

One may readily draw an analogy from this quotation to a religious institute, wherein there is dominative power which does not proceed from the power of the Church, and which is therefore private. It seems, however, that a certain dominative power mentioned in canon 501, § 1, does proceed from the power of the Church. If this is true, that dominative power must be public power; and if it is public power, it must be the power of jurisdiction.

SECTION 2. PUBLIC DOMINATIVE POWER

Not all juridic elements are immutable. Canon law, however, like Roman law before it, is notably traditional and conservative, and occasionally it can happen that a term is preserved while, by a change of times, the substance of the institute to which the term referred changes. This is at least partially the condition of the term "dominative power" in canon 501, § 1:

> Superiores et Capitula, ad normam constitutionum et iuris communis, potestatem habent dominativam in subditos; in religione autem clericali exempta, habent iurisdictionem ecclesiasticam tam pro foro interno, quam pro externo.

Authors and commentators sometimes hesitate to make any statement that some previous author has not already made, but from such a practice too much value is often placed on extrinsic authority and too little on intrinsic. Arcadius Larraona, however, did not hesitate to introduce and substantiate a juridically progressive notion. In his dissertation on public dominative power he proposed the introduction of the notion of such a power as resulting from an accurate inspection of the present canonical legislation, in which for the first time, officially and formally,

[6] Fuertes, *loc. cit.*

religious congregations were introduced as *Religiones* of the true name.[7]

The basic reason which moved the author to this notion is the vast realm of power which is designated in canon 501, § 1, by the name of dominative power. Every power of rulership belonging to non-exempt religious congregations, even inasmuch as they assume a public character, seems to be called dominative in this canon. From an inspection of modern legislation it is certain that public power belongs to some non-exempt religious congregations and, therefore, it is necessary to style some of the power mentioned in the first clause of canon 501, § 1, as *public dominative power.*[8]

Larraona in his thesis treats directly of clerical religious congregations of pontifical approval only. He states generally that, if not all, at least some principles which are generally and truly common can be applied with no difficulty to other societies.[9] What he intends to say by this is simply that, when the superior of a society is capable of possessing jurisdiction according to the law, the Church gives that superior some jurisdiction which is not the dominative power which he already has by reason of being a superior.

One of the author's principal arguments is that some imperfect societies have a public character and that they have, therefore, some public power.[10] An argument of equal or superior value is this: canon 501, § 1, states that superiors have dominative power according to the norm of the constitutions. If one pauses at the word "superiors," dominative power is already implied and necessitated. But the

[7] "De Potestate Dominativa Publica in Iure Canonico," *Acta Congressus Iuridici Internationalis* (5 vols., Romae: Apud custodiam librariam Pont. Instituti Utriusque Iuris, 1935-1937), IV, 145-180.

[8] *Ibid.*, p. 148. The name is well chosen because, while its acts have the species of dominative power by reason of the fact that the society is imperfect, the power is actually conferred by the Church and is, therefore, *public* dominative power or imperfect jurisdiction.

[9] *Ibid.*, pp. 150, 151.

[10] *Ibid.*, pp. 152-167.

canon continues that superiors have dominative power according to the norm of the constitutions *and the common law*. These are the words which substantiate *public* dominative power. The Code, of course, could have been merely remarking the obvious in referring to the dominative power of superiors instead of legislating. But when the Code states that superiors have dominative power according to the norm of the common law, the Code is legislating and is giving to superiors, if they have the capacity, something over and above mere dominative power. Larraona designates this super-added power as public dominative power or imperfect jurisdiction.[11]

It is certainly understandable that the legislator uses the term "dominative power" in this canon. First of all, dominative power is the only power which some superiors, e.g., women, can exercise "according to their constitutions and according to the common law," for the latter excludes women in general from the possession of the power of jurisdiction.[12] Journet, however, states from a theological standpoint:

> Female religious superiors, who cannot receive the sacrament of Order, have no jurisdiction in the strict sense [i.e., no declaratory or canonical power]; but they have a spiritual dominative power, which is a form of jurisdiction coming from Christ, and imparted by the Sovereign Pontiff.[13]

Canonically this must be rejected. One may say that women religious superiors have apparent jurisdiction, or jurisdiction in the broadest sense, but one may not maintain that they have jurisdiction in the strict sense or in the broad sense, i.e., true jurisdiction. The acts which these superiors

[11] "Ideo, potestas dominativa quatenus publica est et aliqua ex iurisdictione habet, non immerito dici potest iurisdictio imperfecta seu inchoata." —*Ibid.*, p. 167. In the footnote, the author cites Nicolaus Gil, who confirms this same view in his own dissertation, *De Potestate Dominativa* (Romae, 1932), pp. 90, 91.

[12] Can. 118.

[13] *The Apostolic Hierarchy*, p. 187.

perform may have the external species of jurisdiction, but the power whereby the acts are performed is not jurisdiction, for women religious are excluded from the possession and, consequently, the exercise of ecclesiastical jurisdiction.[14] Furthermore, with the exception of the case of the papacy, power must be conferred by the Church through an injunction or canonical mission in order to be considered in canon law as the power of jurisdiction. Canonically, therefore, women religious superiors have no ecclesiastical jurisdiction because: 1) their power cannot be a type of power which they are incapable of possessing; 2) their power is not conferred by the Church through the agency of an injunction or canonical mission.

The second reason that the legislator uses the term "dominative power" in canon 501, § 1, is that the "dominative power" in the first clause of the canon is, at the same time, being contrasted with the complete jurisdiction which is mentioned in the second clause of canon 501, § 1. In other words, to religious who are capable of possessing jurisdiction pertains some public ecclesiastical power, which in no way may be confused with mere dominative power, and in the canon cited this power is called dominative by way of opposition to that which, beyond dominative, is present in clerical exempt religious superiors, namely, jurisdiction in the strict sense.

The Commission for the Authentic Interpretation of the Code was asked whether the prescriptions of canons 197, 199, 206-209, concerning the power of jurisdiction, are to be applied, unless the nature of the matter or the text or context of the law prevents it, to the dominative power which superiors and chapters have in religious institutes and in societies of men or women living in common without public vows. The response was in the affirmative.[15] The Commission was necessarily speaking of mere dominative power. Public dominative power is jurisdiction, though im-

[14] Cf. cans. 490; 108, §§ 1-3; 118.
[15] *AAS*, XLIV (1952), 497; *Digest*, III, 73.

perfect, and the canons which govern jurisdiction already apply. Thus, Larraona states:

> *Quoad forum internum et externum.* Etsi haec divisio potestatis ecclesiasticae, in Codice videatur tantum potestati iurisdictionis applicari (c. 196), tamen ipsa aptanda etiam necessario est potestati dominativae publicae, quatenus publica est indeque ad potestatem iurisdictionis accedens.[16]

If one refrains from concentrating on names and terms and thinks of the notions behind the names, public dominative power is truly a power of jurisdiction, with the higher functions proper to strict jurisdiction excepted. Therefore, that public power which exists in certain religious congregations should be called jurisdiction in the broad sense.

Canon 501, § 1, should not be endowed necessarily with such force that, because of its wording, one should almost change the concept of things. If it is established that the power which is there designated as dominative comprehends power which in other places is listed under jurisdiction, that power should admit of being called jurisdiction in the broad sense, and to it should be applied whatever jurisdiction is determined in the Code and whatever is not exclusively proper to jurisdiction in the strict sense.

The doctrine that there is mention of public dominative power in the Code, which is actually imperfect jurisdiction, is consonant with the principles of jurisdiction established in the previous chapters; it is consonant with other passages in the Code; it is, finally, in accord with the classical acceptance of jurisdiction, with its note of publicity, which distinguished it from dominative power, so much so that jurisdiction would exist if the power was public, and dominative power would exist if it remained private.[17]

Article II. The Faculty of Assisting at Marriage

The doctrinal evaluation assigned to the faculty of assist-

[16] *"Art. cit."* pp. 175, 176.
[17] Tirado, *De Iurisdictione Acceptione*, p. 225.

ing at marriage prior to the Code was by no means unanimous. The authors who considered this faculty as something completely devoid of jurisdiction maintained that their opinion was the commonly accepted opinion. While the truth of this contention may be questioned in view of the number of authors who upheld the contrary opinion, this much is certain: 1) the majority of the authors did not consider the faculty of assisting at marriage as a jurisdictional power, and 2) the very nature of the act which flows from the faculty confirms their view.[18]

With the advent of the decree *Ne temere* and the Code itself, there is some basis for a revival of the question. The rôle of the priest who assists at marriage today consists in something more than a mere presence. The priest is required not only to be present freely and not through force or grave fear, but also to request and receive the consent of the parties.[19] A few authors deduce from this that under the law the faculty of assisting is a power of jurisdiction. Most of the authors, however, agree that these changes, although of great importance, in no way alter the nature of the act. This is certainly true. The fact that the official qualified witness to a marriage is required to do certain things for the purpose of avoiding subsequent inconveniences does not effect any substantial change in the nature of the act of assistance. It must also be maintained, by the same token, that the delegation of this faculty is not changed and remains the delegation of a non-jurisdictional faculty.

The question on the nature of this faculty of assisting is not without practical consequence. On the answer depends whether everything established in the Code concerning the power of jurisdiction, principally in reference to its possible delegation and suppletion, can be applied to the faculty of assisting at marriage.[20] Furthermore, on the same answer depends whether the faculty of assisting at

[18] Cf. *supra*, pp. 60-64.

[19] Cf. S.C.C., 2 aug. 1907—*Fontes*, n. 4340; can. 1095, § 1, 3°.

[20] Cf. cans. 196-209.

marriage is precluded through a suspension from jurisdiction.[21]

SECTION 1. THE NATURE OF THE FACULTY AND ITS RELATION TO JURISDICTION

The answer to the question on the nature of the faculty appears indeed to offer a difficulty. An entire dissertation written on the intimate nature of matrimonial assistance culminates in the conclusion that the assistance is not an act of jurisdiction but may be called jurisdiction in some broader sense.

> Quamobrem, sententia clara et succincta negans vel affirmans quoad naturam assistentiae matrimonialis dari nequit, quin adversarius quidam, armis validis ex iure ipso et ex doctrina assumptis, contra illam insurgat. Si iurisdictio in sensu strictissimo sumatur, impossibile videtur affirmare assistentiam matrimonialem esse actum iurisdictionis, hodierno iure aeque ac ante decretum *Ne temere.* Si vero quis illam esse actum iurisdictionis affirmaverit, illius assertio non ideo et in continenti est reiicienda, nam iurisdictionem latius intelligit, sensu scilicet qui argumentis et adminiculis non spernendis ex iure et ex doctrina haustis fulcitur.[22]

By means of a comparison, however, between the faculty of assisting and the elements of true jurisdiction a definite stand may be taken. Jurisdiction is the spiritual and public power, given by Christ or the Church by injunction or canonical mission, whereby a man authoritatively acts as a principal second cause in directing the faithful to their supernatural end. Even though one grants that many of these elements are realized in the faculty of matrimonial assistance, and thereby grants the similarity between it and jurisdiction, there is at least one element which is not verified. In the mere instance of assisting at mar-

[21] Cf. can. 2279, § 2, 1°.

[22] O'Connell, *De Intima Natura Assistentiae Matrimonialis* (Romae: Catholic Book Agency, 1940), pp. 86, 87.

riage the priest does not operate as a principal second cause.[23] In fact, his operation more closely resembles mere instrumentality. Therefore, one may say that the *nature* of the *act* of assisting at marriage, though no exercise of the power of orders is involved, relates more intimately to the power of orders than to the power of jurisdiction. The operation as by a mere instrument is certainly more in evidence than the operation as by a principal second cause. Nevertheless, the *exercise* of the *faculty* of assisting at marriage is quite similar to the exercise of a power of jurisdiction, inasmuch as it is governed by many of the norms for the exercise of jurisdiction. Accordingly the faculty is not to be identified with the power of jurisdiction, but its exercise is similar to that of jurisdiction.

Evidently, then, there is some similarity between the power of jurisdiction and the faculty of assisting at marriage. But there are at least two false theories concerning their relationship. The first of these maintains that everything in the Code which applies to jurisdiction may be applied also to the faculty of assisting. The second contends that no canon on jurisdiction avails also for the faculty of assisting, unless this is expressly mentioned in the Code.

The first theory is obviously false from the fact that canon 199, § 1, which establishes that ordinary power may be delegated habitually, cannot be applied to the faculty of assisting at marriage, except in the sole case of its general delegation to the assistant or curate (*vicarius cooperator*) for the parish to which he is assigned.[24]

The second theory is also false, but not quite as obviously so as the first. In the Code, under the title *De Potestate Ordinaria et Delegata,*[25] are presented general norms, which are of practical necessity, dealing with many facets of ec-

[23] It must be noted that the question in point is not about those things which precede the marriage, some of which may be acts of jurisdiction; the question concerns the mere instance or act of assisting.

[24] Can. 1096, § 1.

[25] Book II, Title V, cans. 196-210.

clesiastical power, e.g., its division, delegation, extension, cessation, etc. It is true that no power other than that of jurisdiction and orders is mentioned therein. Nevertheless, the Code treats of matrimonial assistance as a faculty which derives either from an office or through an act of delegation. Therefore, there is need of norms for regulating this faculty in reference to its delegation, cessation, and so on. Some of these norms are present in the Code, where assistance is treated specifically,[26] but these, for the most part, are norms which establish special dispositions of law, e.g., that a delegation must be made to a determinate person for a determinate marriage and not habitually, except in the case of the specified parochial assistants.[27] Many other norms, which are equally necessary, receive no mention in this chapter of the Code, e.g., the rules for subdelegation or for the cessation of the faculty of assisting. No one would accuse the legislator of the omission of norms for such an important matter. Therefore, one must conclude that, beyond the few norms in the Code which deal specifically with the faculty of assisting, there are other general norms which are destined by the legislator for application to the faculty of assisting at marriage.

There are other reasons which militate for the view that the canons on jurisdiction generally apply to matrimonial assistance. One of these is the fact that there are authentic interpretations which are nothing more than applications of the norms of canon 199 to the faculty of assisting at marriage. The Commission for the Authentic Interpretation of the Code answered the following two questions in the affirmative: 1) whether an assistant or curate who has received a general delegation for all marriages can subdelegate the faculty to a definite priest for a definite marriage, and 2) whether a pastor in the act of delegating can give to the one delegated the authority to subdelegate that faculty to a determinate priest for the same marriage.[28]

[26] Cans. 1094-1099. [27] Can. 1096, § 1.

[28] *AAS*, XX (1927), 61, 62; *Digest*, I, 541.

One might object to such reasoning by saying that this reply of the Commission entailed an extensive interpretation, and by adding, of course, that before its promulgation delegations of this sort were invalid. Authentic interpretations, however, should be presumed to be declarative, not extensive. One might also object incidentally that there can never be an act of delegating apart from the fact that the very act of delegating is in itself an act of jurisdiction. A delegation, however, does not necessarily involve jurisdiction, either as to the object of the act or as to its exercise. The Code itself indicates that the object of a delegation may be something non-jurisdictional.[29] The Commission for the Authentic Interpretation of the Code indicated that not every act of delegation needs to be in itself, i.e., apart from its object, an act of jurisdiction.[30]

The arguments presented are adequate for refuting the two false theories and for maintaining that the canons which deal with the power of jurisdiction are valid also for the faculty of assisting at marriage, in so far as the nature of the matter allows and the special canons on the faculty itself permit. As an example of the application of this principle, the case of a putative pastor assisting at a marriage may be suggested. There is no special canon relative to the supplying of the faculty of assisting, so that the nature of the matter permits an application of the norms for jurisdiction; accordingly canon 209 is made applicable for the case and the faculty of assisting is actually supplied. One author, however, though he reaches the same conclusion, differs in his reasoning thus:

> However, for the reason that the principles governing the delegation of jurisdiction established in

[29] E.g., can. 199, § 4, which indicates that delegated judges may subdelegate non-jurisdictional acts.

[30] *AAS*, XLIV (1952), 497; *Digest*, III, 73. This reply of the Commission applied the norms of certain canons, namely, of canons 197, 199, 206-209, to the consideration of purely dominative power, thereby indicating that the very act of delegation, when performed by one who lacks jurisdiction but has a purely dominative power, cannot be an exercise of jurisdiction.

> Canon 199 are applicable in the matter of delegating assistance at marriages, it does not follow that the Code's principles for supplying jurisdiction (Canon 209) can be applied to assistance at marriages. We have stated that a marriage at which a putative or an invalidly appointed pastor assists is valid. For said marriage is valid not because the Church supplies delegation in the case of invalid assistance at marriage, but because of the supplying of jurisdiction to the pastor, who becomes thereby the true pastor for the aforesaid assistance at marriage.[31]

This is a highly technical distinction and it is not without imperfections. The idea which the author seemingly wishes to convey is that jurisdiction is not supplied for the *act* of assistance, but is supplied to the *man* in order to enable him validly to exercise the faculty of assisting. One may immediately question the validity of the author's remarks on the following basis: if jurisdiction is supplied to the putative pastor, so that he becomes automatically empowered with the faculty of assisting at marriage, an explanation is lacking in reference to a putative delegate who is not a pastor.[32]

The author places the stress of the argument on a jurisdictional aspect, namely, that since *jurisdiction* is supplied to the putative pastor, he becomes empowered for this act of assisting, so that there is no longer any need of supplying *delegation* for the act. The metaphysical reality of how the faculty is exercised validly is something which is not known with absolute certainty. But what is known with certainty is that the priest here considered remains a *putative* pastor with a supplied "something" for the valid as-

[31] Cicognani, *Canon Law* (2. ed., authorized English version by Joseph M. O'Hara and Francis J. Brennan, Westminster, Md.: The Newman Press, Reprint, 1949), p. 764.

[32] On March 26, 1952, the Commission for the Authentic Interpretation of the Code gave an affirmative answer to the following inquiry: "An praescriptum can. 209 applicandum sit in casu sacerdotis, qui, delegatione carens, matrimonio assistit."—*AAS* (1952), 497; *Digest*, III, 76.

sistance at the marriage. Furthermore, it is not precise to say "the Church supplies delegation in the case of *invalid* assistance at marriage," because there is no question of invalid assistance in the case of a supplied delegation. The supply is antecedent to, or at least concomitant with, the act and does not occur after the fashion of a sanation. Moreover, it is inaccurate to infer that canon 199 is the only canon which may be applied to the faculty of assisting at marriage. Certainly other canons on jurisdiction also apply, e.g., a delegate has the obligation of proving his delegation, a pastor could revoke a delegation which he has made, etc.[33]

In final reference to the supplying of jurisdiction, another author may here be quoted.

> Assistentia matrimonio . . . licet non sit actus iurisdictionis stricto sensu dictae, tamen est certe actus potestatis seu iurisdictionalis; idcirco quae generatim dicuntur de iurisdictione, dicenda quoque sunt de assistentia, ita ut praescriptum can. 209 procul dubio applicandum sit etiam assistentiae matrimonio.[34]

SECTION 2. THE EXERCISE OF THE FACULTY UNDER SUSPENSION

This question concerns the manner in which a suspension affects the faculty of assisting at marriage. The parts of canon 2279 which are applicable follow:

> § 1. Suspensio *ab officio* simpliciter, nulla adiecta limitatione, vetat omnem actum tum potestatis ordinis et iurisdictionis, tum etiam merae administrationis ex officio competentis, excepta administratione bonorum proprii beneficii.
> § 2. Suspensio:

[33] Cans. 202, § 2; 207, § 1. Cf. cans. 196-209 for other applications.

[34] Cappello, *Tractatus Canonico-Moralis de Sacramentis*, Vol. V, *De Matrimonio* (6. ed., Taurini-Romae: Marietti, 1950), n. 670, 1, p. 654; cf. also Gasparri, *Tractatus Canonicus de Matrimonio* (2 vols., Editio nova ad mentem Codicis I. C., Romae, 1932), II, n. 969, p. 123.

> 1°. *A iurisdictione* generatim, vetat omnem actum potestatis iurisdictionis pro utroque foro tam ordinariae quam delegatae.

The suspension from office presents little difficulty. If the faculty of assisting is not jurisdiction, it is certainly an administrative act inherent in the office in some respect, but under the penalty of nullity it would be prohibited by such a suspension only after a declaratory or condemnatory sentence.[35]

The suspension from jurisdiction similarly offers little practical difficulty. Some authors consider the faculty of assisting at marriage as a power of jurisdiction, or at least they speak of it as being jurisdictional.[36] A few of these authors accordingly insist that the exercise of this faculty is prohibited by way of a suspension from jurisdiction and that, according to canon 1095, § 1, 1°, and by reason of the fact that the suspension from jurisdiction is a part of the suspension from office, the marriage in point is invalid. Since the more lenient interpretation, however, should be applied in this matter,[37] it would be better to interpret strictly the suspension as it is mentioned in canon 1095, § 1, 1°, so that no partial suspension would be envisioned by it. Therefore, even if one insists that assistance at marriage is an act of jurisdiction, it is not prohibited under the penalty of nullity by way of the suspension from jurisdiction. The following is an example of the insistence that the faculty of assisting is, in its exercise, an act of jurisdiction:

> Diese Frage ist zweifellos zu verneinen, da die Trauung ein Akt der *iurisdictio voluntaria* ist.

[35] Can. 1095, § 1, 1°.

[36] E.g., Badii, *Institutiones*, I, 252; Coronata, *Institutiones Iuris Canonici, De Sacramentis Tractatus Canonicus* (2. ed., 3 vols., Taurini-Romae: Marietti, 1947-1951), III, 742; Boucaren-Ellis, *Canon Law*, p. 189; Regatillo, "Consultas," *Sal Terrae* (Santander, 1912-), XXIV (1935), 923; XXXVII (1949), 303; Triebs, *Praktisches Handbuch*, p. 570.

[37] Cf. cans. 19; 2219, § 1.

> Der Gesetzgeber sagt das nicht besonders, wohl deswegen weil es selbstverständlich ist.[38]

The vast majority of the authors, including even most of those who apply the term "jurisdictional" to the faculty of assisting at marriage, considers the faculty of assisting at marriage, in its exercise, as something other than an act of true jurisdiction.[39] Therefore, the general opinion is that this faculty has no connection whatsoever with the suspension from jurisdiction. An example follows:

> Quidam AA. docent ius assistendi iis poenis indiscriminatim amitti, quae iurisdictione privant, si poena per sententiam lata vel declarata fuerit. Id, ex dictis non potest admitti: tum quia Codex expressis verbis enuntiat in can. 1095, § 1, casus in quibus parochus et loci Ordinarius privantur iure assistendi, tum quia assistentia non est actus iurisdictionis proprie dictae ideoque parochus (vel Ordinarius) *a iurisdictione* suspensus seu ea privatus, valide *per se* assistere potest matrimoniis.[40]

In view of the principles of jurisdiction already enunciated and the opinions of the authors on the nature of the act of assisting at marriage, the practical solution is obvious. The priest who is suspended simply from jurisdiction assists validly at any marriage at which he could otherwise assist validly, for two reasons: 1) in the realm of penalties, the more lenient interpretation must be made,[41]

[38] Triebs, *op. cit.*, p. 570.

[39] E.g., Cappello, *De Matrimonio*, p. 654; Claeys Boúúaert-Simenon, *Manuale Iuris Canonici* (3 vols., Vol. II, 3. ed., Gandae et Leodii: Prostat apud auctores in Seminariis Gandavensi et Leodiensi, 1947), II, 312; Sipos, *Enchiridion*, p. 510; Savaré, *De Errore Communi circa Assistentiam ad Matrimonium* (Romae: Universitas Gregoriana, 1937), p. 60.

[40] Cappello, *De Matrimonio* p. 648; cf. also Vermeersch-Creusen, *Epitome*, II, 275; III, 290; Sipos, *Enchiridion*, p. 511; Beste, *Introductio in Codicem*, p. 946.

[41] Can. 2219, § 1. The penal suspension from jurisdiction, even with a condemnatory or also a declaratory intervening sentence, is at most a *partial* suspension that is not the equivalent of the full penal suspension from office itself, which is postulated if the prohibition is to

and 2) in this particular matter there is a positive doubt which is intrinsically and extrinsically probable, so that the Church would supply anything that is necessary for the validity.[42]

There are other questions which could be considered in this matter,[43] but their discussion is not needed for demonstrating that the act of assisting at marriage is not an exercise of the power of jurisdiction, that the canons on jurisdiction apply to the faculty of assisting at marriage, unless the nature of the matter or the special canons governing this faculty demand otherwise, and that one who is suspended from jurisdiction assists validly at any marriage for which he would otherwise be competent, even after a declaratory or condemnatory sentence.

ARTICLE III. THE ADMINISTRATION OF ECCLESIASTICAL GOODS

This is probably the most complex item of discussion in the entire chapter, and it is such with good reason. There are any number of divers notions bearing on the subject of the administration of ecclesiastical goods. The notion of administration itself may be considered as distinct from acquisition and alienation; according to the adage, "*Quod gubernatio est personis, id administratio est bonis,*" administration is sometimes viewed as a power completely apart from that of jurisdiction. Other notions which also influence the analysis of administration are the distinctions between the following: *dominium humile* or ownership and *dominium altum* or the right of eminent

obtain as forbidding and also invalidating the act of assistance at marriage.

[42] Can. 209; cf. Rainer, *The Suspension of Clerics,* The Catholic University of America Canon Law Studies, n. 111 (Washington, D.C.: The Catholic University of America, 1937), p. 74.

[43] E.g., there is a controversy whether a suspension from office, when it is inflicted or declared by way of a particular precept, suffices to prohibit the assistance at marriage. Cf. cans. 1933, § 4; 2225; 2279, § 1.

domain; public administration and private administration; jurisdiction and ownership; clerical administration and lay administration; ordinary administration and extraordinary administration; etc. Moreover, the vast historical background is not to be overlooked.[44]

In view of this condition of things, the more or less equal division of the authors and commentators on the question whether the administration of ecclesiastical goods is an act of jurisdiction is understandable. Those authors who are staunch proponents of the far-reaching import of public ecclesiastical law will generally follow the affirmative view, because public ecclesiastical law is vitally interested in defending and vindicating the rights of the Church in relation to civil society, and the possession and administration of goods is one of these rights. Those authors who are interested principally in commenting generally on all the institutes of canon law will often follow the negative view, possibly because it is the path which best reconciles one's difficulties in adjusting the administration of ecclesiastical goods with the fact that laymen and women religious, who are incapable of possessing jurisdiction according to the general law, actually do administer ecclesiastical goods in many instances.

No one would presume to solve such a complicated question in so brief a treatise as the present one. Nevertheless, an opinion, together with the arguments inducing it, may be advanced. There are three possible approaches to the problem, two of which are basic: 1) one could consider every act of administration of ecclesiastical goods as an act of jurisdiction, and then administration in itself is an act of jurisdiction; 2) one could consider no act of such administration as an act of jurisdiction, and then administration in itself is not an act of jurisdiction, and 3) one could consider some acts of such administration as acts of juris-

[44] For a brief summary of this background, cf. Sigur, "Lay Co-operation in the Administration of Church Property," *The Jurist*, XIII (1953), 171-185.

diction, and other acts as not. If one subscribes to the last of these views, one must still determine whether a given instance of the administration of ecclesiastical goods is in itself an act of jurisdiction, so that the decision thus reached then reduces this third approach to one of the first two.

It is true that ecclesiastical jurisdiction derives from the divine positive law and from the special promise and concession of Christ. But whether all administration of ecclesiastical goods derives in the same manner is not so evident. One must grant that apart from ecclesiastical society, or simply apart from ecclesiastical goods, the administration of goods derives from the natural law. The question that remains is whether there is an essential difference between the administration of ecclesiastical goods and the administration of goods other than ecclesiastical.

A temporal society functions with a power which is temporal in itself. A spiritual society functions with a power which is spiritual in itself. Therefore, spiritual power, or the power which a spiritual society exercises over anything, is essentially distinct from the power of a temporal society. But one of the objects of the exercise of ecclesiastical power, which is spiritual power, is temporal goods. Therefore, the power which the Church exercises over temporal goods is one of the two powers in its objective hierarchy, namely, the power of orders or the power of jurisdiction. Obviously, no relation to the power of orders is involved; therefore, the power of the Church over its temporal goods is the power of jurisdiction. Ecclesiastical jurisdiction, therefore, may be considered as the power which the Church exercises over things spiritual in themselves and over things temporal in themselves.[45] These temporal goods become spiritual thus:

> Natural resources, acquired virtues and dispositions, things in themselves temporal or cultural—such as churches, religious houses, benefices, treasures of art, the languages needed for worship or for preaching, the liturgical chant—all these, on

[45] Cf. can. 726.

> account of the direct use of them made by the Church and the immediate purpose to which they are referred, at once become spiritual.[46]

The ecclesiastical goods just considered are things which are spiritual normally, i.e., for the greater duration of their existence, by reason of their object. One could, therefore, incidentally introduce the objection that the Church does not exercise ecclesiastical jurisdiction over such things as may be objects of the mixed forum, inasmuch as a temporal society, with mere temporal power, is equally competent.[47] However, besides the direct power of the Church over things spiritual in themselves and over things temporal in themselves but normally spiritual, the Church exercises spiritual jurisdiction formally over things which become spiritual only incidentally and on occasion. Journet subscribes to this notion by quoting the following commentary:

> The object of the jurisdiction, in the case in point, is the temporal only in so far as it enters the religious sphere, and thus ceases to be purely temporal. Such is the *indirect* power.... By reason of the object on which it bears, the indirect power is sometimes qualified as temporal; but in reality, in its nature, in its origin and aim, it is truly spiritual, and it is a power of jurisdiction properly so called.[48]

Authors, therefore, while retaining the notion that administration is a spiritual power, denote that power, when it relates to the administration of goods, by various names, e.g., direct extraordinary power, indirect power, etc. Another author, for instance, expresses the same idea as follows:

> This direct power is nothing other than a necessary sequel of spiritual power, which alone belongs directly and immediately to the Pope; it

[46] Journet, *The Apostolic Hierarchy*, p. 208.

[47] Can. 1553, § 2.

[48] Journet, *op. cit.*, p. 262. The author is quoting Choupin, *Valeur des Décisions Doctrinales et Disciplinaires du Saint-Siège* (3. ed., Paris, 1928), p. 261.

> is the necessary extension of this spiritual power to certain temporal goods, or better, it is the spiritual power itself, as it extends to things of themselves temporal but truly necessary for the spiritual end.
>
> It differs from the direct power of the Church not by origin, for both are from God, nor by essence, since both are truly spiritual or rather they constitute one and the same spiritual power, but only by the object on which it is exercised: the spiritual power of the Church is called indirect as it concerns things in themselves and ordinarily temporal, to which accidentally a spiritual relation attaches so that in that way they become spiritual and enter the religious domain. Wherefore, some authors, not unduly, term that power *direct extraordinary* power, for it touches those things directly, not as temporal, but by a spiritual notion which is in them or attaches to them.[49]

Within the generic notion of the administrative power of the Church must be necessarily included the administration of temporal goods.[50] The Church is essentially a spiritual society, but it needs temporal goods also as means to its end. These temporal goods become spiritual and sacred by reason of the end toward which they are directed, whether it is the worship of God or the sustenance of persons consecrated to Him. Therefore, in no way is it repugnant that the power of the Church, which is called and is spiritual, comprehends within it the administration of temporal goods, which, inasmuch as they are means to a spiritual end, share in the notion of its spirituality. No one would even think, much less say, that Christ, when He es-

[49] Depoorter, "De Potestate Indirecta Ecclesiae in Rebus Temporalibus," *Collationes Brugenses*, XLVIII (1952), 416. The translation is the writer's.

[50] Cf. Bachofen, *Summa Iuris Ecclesiastici Publici* (Romae, 1910), p. 48; Bargilliat, *Praelectiones*, I, 46; Cocchi, *Commentarium*, VI, 388; Coronata, *Compendium Iuris Canonici ad usum scholarum* (3 vols., Taurini-Romae: Marietti, 1949, 1950), I, n. 527, p. 312 (hereafter cited *Compendium*); Chelodi, *Ius Canonicum de Delictis et Poenis et Iudiciis Criminalibus* (5. ed., recognita et aucta a Pio Ciprotti, Trento: Libreria Moderna Editrice, 1943), p. 93.

tablished the objective hierarchy, did not include such power in one of its species of power, namely, in the power of jurisdiction. This establishes no more, however, than that the administrative power of the Church is in some way jurisdictional.

One may attempt to deduce from the Code itself that the administration of the Church's temporal goods is an exercise of jurisdiction: temporal goods which belong to the Church are ecclesiastical goods,[51] and the Roman Pontiff is the supreme administrator of all ecclesiastical goods;[52] since he operates by his primacy of jurisdiction, his administration of ecclesiastical goods is an exercise of the power of jurisdiction.[53] The local ordinary has the duty of supervision over all ecclesiastical goods of his territory which have not been removed from his jurisdiction.[54] With certain limitations, the vicar-general enjoys the jurisdiction which the local ordinary has over both the spiritual and temporal affairs of the entire diocese.[55] Therefore, within the jurisdiction of the local ordinary resides in some way the administration of the ecclesiastical goods of the diocese, whether he himself with his council administrates,[56] or whether it pertains to him to supervise and constitute norms for the administration of these goods.[57]

Everything just stated is patently true. It indicates that the Holy Father exercises jurisdiction over ecclesiastical goods, but it does not prove that every act of temporal administration is an act of jurisdiction.[58] The Holy Father's supreme administration may be considered as his right of eminent domain[59] and it is true jurisdiction. But bishops

[51] Can. 1497, § 1.

[52] Can. 1518.

[53] Can. 218, § 1; cf. also *supra*, pp. 112-114.

[54] Can. 1519, § 1.

[55] Cans. 368, § 1; 335, § 1.

[56] Can. 1520.

[57] Can. 1519, §§ 1, 2.

[58] Cf. Vromant, *De Bonis Ecclesiae Temporalibus* (3. ed., Bruxelles: Éditions de Scheut, 1953), p. 45.

[59] Cf. can. 1499, § 2.

and all other inferiors lack this supreme administration. Therefore, one would temerariously draw the conclusion that every act of administration of goods is an act of jurisdiction, regardless of the agent.[60]

Nevertheless, the power of administration must be considered fundamentally either as a jurisdictional power in itself or as a non-jurisdictional power in itself. If the affirmative view is preferred, the major discrepancies that remain are: 1) laymen, who are incapable of possessing jurisdiction, administer ecclesiastical goods; 2) women religious, also incapable of possessing jurisdiction, administer ecclesiastical goods. If the negative view is taken, the problems concerning administration by laymen and women religious are somewhat explained.

In exemplification of the solution of a difficulty by one who maintains the affirmative view, the following summary is offered. First, the canonical principle that laymen are incapable of possessing jurisdiction is recognized; secondly, certain powers, e.g., some faculties of the right of patronage, are cited as exceptions made by the Code to its own principle; finally, the dubious contention is advanced that acts of administration cannot be acts of jurisdiction in one person and not in another, and that they are all, therefore, acts of jurisdiction. It follows, then, that lay incapacity for possessing jurisdiction is not absolute but only relative, and that, in certain matters granted by the Code, laymen and women religious do exercise ecclesiastical jurisdiction.[61] This argument is meritorious, but not without flaw. It would demand that women religious, lay men and,

[60] Cf. Nebreda, "Quaestiones Selectae de Iure Administrativo Ecclesiastico," *Commentarium pro Religiosis*, VII (1926), 191-198; Sigur, "Lay Cooperation in the Administration of Church Property," *The Jurist*, XIII (1953), 187.

[61] Schröcker, *Die Verwaltung des Ortskirchenvermögens nach kirchlichem und staatlichem Recht* (Paderborn: Ferdinand Schöningh, 1935), pp. 42-48 (hereafter cited *Die Verwaltung des Ortskirchenvermögens*). In the *Görres Gesellschaft Veröffentlichugen der Sektion für Rechts-und Staatswissenschaft* this work is listed as Heft 70.

possibly, lay women exercise ecclesiastical jurisdiction and, therefore, participate essentially in the hierarchy in which clerics alone can be enrolled.[62] This argument and explanation could be immediately accepted, however, provided that jurisdiction is understood in some broader sense than that which canons 108 and 118 specify, namely, in some general sense relating to acts promoting the end of society.[63]

As an example of how a difficulty of the affirmative view may be explained by one who maintains the negative view, the following conclusion is presented:

> Ad hoc nullatenus requiritur potestas *iurisdictionis,* sed sufficit potestas *dominativa,* potestas quae ordinatur ad conservationem, ad promotionem boni communis totius Religionis.[64]

If one follows strictly, however, either the affirmative or the negative opinion, one still encounters dilemmas. But if a third opinion is advanced, which is a slight accommodation of the negative view, practically all of the difficulties seem obviated. This third approach, which maintains that the administration of ecclesiastical goods is not in itself an act of true jurisdiction, except in the one possible case of the eminent domain of the Holy Father, finds no difficulty in permitting to laymen and to women religious the exercise of acts, which usually appear as acts of jurisdiction, but which in them are purely administrative acts, acts of apparent jurisdiction, or acts of jurisdiction in the broadest sense. In other words, one would consider the majority of the acts of administration as jurisdictional acts, since they are performed either by agents who are capable of possessing jurisdiction or by agents who already possess

[62] Cans. 108, §§ 1-3; 118.

[63] In view of recent developments on lay participation in the *magisterium,* even to the point of using the term "canonical mission" in this regard, this notion may not be too farfetched.

[64] Huot, "Bonorum Temporalium apud Religiones Administratio Ordinaria et Extraordinaria," *Commentarium pro Religiosis et Missionariis,* XXXIV (1955), 189. For historical background and extensive argumentation, cf. *op. cit.,* XXXIII (1954), 60-76, 312-328; XXXIV (1955), 55-64, 175-192, 266-273, 365-373.

ecclesiastical jurisdiction and whose administration, therefore, either constitutes a power of jurisdiction or is subsumed under the existing power of jurisdiction; the minority of the acts of administration, namely, those executed by laymen and others who are incapable of possessing jurisdiction, would be considered accordingly as non-jurisdictional acts: 1) because acts of administration are not in themselves acts of jurisdiction, and 2) because, if some agents lack jurisdiction, there is no power of jurisdiction in them under which the acts of administration can be subsumed.

The following quotation is noteworthy:

> Si insuper Ecclesia alicui non contulit potestatem iurisdictionis, actus ab eo positi non sunt actus iurisdictionis. Attento vero praescripto can. 118 non facile est admittendum Ecclesiam lege generali laicis conferre iurisdictionem.[65]

The author insists that if a subject is incapable of the possession of jurisdiction, he cannot possibly exercise jurisdiction, at least not the jurisdiction specified in canon 118. Another author similarly demonstrates that, while the laity participate in the *magisterium* of the Church, they exercise no jurisdiction.[66]

This much, therefore, can be said with certainty: 1) if one grants that an act of administration is not in itself an act of jurisdiction, there is no contradiction in the notion of lay administration; 2) if one insists that an act of administration is in itself an act of jurisdiction, one must either understand jurisdiction in some sense broader than that signified in canons 108 and 118, or admit that laymen and women religious exercise true ecclesiastical jurisdiction by way of exception to the general law.[67] If one attempts any other explanation, one cannot avoid the en-

[65] Jone, *Commentarium,* I, 130, 131. Cf. also *ibid.,* II, 624.

[66] Champoux, *The Juridical Position of the Laity in the Church,* p. 58.

[67] If one admits this last possibility, the entire economy of ecclesiastical jurisdiction suffers a significant alteration, which seems juridically inadmissible.

velopment in a contradiction, regardless of the clever semantics employed. If one, for instance, insisted that the administration of ecclesiastical goods is an act which is in itself jurisdictional and that certain societies absolutely lack jurisdiction, one could propose the following justifications: 1) since administration of ecclesiastical goods is something jurisdictional in itself, once the said administration is performed by one who possesses jurisdiction the act is an act of true jurisdiction . . . it is only by reason of the ecclesiastical approval of a society and by reason of the fact that every society possesses dominative power for the administration of its goods, that the Church entrusts some administration of ecclesiastical goods, under proper supervision, to certain societies which lack the power of jurisdiction; or 2) for practical reasons, the Church shares with certain societies an act which is in itself jurisdictional, since these societies, though they lack jurisdiction, have dominative power, which the Church judges by extension as adequate for the administration, inasmuch as it is supervised by persons truly possessing ecclesiastical jurisdiction; or 3) the Church entrusts a jurisdictional act, which, while retaining its jurisdictional appearance, is disqualified by law from preserving its jurisdictional nature and name . . . the act has the external species of jurisdiction but does not proceed from jurisdiction. Each of these attempted justifications is specious, for each contains the inherent contradiction that the act of administration, which is considered as an act of jurisdiction in itself, becomes in certain instances an act which is considered in itself not as an act of jurisdiction.

In summary, sufficient and logical arguments indicate that the power which the Church exercises in general over its temporal goods should be considered as a part of the executive power of jurisdiction. It does not necessarily follow, however, that each particular act of administration is in and of itself an exercise of jurisdiction. On the contrary, the fact that the Church exercises ecclesiastical jurisdiction over its temporal possessions in no way postulates that, in each case wherein an act of mere administration is placed, the Church is delegating some ecclesiastical jurisdiction for the execution of some simple act of administration. The situation recalls this analogy: the Church teaches by reason of the power of jurisdiction; but each time one teaches another some doctrine of the Church, one does not necessarily exercise the power of jurisdiction. If the one who teaches possesses ecclesiastical jurisdiction, certain acts of teaching in that case may proceed from jurisdiction; if the one who teaches enjoys and can enjoy no ecclesiastical jurisdiction, no act of teaching in that case can proceed from jurisdiction or be considered as jurisdictional. Similarly, in the case wherein one possesses or can possess jurisdiction, certain acts of administration may proceed from that jurisdiction; in the case wherein one can possess no jurisdiction, no act of administration can proceed from jurisdiction or be considered as jurisdictional.

The better opinion seems to be that, while the Church enjoys jurisdiction over its temporal goods, an act of administration is not in itself an act of jurisdiction. The act may be and often is subsumed, as it were, under the jurisdiction of the agent, or may even constitute a power of jurisdiction in certain agents. This opinion seems to agree both with the nature of administration and with the positive legislation on the matter. On the other hand, if one insists on qualifying every act of administration as an act of jurisdiction, then jurisdiction must be understood in some sense broader than that specified in canons 108 and 118; jurisdiction would then signify some general contributory promotion of the end of the society.

At this point brief surveys of several related questions may be appended, the first of which is the effect of a suspension on the administration of goods. In reference to the suspension from office, the administration of ecclesiastical goods is prohibited by reason of its inclusion under either jurisdiction or mere administration as attaching to the office.[68] Therefore, if one considers the administration of ecclesiastical goods as an act of jurisdiction, it is included under the term "jurisdiction" and is prohibited. If one considers such administration not as an act of jurisdiction, but as an act of "mere administration" belonging to the office, it is included in that term and likewise prohibited.[69]

In relation to the suspension from jurisdiction, the administration of ecclesiastical goods would be lawful on the grounds of the positive and probable doubt whether such an act is true jurisdiction.[70]

Finally, and by way of incidental conclusion in relation to other faculties, rights, and offices in the Code, one needs only to apply the essential elements of jurisdiction to the particular matter to see whether true jurisdiction is involved. The doctrine of subjective rights must certainly be recalled and retained.[71] Many faculties which a pastor, for example, enjoys are mere subjective rights.[72] Many rights which are established by the legislator do not imply the true power of imperium, but the mere faculty to use those rights, even though the legislator may demand the exercise of a particular right as a substantial part of the form of certain juridic acts to which are attached certain juridic effects which are socially public. Many acts have the external appearance of acts of jurisdiction, but do not proceed from the power of jurisdiction. The acts which are designated by the Code as "authorized (*legitimi*) eccle-

[68] Can. 2279, § 1. This administration cannot be considered not prohibited by reason of its inclusion under the concept of the administration of the goods of one's own benefice, which administration is something totally distinct and as such forms the object of canon 2280.

[69] Coronata, *Institutiones Iuris Canonici ad usum utriusque cleri et scholarum*, Vol. IV, *De Delictis et Poenis* (3. ed., Taurini-Romae: Marietti, 1948), pp. 247, 248.

[70] Cf. *supra*, pp. 145-147.

[71] Cf. *supra*, pp. 129, 130.

[72] E.g., can. 462.

siastical acts" are not all acts of jurisdiction.[73] Therefore, in each individual case, in order to determine whether an act is one of jurisdiction, one must look to the concept of jurisdiction to see if all its elements are verified. If an act proceeds from power, spiritual and public, given by Christ or the Church by injunction or canonical mission, whereby a man authoritatively functions as a principal second cause in directing the faithful to their supernatural end, that act is an exercise of the power of jurisdiction.

[73] Cf. can. 2256, 2°.

CHAPTER VII

THE JURISDICTION OF PASTORS IN THE EXTERNAL FORUM

The presentation and elucidation of notions concerning jurisdiction and the external forum is at an end. All that remains is an application of the concepts and principles already enunciated to the subject of parochial jurisdiction in the external forum, and an investigation of the views of the authors. It may be useful at this point to recall the primary intention of this dissertation, namely, the justification of the validity and propriety of its title phrase. The preamble of that justification was previously announced in the theological treatment of parochial jurisdiction;[1] the text of that justification, from an entirely canonical standpoint, is offered in this chapter.

There is no need to investigate every function of the pastor in order to determine whether each is an exercise of jurisdiction.[2] An application of the few and proper principles of jurisdiction and forum should suffice in any given case to establish whether the particular function is an act of jurisdiction and to which forum it pertains. Nothing astonishing, therefore, should be anticipated in this final chapter, since it consists merely in an application of the foregoing principles to the notion of parochial power, which the reader may already have effected mentally, and in a brief survey of some extrinsic arguments.

ARTICLE I. THE NOTION OF PASTOR

Among the three substantives employed in the title of this thesis, namely, "jurisdiction," "pastors," and "forum,"

[1] Cf. *supra*, pp. 80-83.

[2] There are many specialized works on pastoral functions, e.g., Kelly, *The Functions Reserved to Pastors;* Koudelka, *Pastors, Their Rights and Duties*, The Catholic University of America Canon Law Studies, n. 11 (Washington, D.C.: The Catholic University of America, 1921).

the only one which can be considered as a constant is the term "pastors." Inasmuch as there is this uniformity concerning the term, a spacious commentary on the institute is superfluous. In almost every commentary on the Code the term receives adequate treatment. Moreover, there are many expert works wherein it receives special treatment.[3] Accordingly, therefore, only a descriptive and condensed version is here presented.

The pastor, as defined by canon 451, § 1, is the priest or the moral personality upon whom a parish is conferred in title with the care of souls, which is to be exercised under the authority of the local ordinary.

> Parochus est sacerdos vel persona moralis cui paroecia collata est in titulum cum cura animarum sub Ordinarii loci auctoritate exercenda.

This definition contemplates the pastor in the strict sense. In order that a man be validly designated as a pastor, it is necessary that he be a priest.[4] Nevertheless, a moral personality, such as an ecclesiastical corporation, a chapter, an order, a congregation, or a monastery, can be designated in such a way that the moral personality itself is the pastor;[5] in those cases, wherein the moral personality holds title to the parish as pastor, the law requires that a vicar, who is a priest, be appointed to exercise the actual care of souls.[6]

[3] E.g., Kelly, *op. cit.*, pp. 53, 54; Koudelka, *op. cit.*, pp. 11-16; Freking, *The Canonical Installation of Pastors*, The Catholic University of America Canon Law Studies, n. 273 (Washington, D.C.: The Catholic University of America Press, 1948), pp. 3-5, 72-75; Donovan, *The Pastor's Obligation in Prenuptial Investigation*, The Catholic University of America Canon Law Studies, n. 115 (Washington, D.C.: The Catholic University of America, 1938), pp. 59-68; Fanfani, *De Iure Parochorum ad normam Codicis Iuris Canonici* (Taurini-Romae, 1924), pp. 72-76 (hereafter cited *De Iure Parochorum*); De Meester, "De Rectoribus Ecclesiarum," *Collationes Brugenses*, XXIV (1924), 56-59, "Notio Parochi," *Collationes Brugenses*, XXII (1922), 477-480.

[4] Can. 453, § 1.

[5] Cf. can. 452, § 1.

[6] Cans. 452, § 2; 471.

The element which constitutes a priest as a pastor is the appointment in his own right to the care of a determinate group of souls by competent ecclesiastical authority.[7] The Sacred Congregation of the Council distinguishes pastors from certain parochial vicars in that the former hold their parishes *in title,* while the latter, even if they possess full parochial powers, receive their parishes *in administration* only.[8] The expression "in title" has the multiple connotation of cause, perpetuity, and juridic right.[9]

Besides pastors in the strict sense, there are parochial vicars, whom the law recognizes as being equivalent to pastors in relation to rights and duties.[10] One may argue from canons 453, § 1, and 451, § 2, that the law implicitly demands that these parochial vicars be priests, inasmuch as they have the rights and duties of pastors and in the law fall under the name of pastors; therefore, the requirement of the priesthood for valid parochial appointment affects them also.

Those parochial vicars who have all the rights and duties of pastors and, therefore, must be regarded as equivalent to pastors, are the following: 1) Quasi-pastors, i.e., those in charge of missionary parishes in a vicariate or prefecture Apostolic;[11] 2) actual vicars, i.e., those in charge of parishes held in title by moral persons;[12] 3) administrators,

[7] For the purposes of this dissertation it matters not whether the pastor is secular or religious, removable or irremovable, territorial, personal, or cumulative in his character.

[8] S.C.C., *Blesen.,* 12 nov. 1927— *ASS,* XX (1927), 84; *Digest,* I, 245.

[9] Cf. Reiffenstuel, *Jus Canonicum Universum,* Lib. II, tit. XXVI, n. 127; Schäfer, *Die Kirchennämter nach dem Codex Iuris Canonici,* II Teil, *Pfarrer und Pfarrvikare nach dem Codex Iuris Canonici* (Münster, 1922), pp. 10, 11; Coronata, *Compendium,* I, 449; Agius, *Summarium Iurium et Officiorum Parochorum* (Neapoli: M. D'Auria, Pontificius Editor, 1953), p. 5.

[10] Can. 451, § 2, 1°, 2°. Cf. Stocchiero, "De Jurisdictione Vicariorum Paroecialium," *Jus Pontificium,* XI (1931), 144-150, 221-231.

[11] Cans. 451, § 1, 1°; 216, §3.

[12] Can. 471.

i.e., those in charge of vacant parishes;[13] 4) substitutes, i.e., those in charge of parishes in the absence of the pastors;[14] 5) adjutants, i.e., those assigned in aid of pastors who have suffered some total permanent disability;[15] 6) assistants, when they take charge of a parish that has fallen vacant according to canon 474, 2°.[16]

Since the power of dispensing enjoys great prominence among the powers of the external forum, other persons who enjoy the pastor's power of dispensing are here enumerated, even though these persons are not directly connected by law with a parochial benefice: 1) Military chaplains for the armed forces;[17] 2) ships' chaplains, except in matrimonial matters;[18] 3) rectors of seminaries, except in matrimonial matters;[19] 4) rectors of subsidiary churches or chaplaincies, when the sparse or fluctuating population or the absolute want of an endowment makes the elevation of certain churches to the status of parishes inadvisable.[20]

[13] Can. 472.

[14] Cans. 465, §§ 4, 5; 474; 1923, § 2. They have full parochial powers unless the ordinary or pastor has made some reservations.

[15] Can. 475. They have all parochial rights and duties, except for the obligation of the Mass for the people, unless they are replacing the pastor only partially, in which case their rights and duties are determined in the letter of their appointment.

[16] According to canon 476, § 6, an assistant could possibly enjoy full delegated parochial power, but only in the exceptional case where neither the diocesan statutes, nor the letter of the ordinary, nor the commission of the pastor himself have set any limitations. An assistant could also conceivably be designated the substitute or adjutant according to the norms of canons 474 and 475.

[17] Can. 451, § 3; cf. *Digest,* II, 586, 588.

[18] *AAS,* XLIV (1952), 698; *Digest,* III, 92; cf. also Wycislo, "Apostolic Constitution on Migration," *The Homiletic and Pastoral Review* (New York, 1900-), LIII (1953), 318-326.

[19] Can. 1368.

[20] Declaration of the Sacred Consistorial Congregation, 1 aug. 1919—*AAS,* XI (1919), 346, 347; *Digest,* I, 146, 147; Vermeersch-Creusen, *Epitome* I, 399. Inasmuch as this declaration affects territories formerly subject to the Sacred Congregation for the Propagation of the Faith, it applies in this country and refers to those

No other priests, whether rectors of churches or chapels, or chaplains of hospitals, religious communities, pious houses, or prisons, come under the name of pastor in the common law. Consequently, those priests do not enjoy the dispensatory power which is conceded to pastors by the law.[21]

ARTICLE II. THE NOTION OF PAROCHIAL JURISDICTION

It seems so futile for authors to hesitate or even to refuse to predicate jurisdiction in the external forum for pastors. Everyone realizes that pastors lack the complete jurisdictional powers of the external forum, such as those of a bishop;[22] but pastors do share some of that power. If it pertained to the office of pastor to grant but one dispensation in the external forum, he would then possess some true jurisdiction in the external forum. The wasted verbiage of the authors in their hesitation or refusal to recognize such jurisdiction for pastors results in many inconsistencies and even in manifest contradictions.

The point is simply this: if the bishop, with his complete jurisdiction, has ten units of ecclesiastical power in his episcopal power station, as it were, and the pastor, with his incomplete jurisdiction, has two units of ecclesiastical power in his parochial sub-station, as it were, there is absolutely no sense in hesitating or refusing to acknowledge the two units of the pastor. The presiding judge of the episcopal curia has imperfect jurisdiction, that is, he possesses that part of the complete episcopal jurisdiction which is called judicial power, and everyone admits that this in-

cases wherein a priest, even though he be an assistant, is appointed in charge of a parochial entity known as a mission.

[21] A specialized work in this regard, soon to be published, is Huhmann, *The Pastor's Power of Dispensing*, Typewritten doctoral dissertation (Romae: Pontificium Athenaeum Angelicum, 1956).

[22] E.g., pastors are not included among those who possess the jurisdiction in the external forum as indicated by canon 2253, 1°, since the phrase, as it appears in that canon, must be understood as contemplating a complete jurisdiction in the external forum.

complete jurisdiction is jurisdiction of the external forum. But when it comes to the pastor who has imperfect jurisdiction, that is, certain governmental and administrative powers, which are species of the executive power of jurisdiction, together with certain dispensatory powers, which constitute a degree of legislative power, some authors seem to lay themselves open to all sorts of frenzied circumlocutions and tergiversations in order to avoid the expression "jurisdiction of pastors in the external forum." The power both of the presiding judge and of the pastor should be designated, according to the classifications employed in this dissertation, as jurisdiction in the broad sense, that is, partial but true jurisdiction, as opposed to jurisdiction in the strict sense, that is, complete jurisdiction.[23]

SECTION 1. ITS CHARACTERISTICS

True ecclesiastical jurisdiction is public power.[24] Beyond the mere dominative power which a pastor enjoys,[25] some of the powers which a pastor possesses, namely the powers of jurisdiction, are public powers.[26] In this sense, therefore, the pastor may be considered as a public person.[27]

Furthermore, the parish itself, though it is not a juridically perfected society, must be regarded as an essential element of the juridically perfect society, the Church.[28] Therefore, not only the power to which the parish is subjected, but also some of the power which its immediate superior exercises over it, is public power.

[23] Cf. *supra*, pp. 80-83.

[24] Cf. *supra*, p. 125.

[25] Cf. *supra*, p. 132.

[26] Even the pastor's ordinary jurisdiction in the internal forum is public power, simply because it is true jurisdiction; cf. cans. 196; 873, § 1; 892, § 1.

[27] Moreover, the pastor is by reason of his office a public ecclesiastical notary, who has the right and duty to keep the parochial registers and to transcribe authentic copies from the original instruments; cf. S.C.C., *Platien.*, 3 iul. 1909—*AAS*, I (1909), 657-660; cans. 470, §§ 1-4; 777, § 1; 798; 1659, § 2; 1813, § 1, 4°, etc.

[28] Cf. *supra*, pp. 130-132.

> Societates particulares quandoque sunt velut partes constitutivae ipsius societatis completae et perfectae, sunt partes organismi societatis, sunt subiecta iuris publici et tunc valet aequatio: societas publica, potestas publica.
>
> Quandoque societates particulares, quae intra societatem perfectam vivunt, comparantur ad constitutionem societatis non tamquam pars organizationis politicae, sed tamquam elementum materiale, tamquam individua. Elementa enim essentialia in qualibet societate sunt, organizatio politica seu elementum formale, et populus seu elementum materiale, passivum. . . .
>
> Cum una sit potestas publica, potestas suprema ut diximus, si in aliqua particulari societate adest potestas publica, illa potestas erit pars potestatis supremae et habetur velut a fonte, ab ipsa suprema potestate.[29]

But since both the exercise of some of that power and also its effects are juridically public, or capable of juridic proof, some of that power is jurisdiction in the external forum.[30]

The local ordinary possesses complete power, and the pastor enjoys incomplete power; but just as a diocese is an integral part of the juridically perfect society which is the Church, and the bishop's power is public, so also the parish is an integral part of the diocese, and at least some of the pastor's power is public. Thus, Larraona states:

> Nec parochi figuram explicamus si dicamus ipsum in foro interno frui potestate iurisdictionis, in foro vero externo (seu si malumus extra forum internum) nuda potestate dominativa illi simili per quam confraternitas gubernatur.[31]

And in a note he adds that, although the pastor's power in the external forum is not jurisdiction in the strict sense,

[29] Fuertes, "De Potestate Dominativa in Religionibus non Exemptis," *Commentarium pro Religiosis et Missionariis*, XXXII (1953), 204, 205.

[30] E.g., a pastor may grant a dispensation by means of a rescript; cf. Cicognani, *Canon Law*, p. 828.

[31] "De Potestate Dominativa Publica in Iure Canonico," *Acta Congressus Iuridici Internationalis*, IV, 179.

it is doubtlessly a true and public power.[32] Furthermore, he admits that a religious society, e.g., a non-exempt clerical congregation of pontifical approval, or a parish, is a society not in the same degree as public as a diocese, or as some other territorial institute equivalent to a diocese, or as an exempt religious institute. Also admitting that pastors and even the major superiors, or the heads of non-exempt clerical institutes, are not ordinaries or prelates properly so called, he nevertheless continues:

> Tamen haec et similia instituta sunt evidenter, et sub pluribus respectibus, non mere privata sed publica; imo, character publicus adeo in ipsis elucet, ut characteri privato praeponderet.[33]

Parochial jurisdiction is ordinary and proper jurisdiction.[34] Obviously, the pastor may possess over and above these powers certain other powers delegated by his local ordinary. The pastor may delegate his ordinary jurisdiction to another priest within the limitations expressed in the law.[35] A pastor cannot, for example, delegate jurisdiction to hear confessions;[36] nor can he delegate the faculty of preaching.[37] Of course, if one does not consider the faculty of preaching as a power of jurisdiction in the external forum, it follows that, since the only legal restrictions on parochial jurisdiction are then related to the internal forum, and since assistance at marriage is not to be considered as jurisdiction at all, the pastor may delegate all of his jurisdiction of the external forum, and also that jurisdiction of the internal forum which is not legally restricted.

All parochial jurisdiction, of course, is to be exercised under the authority of the local ordinary.[38] Beyond the

[32] *Ibid.*, note 107.

[33] *Ibid.*, p. 150.

[34] Cf. *supra*, pp. 81, 82.

[35] Can. 199, § 1.

[36] Cf. can. 874, § 1; *AAS*, XI (1919), 477; *Digest*, I, 410, 411.

[37] Cf. cans. 1327; 1328; 1337; *AAS*, IX (1917), 328; *Digest*, I, 623.

[38] Can. 451, § 1.

essential notions of constitution in and removal from office, this means much the same as what is intended when another canon states that the vicar-general should take care not to use his powers contrary to the mind and the will of the bishop.[39] In other words, if the pastor or the vicar-general exercises his power contrary to the mind and the will of the bishop, the exercise is, for the most part, valid, but grossly imprudent.[40] Moreover, the phrase implies certain potential exemptions of persons, and also limitations of power and of the fruits of the benefice. But, as Chelodi (1880-1922) and others have indicated, the pastor's power, as defined and sanctioned in the common law, cannot be arbitrarily removed or so limited that it becomes almost inane.[41] Nevertheless, since the bishop retains immediate and ordinary jurisdiction over the entire diocese, he can always delegate another for individual acts or functions, even though the pastor is unwilling; he can also remove from the parochial jurisdiction families of religious and pious houses not exempt by law.[42]

> The Church has always considered this subordination of priests to bishops as essential to her constitution. Hence the severe measures taken from the beginning to prevent the organization of parishes from endangering unity in the diocese and the concession of power to parish priests from infringing upon the divine right of bishops.[43]

The care of souls, which implies parochial rights, duties, and true jurisdiction, is obtained by the pastor when, after

[39] Can. 369, § 2.

[40] In reference to the vicar-general, the case delineated in canon 44, § 2, is excepted.

[41] *Ius Canonicum de Personis*, p. 351.

[42] Can. 464, § 2; cf. Larraona, "De Potestate Paroeciali relate ad Religiosos," *Commentarium pro Religiosis*, VIII (1927), 36-41. The doctors warn that such delegations and exemptions, through the agency of the bishop, should be effected only rarely and with a just cause, lest the rights of pastors be injured. Cf. Wernz-Vidal, *Ius Canonicum*, II, 926; Bargilliat, *Praelectiones*, II, 5.

[43] Ayrinhac, *Constitution of the Church in the New Code of Canon Law* (London, New York, Toronto, 1929), p. 302.

the canonical mission, he takes possession of the parish according to the norms of law.[44]

From these characteristics as also in consequence of an inspection of any jurisdictional power which pastors exercise in either forum, it is seen that the elements of true ecclesiastical jurisdiction are verified. Parochial jurisdiction is the public and spiritual power, conferred by the Church by a canonical mission, whereby a pastor functions as a principal second cause in directing his subjects toward their supernatural end. Each time that this jurisdiction is so exercised that it is subject to juridic proof, it is parochial jurisdiction in the external forum.

SECTION 2. ITS INSTANCES

The consideration of all possible parochial functions, in order to determine whether each is an act of jurisdiction in the external forum, is impractical. When one determines that any function is an exercise of true jurisdiction, it pertains to the external forum or internal forum depending on whether it is capable of juridic proof. Nevertheless, several such powers of the external forum are here mentioned, the most significant and generally recognized of which is the power of dispensing.

It approaches the superfluous to remark that the power of dispensing implies true ecclesiastical jurisdiction, and that such a power may be exercised in either forum, unless it is otherwise restricted. Cicognani remarks: "Dispensations also *establish law* in a particular case and can indeed be granted in the form of a rescript."[45] And he continues: "A dispensation . . . is essentially an act of jurisdiction. Hence the employment of dispensatory power requires an act of the will posited wittingly and willingly by a lawful superior."[46] In reality, the power of dispensing

[44] Cf. cans. 461, 1443-1445; 1406, § 1, 7°.

[45] *Canon Law*, p. 828.

[46] *Ibid.*, p. 830. Cf. also Bouscaren-Ellis, *Canon Law*, p. 433; Kelly, *The Jurisdiction of the Simple Confessor*, p. 201; Berutti, *Institutiones*, Vol. II, Pars I, p. 305; D'Angelo, "Annotatiunculae

represents a degree and implies a measure of legislative authority, for a dispensation is a fracture of the bond of the law or a relaxation of the will of the legislator in a particular case, and it requires the intervention of some species of legislative authority.[47]

While it is true that neither ordinaries nor pastors dispense generally from the universal laws of the Church, both are expressly granted certain powers in this respect.[48] The express concessions made to pastors by the law have already been enumerated;[49] other powers may be expressly delegated to pastors by their ordinaries.[50] But the necessity of the express concession, as demanded by canon 83, does not mean that concessions of other powers of dispensing may not be implicit.[51]

> *Ex implicita concessione* vero iis [i.e., parochis] respective eadem adscribenda est facultas quam competere diximus Ordinariis; ea scilicet, quae includitur in potestate explicite ipsis concessa, qua effectus in causa, conclusio in principio, species in genere, vel conditio sine qua potestas explicite concessa intelligi vel exerceri nequeat.[52]

Public preaching and teaching on the part of the pastor should be considered as exercises of jurisdiction in the external forum. If one admits that public preaching can be an exercise of jurisdiction,[53] it follows that, since it is sub-

in Modos quibus Leges Canonicae Cessant 'ab extrinseco,'" *Apollinaris*, I (1928), 256; Abbo-Hannan, *The Sacred Canons*, I, 111.

[47] Cf. can. 80; Saucedo, "Exercitium Jurisdictionis et Superiores Laici ex Ordine Hospitalario S. Joannis de Deo," *Commentarium pro Religiosis*, XIII (1932), 296.

[48] Cf. cans. 81; 83.

[49] Cf. *supra*, pp. 64, 65; cans. 1245, § 1; 1043-1045; 1125.

[50] Cf., e.g., can. 82.

[51] Cf., e.g., cans. 66, § 3; 200, § 1. The opposite of *express* is *tacit*, not *implicit*, which is opposed to *explicit*.

[52] Michiels, *Normae Generales Juris Canonici* (2. ed., 2 vols., Parisiis-Tornaci-Romae: Desclée et Socii, 1949), II, 720.

[53] It appears that such preaching often fulfills all the requirements necessary to be regarded as jurisdiction, even as to the canonical injunction; cf. cans. 1327; 1328.

ject to juridic proof, it is an exercise of jurisdiction which pertains to the external forum. There is no question of the pastor's prerogative and duty to preach and teach by reason of his office; the care of souls demands this.[54] And just as the preaching of the Holy Father must be considered as an exercise of jurisdiction,[55] so the preaching of the bishop and of the pastor should also be considered as an exercise of jurisdiction.[56]

Many authors, however, do not agree to this, just as many authors also do not admit that the administration of ecclesiastical goods can be jurisdictional. One author designates the faculty received by way of a canonical mission or by way of a commission for preaching publicly as jurisdiction,[57] but later states:

> Preaching may not be considered as an act of the powers of orders or of jurisdiction, but certainly it can be included among the acts of mere administration of which the priest is competent by reason of his office.[58]

The incongruities on this and other subjects related to the power of jurisdiction merely bear witness to the intricacy of the notion of jurisdiction. Authors who use the term "jurisdiction" in various significations are inevitably courting apparent contradictions. According to the terminology of this dissertation and the principles of jurisdiction and forum established herein, the lawful public preaching by an agent who either possesses true jurisdiction or is capable of possessing it must be designated as jurisdiction in the broad sense. Even those who deny this must admit that such preaching relates in some way to the power of juris-

[54] Cf. cans. 464, § 1; 1329-1333.

[55] Cf. *supra*, p. 112; cans. 218, § 1; 1327, § 1.

[56] Cf. cans. 1327, § 2; 1329-1333.

[57] Allgeier, *The Canonical Obligation of Preaching in Parish Churches*, The Catholic University of America Canon Law Studies, n. 291 (Washington, D.C.: The Catholic University of America Press, 1949), p. 36.

[58] *Ibid.*, p. 89.

diction, inasmuch as the *magisterium* is a species of jurisdiction.

If one has not already adverted to the problem of lay participation in the *magisterium* and its consequent jurisdictional implications, one may do so now. As Bouscaren-Ellis indicate:

> There is a *theoretical* difficulty about lay people teaching the catechism publicly, because such teaching might seem to require a canonical mission, and that would imply jurisdiction. On the other hand lay persons are incapable of ecclesiastical jurisdiction (cf. c. 118). Practically it is certain both from this canon [1333] and from many other sources that the help of lay persons of both sexes in teaching catechism even publicly is not only welcomed but earnestly solicited. For centuries lay catechists have been employed in the mission fields. Recent documents on Catholic Action invite the laity to co-operate with the hierarchy very especially in this work. Perhaps the answer to the theoretical difficulty is this. Lay persons thus working with the approval of the hierarchy have a canonical mission only in the broad sense; a mandate, without jurisdiction. They work *ex iurisdictione,* though not *cum iurisdictione.*[59]

The designation of the operation of the laity and of others who by the common law are incapacitated for the exercise of jurisdictional acts as being "out of jurisdiction" rather than "with jurisdiction" is in perfect accord with the propositions embodied above. The explanation is substantially the same as that of the lay administration of ecclesiastical goods. Since some persons perform certain acts which have the external species of jurisdiction, and since those persons are excluded from the exercise of that ecclesiastical jurisdiction which is specified in canons 108 and 118, their acts simply cannot be jurisdictional in the

[59] *Canon Law,* pp. 688, 689; cf. also Coronata, *Institutiones,* Vol. II, *De Rebus* (4. ed., Taurini-Romae: Marietti, 1951), 259; Schröcker, *Die Verwaltung des Ortskirchenvermögens,* p. 43; De Meester, *Juris Canonici et Juris Canonico-Civilis Compendium* (3 vols. in 4, Brugis, 1921-1928), III, 193, 194 (hereafter cited *Compendium*).

sense of the canons cited. If one wishes to use the term "jurisdiction" in some extremely broad sense, or in a sense other than that envisioned by the canons mentioned, one may then consider such activity of laymen as jurisdiction.[60] But if jurisdiction is to be considered as the power delineated in canons 108 and 118—and it should be so considered —then the previously given explanation must apply. Laymen and others, though they do not possess the power of jurisdiction, may function "out of jurisdiction," or under the supervision and with the approval of ecclesiastical authority, but not "with jurisdiction," or with any certain ecclesiastical power which they cannot conceivably possess. In other words, the function of the laity in the matter of public teaching is much the same as their rôle in the administration of ecclesiastical goods. One who possesses some ecclesiastical jurisdiction, however, such as the pastor, may well perform these acts "with jurisdiction," inasmuch as they are at least subsumed under or assimilated within an existing power of jurisdiction.

A logical progression from this consideration is to that of parochial administration or the administration of the ecclesiastical goods as performed by the pastor.[61] According to the previous explanation, such administration should be considered as an exercise of true ecclesiastical jurisdiction.[62] In so far as this administration and its effects are subject to juridic proof, it may be considered as an exercise of parochial jurisdiction in and for the external forum. Many authors, of course, reject or hesitate to recognize this theory by reason of their particular concept of ecclesiastical jurisdiction, or of the external forum, or of both. An example of the hesitation spoken of follows:

> Iurisdictio ordinaria competit . . . parochis et vicariis actualibus seu perpetuis pro subditis in foro

[60] Cf. *supra*, pp. 153-157.

[61] Cf. McReavy, "The Administration of Parochial Property," *The Clergy Review* (London, 1931-), XXIX (1948), 1-11.

[62] Cf. *supra*, pp. 147-157; cf. also cans. 1476; 1182, §§ 1-3.

> interno, et *secundum quid* in foro externo, sc. relate ad paroeciae administrationem.[63]

This semblance of an equivocation seems in itself to pave the way for the following article.

Article III. Doctrinal Views Regarding Parochial Jurisdiction

The authors prior to the Code commonly and rightly denied to pastors the perfect jurisdiction of the external forum, which included the threefold legislative, judicial, and coercive power. They never excluded from the realm of parochial jurisdiction, however, an imperfect power of the external forum, which they designated as administrative, disciplinary, domestic, dominative, economic, paternal, etc. Such designations are understandable when one considers the historical reason for the denial of jurisdiction in the external forum in respect to pastors. That reason was reflected in the aim to combat parochialism, which so exaggerated the rights of pastors that it considered them as true prelates with perfect or complete power in the external forum. Some recent authors retain the doctrine of the classical canonists both as to concept and as to terminology. But the majority of the authors, modern and ancient, designates parochial jurisdiction as administrative, dominative, economic, etc., not for the reason that it is not jurisdiction at all, but rather for the purpose of distinguishing it from the perfect power of rulership, which is proper only to prelates or ordinaries.

There is no question of the existence of parochial power in the internal forum, whether sacramental or extra-sacramental, since all authors designate it as the power of juris-

[63] De Meester, *Compendium,* I, 307, 308. In a later passage in the same work the author denies jurisdiction in the external forum to pastors, because they cannot enact laws, inflict censures, and dispense from the universal law, but he remarks in the same paragraph that they have *de facto,* by disposition of the law, acquired certain powers of dispensing even in the external forum; cf. *ibid.,* II, 265, 266.

diction. Relevant to the internal forum, jurisdiction has the notion of the power of judging when it designates the faculty of receiving sacramental confessions. The confessor, in virtue of this power, authoritatively weighs the matter which is necessary, or at least sufficient, for absolution; forms a judgment on the penitent's dispositions; imposes a penance which is to be accepted and fulfilled by the sinner, and finally pronounces the sentence of absolution. The process closely resembles a trial in the external forum, even if the confessor should refuse absolution.

The attitude of modern authors toward the subject of parochial jurisdiction in the external forum differs little from that of their predecessors. The modern heritage, therefore, is simply the admission or denial of such jurisdiction according to one's own particular notions on the subject. The contention, however, which supported as common among the pre-Code authors the doctrine which denied to pastors a jurisdiction in the external forum, was shown to be false.[64] That same contention, as applying to modern authors, is also false. Today, just as prior to the Code, some authors sustain the negative view, while others uphold the positive view. Today also, just as prior to the Code, the authors who sustain the negative opinion do so because of their unduly restricted understanding of the power of jurisdiction, or because of their peculiar notion of the ecclesiastical forum. Consequently, if such restricted notions can be indicated in the works of those authors who support the negative view, then more arguments are thereby furnished for the general acceptance and the propriety of the expression "jurisdiction of pastors in the external forum."

One author, for instance, states: "Nulla jurisdictione in foro externo potiuntur parochi." And in the next sentence he explains the statement thus: "Neque sunt judices

[64] Cf. *supra*, pp. 52-60. The old authors were often misquoted and more often misinterpreted; even contrary evidence was found in these very authors.

fidei, neque potestatem legislativam habent, neque possunt censuras ferre, et nulla ipsis competit potestas dispensandi in votis."[65]

Another author arrives at the same conclusion thus:

> At, ordinaria potestas seu iurisdictio parochorum, *nonnisi in foro interno* . . . exerceri potest. . . . Sane, iurisdictio fori externi importat potestatem legislativam, iudicialem et coactivam.[66]

Still another author remarks:

> Ahora bien: ese poder no puede llamarse *jurisdicción verdadera* en el fuero *externo*, porque ésta se ordena directa e inmediatamente a la promoción del bien común, mediante el ejercicio perfecto del poder legislativo, ejecutivo y judicial, y la potestad del párroco no es de tal naturaleza, sino que se ordena al bien privado e interno de los feligreses.[67]

This restricted notion of jurisdiction in the external forum continues today, as is manifest from the following:

> La giurisdizione di foro esterno che importa potestà legislativa, giudiziaria e coativa, non compete al parroco perchè questi non ha per ufficio la potestà di fare leggi, di conoscere giudizialmente le cause, e di comminare pene ecclesiastiche, esorbitando tale potestà dalla natura dell'ufficio parrocchiale.[68]

It is evident that these authors, and others who speak similarly, understand jurisdiction not in the broad sense, which should be retained according to the classical definition and usage, but rather in the strict and more eminent

[65] Bargilliat, *Praelectiones*, II, 51.

[66] Fanfani, *De Iure Parochorum*, p. 186.

[67] Montero y Gutiérrez, *Instituciones de Derecho Canónico* (3. ed., Madrid: Imprenta Saez, 1948), pp. 184, 185. Cf. also Badii, *Institutiones*, I, 252; Claeys Boúúaert-Simenon, *Manuale Juris Canonici* (3 vols., Vol. I, 5. ed., Gandae et Leodii: Prostat apud auctores in Seminariis Gandavensi et Leodiensi, 1939), I, 313; Cocchi, *Commentarium*, III, 389, 391; Vermeersch-Creusen, *Epitome*, I, 406, 407; Clarke, *Parish Societies*, The Catholic University of America Canon Law Studies, n. 176 (Washington, D.C.: The Catholic University of America Press, 1943), p. 86.

[68] Da Forchia, "La Cura d'Anime come Istituto Giuridico," *Ius Seraphicum* (Romae, 1955-), II (1956), 297.

sense of designating a more perfect degree of the power of rulership. No one, therefore, can cite these authors in valid refutation of the imperfect jurisdiction of pastors in the external forum.

Some authors, as Cappello, contend that the pastor has disciplinary and administrative power only in the external forum. They deny true jurisdiction to pastors since their powers of jurisdiction are not connatural to, or from the nature of, the parochial office, but merely accessory to it in consequence of a benign concession of the legislator.[69] Certainly the parochial office can be conceived without such powers, for the common law prior to the Code did not grant them to pastors. But even though this is admitted, these powers, whether they be considered ordinary, delegated by the law, or anything else, are nevertheless powers of jurisdiction which may be exercised in the external forum.[70]

From what has been said concerning the complexity of the concept of jurisdiction, one may readily understand that an author could indeed employ the term "jurisdiction" in the strict sense in one instance and then use it in the broad sense in another, and even without any qualification.[71] It is also conceivable that an author could employ the term in different senses even in the same paragraph or sentence.[72] Be that as it may, the contradictions which thereby appear in this matter are usually apparent ones only and not true contradictions. The simple fact of such a diversified usage itself argues for the propriety of the phrase "parochial jurisdiction in the external forum."

There is an ample representation of authors who are quite positive in their claim for the possession of juris-

[69] *Summa Iuris Canonici,* I, 456.

[70] Cf. *supra,* pp. 119, 120, where it is demonstrated that these powers are actually ordinary ones.

[71] Cf., e.g., De Meester, *Compendium,* I, 307, 308, II, 265, 266, and Cocchi, *Commentarium,* III, 389, 411, where this is exemplified.

[72] Cf. e.g., Badii, *Institutiones,* I, 252, and Regatillo, *Institutiones,* I, 396, where this is instanced.

diction in the external forum on the part of pastors. One author makes the following statement:

> Imprimis utrumque forum ad Ecclesiam pertinet, et per Ecclesiam exercetur; immo quandoque eadem persona est competens in foro interno simul et externo: ordinarius loci, et etiam *parochus,* quod ad plures materias.[73]

Another arrives at this conclusion:

> Dicamus propterea, potestatem parochis competentem in foro externo, vi officii, esse *potestatem ordinariam regiminis* seu *iurisdictionis,* quia est participatio potestatis regiminis "quae ex divina institutione est in Ecclesia," quamquam gradu utique imperfecto, remissiorique ac reperitur in veris Ecclesiae praelatis.[74]

Still another author treats the question as follows:

> Potestatem ordinis parochus opus est iam receperit cum sacro presbyteratus ordine; cum parochiali igitur officio recepit potestatem verae iurisdictionis; non tamen normativam seu legiferam nisi admodum coarctatam, dispensandi videlicet peculiaribus in urgentibus adiunctis super matrimonii impedimentis ex can. 1044 ss. et super lege dierum festorum et esurialium intra fines can. 1245, § 1: latiorem autem obtinet potestatem iurisdictionis exequutivam, non quidem coactivam, neque iudicialem fori externi, sed *administrativam* et *fori interni iudicialem* prouti expostulat cura pastoralis; ideoque eam appellant etiam oeconomicam. Quae, quia cum officio cohaeret iure ipso, est ordinaria, et quia etiam socialem publicamque vitam Ecclesiae attingit, ut dispensatio super praecepto festivo aut super impedimentis matrimonii, ut ministerium verbi, administratio beneficii aliaque id genus, non dixerim eam esse tantum fori interni, siquidem potestas iudicialis interno quidem saepitur foro, administrativa tamen foras quoque, idque plerumque, prorumpit.[75]

[73] Capobianco, "De Notione Fori Interni in Iure Canonico," *Apollinaris,* IX (1936), 373.

[74] Tirado, *De Iurisdictionis Acceptione,* p. 215.

[75] Romani, *Institutiones Juris Canonici,* Vol. I, *Jus Constitutionale* (Romae: E Schola Typographica "Pio X," 1941), p. 323.

A Spanish author entertains the question and advances the following three reasons for the affirmative view: 1) the government of a parish is much more complicated than that of a religious community, and if the superiors of some such communities possess jurisdiction in the external forum, so also do pastors; 2) pastors have no legislative, judicial, or coercive power for the reason simply that they do not need it; so also some religious superiors have no legislative power, but that fact does not militate against their possession of jurisdiction in the external forum; 3) the power of dispensing from ecclesiastical law postulates the possession of true jurisdiction; but the Code has empowered pastors to grant certain dispensations in the external forum. The author concludes, therefore, that pastors have some true jurisdiction in the external forum.[76]

Finally, there may here be offered this excerpt from a recent dissertation:

> On peut donc affimer sans crainte que le pouvoir possédé par les curés au for externe est une véritable juridiction, bien qu'à un degré imparfait ou incomplet.[77]

All of the authors just mentioned, therefore, and many more, do not hesitate to admit for pastors a true jurisdiction in the external forum.[78]

[76] Alonso, "Los Párrocos en el Concilio de Trento y en el Código de Derecho Canónico," *Revista Española de Derecho Canónico,* II (1947), 953.

[77] Ménard, *L'Exemption des Séminaires de la Juridiction Paroissiale,* The Catholic University of Ottawa Canonical Series, n. 30 (Ottawa: Les Éditions de L'Université d'Ottawa, 1950), pp. 72, 73. The author fails, however, to draw the necessary distinctions between administrative jurisdiction, subjective rights, and mere administration, thus falling into error on certain points; cf. *loc. cit.*

[78] Cf., in addition, Bouscaren-Ellis, *Canon Law,* pp. 189, 210; Depoorter, "De Potestate Parochorum in Foro Externo," *Collationes Brugenses,* XLIII (1947), 56-59; Chelodi, *Ius Canonicum de Personis,* p. 351; Woeber, *The Interpellations,* The Catholic University of America Canon Law Studies, n. 172 (Washington, D.C.: The Catholic University of America Press, 1942), p. 126; Sipos, *Enchiridion,* p. 252.

From all indications the progression of time is ushering in more and more canonists to the adoption of what is implied in the title phrase of this dissertation, and rightly so. One who understands the concepts of jurisdiction and forum, as they are proposed in this work, is practically impelled to designate certain powers of pastors as of a jurisdictional character in the external forum. Nevertheless, the concept of ecclesiastical jurisdiction is far from being completely stabilized, and, as a result, the writer is among the first to admit that some of the theory contained in this work may later in turn become obsolete. But certainly anything which can contribute to the present fuller understanding of ecclesiastical jurisdiction should be and will be warmly received. The jurisdiction of pastors, both in content and character, has changed in history and will change in the future because of the fact that the Church and its law, the *Ius Canonicum,* are of an organic structure.

One conclusion that may be drawn from this dissertation vividly recalls the fact that the Canon Law is not *lex* but *ius.*[79] The distinction, which perhaps cannot as readily be duly and incisively delineated in the vernacular, emphasizes the fact that the Canon Law is something more than a collection of rules, that it embodies a fundamental governing principle, and that each canonical enactment derives its sanction not from some or any power external to the Church, not from the consent of the governed, but from a divinely constituted power, for it is a great whole, the *Ius Canonicum,* which in its organic structure not only has shown, but throughout the future will continue to show, a healthy growth and a fruitful development.

[79] "Ius generale nomen est; lex autem iuris est species. Ius autem est dictum, quia iustum est. Omne autem ius legibus et moribus constat."—C. 2, D. 1.

SUMMARY AND CONCLUSIONS

1. Prior to the time of Gratian (ca. 1140) the parish priest was considered to possess the care of souls or jurisdiction, and was accordingly presumed to possess the character of a prelate. This appellation as a prelate continued at least to the fifteenth century, and possibly to its insinuated exclusion by the Council of Trent (1545-1563). [Cf. pp. 1-4, 6, 7, 13, 14, 26.]

2. By the time of the Decretals (1234) the power of orders was clearly delineated from the power of jurisdiction, while the care of souls embraced both powers and both forums. [Cf. pp. 4-8.]

3. From the Decretals to the Council of Trent the meaning of the care of souls suffered rapidly successive changes, now meaning jurisdiction even in the external forum, now meaning only the power of orders. Toward the end of this period, the term related more to jurisdiction, which comprehended everything relevant to the administration of justice and equity, as well as the lawful exercise of the power of orders, to the exclusion of the power of orders itself. The perennial meaning of jurisdiction as the general administration of justice and equity had already developed by the time of Emperor Justinian (527-565). [Cf. pp. 1, 2, 8-11, 13, 15-21.]

4. Between 1140 and 1234 the distinction between the *lex dioecesana* and the *lex iurisdictionis* was at its zenith, but afterwards this distinction began its gradual descent to ultimate oblivion. [Cf. pp. 5-8, 30-41.]

5. From the Council of Trent to the promulgation of the Code jurisdiction was employed in two senses: in its extended and more frequent sense it meant either legislative, judicial, and coercive power, or the total ecclesiastical power of rulership, under which some authors included even the administration of goods and the exercise of dominative power; in its restricted sense it meant either the ***potestas***

iuris dicendi or *potestas* joined with *imperium.* The lawful exercise of the power of orders, and, in the case of the sacrament of penance, even the valid exercise thereof, postulated a possession of jurisdiction. [Cf. pp. 30-41.]

6. From the Council of Trent to the nineteenth century exclusive all authors, when considering the entirety of ecclesiastical power, made the essential distinction between the power of orders and the power of jurisdiction. [Cf. pp. 31-35.]

7. The doctrine of the tripartition of ecclesiastical power into the power of orders, of jurisdiction, and of the *magisterium,* contrary to the classical and traditional twofold division, rose and, for all practical purposes, fell in the nineteenth century. [Cf. pp. 35-41.]

8. From the Council of Trent to the promulgation of the Code the doctrinal development regarding the divisions of jurisdiction indicated this manifest anomaly: Authors noted that the acceptance of the term "jurisdiction" differed in ecclesiastical law from that in Roman law, but at the same time diligently endeavored to transpose its Roman law divisions into the realm of ecclesiastical jurisdiction. Accordingly the two divisions of ordinary and delegated jurisdiction and of voluntary and contentious jurisdiction were the most important and most common, though authors differed greatly as to the character and extent of each. [Cf. pp. 41-46.]

9. The commonly accepted meaning of external forum prior to the eighteenth century denoted the contentious or judicial forum. In the eighteenth and following centuries the external forum was generally viewed as that which concerned directly and primarily the public utility of the faithful, while the internal forum referred directly and primarily to the private utility of individual members of the Church. [Cf. pp. 47-52.]

10. The common doctrine among post-Tridentine and pre-Code authors rightly denied to pastors a complete jurisdiction in the external forum. But the contention which sup-

ports as common among those authors the opinion which denied to pastors even an incomplete or an imperfect jurisdiction in the external forum is absolutely false. [Cf. pp. 52-60.]

11. Prior to the Code the jurisdictional character of the faculty of assisting at marriage was debated, and the opinion which came to be regarded as the common one excluded from that faculty any participation in the nature of true jurisdiction. [Cf. pp. 60-64.]

12. As exemplified in the parochial power of dispensing even prior to the Code, pastors did exercise some true jurisdiction in the external forum. [Cf. pp. 64-67.]

13. The ecclesiastical hierarchy embraces the hierarchy of orders and the hierarchy of jurisdiction, which includes, when objectively considered, the *magisterium* as a species of power. [Cf. pp. 73-75, 77-79, 110, 115, 116.]

14. The power of jurisdiction is the active potency whereby a man authoritatively acts as a principal second cause in directing the faithful to their end. [Cf. pp. 76, 77.]

15. If anyone states that pastors have no jurisdiction in the external forum, he must also state, in order to preserve the intelligibility, consistency, and validity of his statement, that pastors have absolutely no jurisdiction. Conversely, if one acknowledges for pastors any jurisdiction, even jurisdiction in the internal forum, he must accordingly recognize some parochial jurisdiction in the external forum. [Cf. pp. 80, 81, 164-169.]

16. Parochial jurisdiction is an ordinary but a vicarious or a derived power in the theological sense; it is an ordinary and a proper power, however, in the canonical sense. [Cf. pp. 80-83, 167-169.]

17. The internal forum and the external forum, which are proper to the juridic life of the Church, are not divisions of but distinctions in the one ecclesiastical juridic order, in which all human acts pertain either to the internal forum alone or to the internal and the external forum simultaneously. The better criterion for distinguishing the

external forum from the internal forum is juridic publicity, or juridic proof, rather than public utility. [Cf. pp. 84-101.]

18. Jurisdiction may signify generically the entire spiritual power of rulership which is in the Church by divine institution. The term has numerous synonyms, as well as multiple applications, in canon law and it may also designate the parts of the complete power of rulership. [Cf. pp. 115-118.]

19. The most precise and comprehensive division of jurisdiction is that of legislative, judicial, and executive power, the last of which comprises a governmental, an administrative, and a coercive power. [Cf. pp. 122-124.]

20. Jurisdiction receives the same broad signification from the present legislation and from modern authors as it received prior to the Code. It may best be described as the power, or active potency, spiritual and public, conferred by Christ or the Church by injunction or canonical mission, whereby a man authoritatively functions as a principal second cause in directing the faithful to their supernatural end. [Cf. pp. 76, 77, 111-121, 124-128.]

21. Besides the purely dominative power mentioned in the Code, there may well be a public dominative power, which is actually imperfect jurisdiction. [Cf. pp. 130-137.]

22. Though the faculty of assisting at marriage and its delegation are not of a jurisdictional nature, the canons regulating the powers of jurisdiction are applicable also to this faculty, in so far as the nature of the matter allows and the special canons on the faculty itself permit. [Cf. pp. 137-144.]

23. A priest who has incurred the suspension from jurisdiction assists validly, even after the sentence, at any marriage for which he would otherwise be competent. [Cf. pp. 144-147.]

24. The administration of ecclesiastical goods is in some way jurisdictional, inasmuch as the Church formally exercises jurisdiction not only over things spiritual in them-

selves, but also over things temporal in themselves. Except for the one possible case of the administration of the Holy Father, however, the administration of ecclesiastical goods is not in and of itself an act of jurisdiction, but may be subsumed under and flow from the jurisdiction of an officer who already possesses jurisdiction, or may even constitute a power of jurisdiction in an agent capable of possessing such power. [Cf. pp. 147-157.]

25. Parochial jurisdiction in the external forum is the incomplete public power of rulership, which is exercised by the pastor under the authority of the local ordinary and which is so exercised as to be capable of juridic proof. The power of dispensing, public preaching and teaching, and the administration of ecclesiastical goods are several parochial powers of jurisdiction which relate to the external forum. [Cf. pp. 164-174.]

26. Modern authors admit or deny a parochial jurisdiction in the external forum according to their particular notions on the matter, but the progression of time is ushering in more and more canonists to the adoption of the decorous and appropriate expression "jurisdiction of pastors in the external forum." [Cf. pp. 174-180.]

BIBLIOGRAPHY

Sources

Acta Apostolicae Sedis, Commentarium Officiale, Romae, 1909-1929; Civitate Vaticana, 1929—

Acta Sanctae Sedis, 41 vols., Romae, 1865-1908.

Bouscaren, T. Lincoln, *The Canon Law Digest*, 3 vols., Vol. I, 7. printing, 1950; Vol. II, 5. printing, 1949; Vol. III, 1954, and Supplements 1953 through 1956, 1954-1957, Milwaukee: The Bruce Publishing Co.

Codex Iuris Canonici Pii X Pontificis Maximi iussu digestus, Benedicti Papae XV auctoritate promulgatus, Praefatione, Fontium Annotatione et Indice Analytico-Alphabetico ab Emo Petro Card. Gasparri Auctus, Romae: Typis Polyglottis Vaticanis, 1917; reimpressio, 1934.

Codicis Iuris Canonici Fontes, cura Emi Petri Card. Gasparri editi, 9 vols., Romae (postea Civitate Vaticana): Typis Polyglottis Vaticanis, 1923-1939 (Vols. VII-IX, ed. cura et studio Emo Iustiniani Card. Serédi).

Collectanea S. Congregationis de Propaganda Fide, 2 vols., Romae: Typographia Polyglotta S.C. de Propaganda Fide, 1907.

Corpus Iuris Canonici, editio Lipsiensis II, post Aemilii Ludovici Richteri curas instruxit Aemilius Friedberg, Lipsiae: Ex officina Bernhardi Tauchnitz, 1879-1881; ed. anastatice repetita, 1928.

Decretales D. Gregorii Papae IX, suae integritati una cum glossis restitutae, cum privilegio Gregorii XIII, Pont. Max., et Aliorum Principum, Romae, 1582.

Decretum Gratiani emendatum et notationibus illustratum cum glossis, Gregorii XIII, Pont. Max., iussu editum, 2 vols., Romae, 1582.

Jaffé, Philippus, *Regesta Pontificum Romanorum ab condita Ecclesia ad annum post Christum natum MCXCVIII*, ed. 2. correctam et auctam auspiciis Gulielmi Wattenbach curaverunt, S. Loewenfeld, F. Kaltenbrunner, P. Ewald, 2 vols., Lipsiae, 1885-1888.

Liber Sextus Decretalium D. Bonifacii Papae VIII, suae integritati cum Clementinis Extravagantibus, earumque Glossis restitutis, Romae, 1582.

Mansi, Joannes, *Sacrorum Conciliorum Nova et Amplissima Collectio*, 53 vols. in 60, Parisiis, 1901-1927.

McNabb, Vincent, *The Decrees of the Vatican Council*, New York, Cincinnati, Chicago, 1907.

Monumenta Germaniae Historica, Epistolarum Tomi I et II, Gregorii Papae Registrum Epistolarum, ed. P. Ewald and L. M. Hartmann, Berolini, 1887-1899.

———, *Epistolarum Tomus V, Epistolae Karolini Aevi, Tomus III*, Berolini, 1899.

Potthast, Augustus, *Regesta Pontificum Romanorum inde ab anno post Christum natum MCXCVIII ad annum MCCCIV*, 2 vols., Berolini, 1874, 1875.

Schroeder, Henry J., *Canons and Decrees of the Council of Trent*, St. Louis: B. Herder Book Co., 1941.

Thesaurus Resolutionum Sacrae Congregationis Concilii, 167 vols., Romae, 1718-1908.

AUTHORS

Abbo, John A.-Hannan, Jerome D., *The Sacred Canons*, 2 vols., St. Louis: B. Herder Book Co., 1952.

Agius, Laurentius, *Summarium Iurium et Officiorum Parochorum*, Neapoli: M. D'Auria, Pontificius Editor, 1953.

Aichner, Simon, *Compendium Juris Canonici*, 6. ed., Brixinae, 1887.

Allgeier, Joseph, *The Canonical Obligation of Preaching in Parish Churches*, The Catholic University of America Canon Law Studies, n. 291, Washington, D.C.: The Catholic University of America Press, 1949.

Ayrinhac, Henry A., *Constitution of the Church in the New Code of Canon Law*, London, New York, Toronto, 1929.

Bachofen, Augustinus, *Summa Iuris Ecclesiastici Publici*, Romae, 1910.

Badii, Caesar, *Institutiones Iuris Canonici*, 3. ed., 2 vols., Florentiae, 1921, 1922.

Barbosa, Augustinus, *De Officio et Potestate Episcopi*, Lugduni, 1628.

———, *De Officio et Potestate Parochi*, Lugduni, 1665.

Bargilliat, Michael, *Praelectiones Juris Canonici*, 37. ed., 2 vols., Parisiis, 1923, 1924.

Begnudelli, Franciscus, *Bibliotheca Juris Canonico-Civilis Practica*, 4 vols., Mutinae, 1757.

Bender, Ludovicus, *Philosophia Iuris*, Romae: Officium Libri Catholici, 1947.

Benedictus XIV, *De Synodo Dioecesana*, 3 vols., Romae, 1783.

Berardi, Carolus, *Commentarium in Jus Ecclesiasticum Universum*, 2 vols. in 1, Mediolani, 1846.

Berengo, Iohannes, *Enchiridion Parochorum seu Institutiones Theologicae Pastoralis*, 2. ed., Venetiis, 1877.

Bertachinus, Ioannes, *Repertorium*, 5 vols., Venetiis, 1570.

Berutti, Christophorus, *Institutiones Iuris Canonici*, 6 vols., Taurini: Marietti, 1936- , Vol. II, Pars I, 1943.

Beste, Udalricus, *Introductio in Codicem*, 3. ed., Collegeville, Minn.; St. John's Abbey Press, 1946.

Blat, Albertus, *Commentarium Textus Codicis Iuris Canonici*, Lib. II, *De Personis*, 2. ed., Romae, 1921.

———, *Opusculum de Potestate Superiorum in Religionibus*, Romae: Pontificium Institutum Angelicum, 1935.

Böckhn, Placidus, *Commentarium in Jus Canonicum*, 3 vols., Salisburgi et invenitur Parisiis, 1776.

Boich, Henricus, *In Quinque Decretalium Libros Commentaria*, Venetiis, 1576.

Bouix, Dominicus, *De Principiis Juris Canonici*, 3. ed., Parisiis, 1882.

———, *Tractatus de Parocho*, 3. ed., Parisiis, 1880.

Bouscaren, T. L.-Ellis, A. C., *Canon Law, A Text and Commentary*, Milwaukee: The Bruce Publishing Co., 1946, Reprint, 1948.

Boverio, Zacharias, *Censura Paraenetica in Quatuor Libros de Republica Ecclesiastica*, Mediolani, 1621.

Buckland, William W., *A Textbook of Roman Law*, 2. ed., Cambridge: University Press, 1932.

Cappello, Felix, *Tractatus Canonico-Moralis de Sacramentis*, Vol. V, *De Matrimonio*, 6. ed., Taurini-Romae: Marietti, 1950.

———, *Summa Iuris Canonici*, 4. ed., 3 vols., Romae: Aedes Universitatis Gregorianae, 1945-1955.

Champoux, Timothy, *The Juridical Position of the Laity in the Church*, Romae: Typis Pontificiae Universitatis Gregorianae, 1939.

Chelodi, Ioannes, *Ius Canonicum de Delictis et Poenis et Iudiciis Criminalibus*, 5. ed., recognita et aucta a Pio Ciprotti, Trento: Libreria Moderna Editrice, 1943.

———, *Ius Canonicum de Personis*, 3. ed., recognita et aucta a Pio Ciprotti, Vincenza: Società Anonima Tipografica, Trento: A. Ardesi, 1942.

Choupin, Lucien, *Valeur des Décisions Doctrinales et Disciplinaires du Saint-Siège*, 3. ed., Paris, 1928.

Cicognani, Amleto G., *Canon Law*, 2. ed., authorized English version by Joseph M. O'Hara and Francis J. Brennan, Westminster, Md.: The Newman Press, Reprint, 1949.

Claeys Boúúaert, F.-Simenon, G., *Manuale Iuris Canonici*, 3 vols., Gandae et Leodii: Prostat apud auctores in Seminariis Gandavensi et Leodiensi, Vol. I, 5. ed., 1939; Vol. II, 3. ed., 1947.

Clancy, Patrick, *The Local Religious Superior*, The Catholic University of America Canon Law Studies, n. 175, Washington, D.C.: The Catholic University of America Press, 1943.

Clarke, Thomas J., *Parish Societies*, The Catholic University of

America Canon Law Studies, n. 176, Washington, D.C.: The Catholic University of America Press, 1943.

Cocchi, Guidus, *Commentarium in Codicem iuris canonici ad usum scholarum*, 4. ed., 8 vols., Taurinorum Augustae: Marietti, 1931-1946, Vol. II, 1937.

Coronata, Matthaeus Conte a, *Compendium Iuris Canonici ad usum scholarum*, 3 vols., Taurini-Romae: Marietti, 1949, 1950.

———, *Institutiones Iuris Canonici ad usum utriusque cleri et scholarum*, 5 vols., Taurini-Romae: Marietti, Vol. II, *De Rebus*, 4. ed., 1951; Vol. IV, *De Delictis et Poenis*, 3. ed., 1948.

———, *Institutiones Iuris Canonici, De Sacramentis Tractatus Canonicus*, 2. ed., 3 vols., Taurini-Romae: Marietti, 1947-1951.

Craisson, D., *Manuale Totius Juris Canonici*, 5. ed., 4 vols., Pictavii, 1877.

Crnica, Antonius, *Commentarium Theoretico-Practicum Codicis Iuris Canonici*, 2 vols., Šibenik: Typis Typographiae "Kačic," 1940, 1941.

De Ancharano, Petrus, *Consilia sive Iuris Responsa*, Venetiis, 1574.

De Angelis, Philippus, *Praelectiones Juris Canonici*, 5 vols. in 9, Romae-Parisiis, 1877-1891.

De Baysio, Guido, *Rosarium seu in Decretorum Volumen Commentaria*, Venetiis, 1577.

De Bellamera, Aegidius (Gilles de Bellemère), *In Secundam Primi Decretalium Libri Partem Praelectiones*, Lugduni, 1548, 1549.

De Luca, Joannes B., *Theatrum Veritatis et Justitiae*, 16 vols., Coloniae Agrippinae, 1706.

De Meester, Alphonsus, *Juris Canonici et Juris Canonico-Civilis Compendium*, 3 vols. in 4, Brugis, 1921-1928.

De Molina, Ludovicus, *De Iustitia et Iure*, 5 vols., Coloniae Allobrogum, 1759.

De Oliva, Felicianus, *Tractatus de Foro Ecclesiae*, Coloniae Allobrogum, 1733.

De Ubaldis, Baldus, *Super Decretalibus ... Commentaria*, Lugduni, 1547.

———, *Margarita Baldi de Ubaldi ... ad Innocentii IV Pont. Max. in V Libros Decretalium Commentarios repertorii loco addita*, Venetiis, 1570.

Devoti, Joannes, *Jus Canonicum Universum Publicum et Privatum*, 3 vols., Romae, 1837.

Donovan, James J., *The Pastor's Obligation in Prenuptial Investigation*, The Catholic University of America Canon Law Studies, n. 115, Washington, D.C.: The Catholic University of America, 1938.

Fagnani, Prosperus, *Commentaria in primum [-quintum] librum Decretalium*, 5 vols. in 4, Venetiis, 1709.

Fanfani, Ludovicus, *De Iure Parochorum ad normam Codicis Iuris Canonici*, Taurini-Romae, 1924.

Ferrante, Joseph, *Elementa Juris Canonici*, Romae, 1854.

Ferraris, Lucius, *Prompta Bibliotheca Canonica, Iuridica, Moralis, Theologica, partim Ascetica, Polemica Rubricistica, Historica*, 2. ed., 8 vols., Bononiae, sed prostant Venetiis, 1752.

Freking, Frederick W., *The Canonical Installation of Pastors*, The Catholic University of America Canon Law Studies, n. 273, Washington, D.C.: The Catholic University of America Press, 1948.

Gasparri, Petrus, *Tractatus Canonicus de Matrimonio*, 3. ed., 2 vols., Parisiis, 1904.

———, *Tractatus Canonicus de Matrimonio*, ed. nova ad mentem Codicis I. C., 2 vols., Romae, 1932.

Giraldi, Ubaldus, *Expositio Juris Pontificii*, 2 vols., Romae, 1769.

Gomez de Salazar, F.-de la Fuente, V., *Lecciones de Disciplina Eclesiástica*, 3 ed., 2 vols., Madrid, 1880.

Gonzales-Tellez, Emmanuel, *Commentaria in Quinque Libros Decretalium*, 5 vols., Maceratae, 1756.

Grégoire, Petrus, *Partitiones Juris Canonici seu Pontificii in V Libros digestae*, Lugduni, 1594.

Hale, Joseph F., *The Pastor of Burial*, The Catholic University of America Canon Law Studies, n. 234, Washington, D.C.: The Catholic University of America Press, 1949.

Heintschel, Donald E., *The Mediaeval Concept of an Ecclesiastical Office*, The Catholic University of America Canon Law Studies, n. 363, Washington, D.C.: The Catholic University of America Press, 1956.

Hinschius, Paul, *System des katholischen Kirchenrechts mit besonderer Rücksicht auf Deutschland*, 4 vols., Berlin, 1869-1888.

Hostiensis (Henricus de Segusio), *Commentaria in Quinque Libros Decretalium*, 2 vols., Venetiis, 1581.

———, *Summa Aurea*, Venetiis, 1570.

Icard, Henricus, *Praelectiones Juris Canonici*, 6. ed., 3 vols., Parisiis, 1886.

Innocentius IV, *In V Libros Decretalium Commentaria*, Venetiis, 1570.

Joannes Andreae, *In VI Libros Decretalium Novella Commentaria*, 6 vols., Venetiis, 1581.

Jone, Heribertus, *Commentarium in Codicem Iuris Canonici*, 3 vols., Paderborn: Officina Libraria F. Schöningh, 1950-1955.

Journet, Charles, *The Church of the Word Incarnate*, Vol. I, *The Apostolic Hierarchy*, translated by A. H. C. Downes, London and New York: Sheed and Ward, 1955.

Kelly, Bernard M., *The Functions Reserved to Pastors*, The Catholic University of America Canon Law Studies, n. 250, Washington, D.C.: The Catholic University of America Press, 1947.

Kelly, James P., *The Jurisdiction of the Simple Confessor*, The Catholic University of America Canon Law Studies, n. 43, Washington, D.C.: The Catholic University of America, 1927.

Koudelka, Charles J., *Pastors, Their Rights and Duties*, The Catholic University of America Canon Law Studies, n. 11, Washington, D.C.: The Catholic University of America, 1921.

Laurentius, Ioseph, *Institutiones Iuris Ecclesiastici*, Friburgi Brisgoviae, 1903.

Laymann, Paulus, *Theologia Moralis*, Venetiis, 1630.

Lombardi, Carolus, *Iuris Canonici Privati Institutiones*, 2. ed., 3 vols., Romae, 1901.

Maroto, Philippus, *Institutiones Iuris Canonici ad normam novi Codicis*, 2 vols., Vol. I, 3. ed., Romae, 1921.

McManus, James, *The Administration of Temporal Goods in Religious Institutes*, The Catholic University of America Canon Law Studies, n. 109, Washington, D.C.: The Catholic University of America, 1937.

Ménard, Pierre, *L'Exemption des Séminaires de la Juridiction Paroissiale*, The Catholic University of Ottawa Canonical Series, n. 30, Ottawa: Les Éditions de L'Université d'Ottawa, 1950.

Michiels, Gommarus, *Normae Generales Juris Canonici*, 2. ed., 2 vols., Parisiis-Tornaci-Romae: Desclée et Socii, 1949.

Montero y Gutiérrez, Eloy, *Derecho Publico Eclesiástico y Normas Generales*, 2. ed., Madrid: Imprenta Saez, 1948.

———, *Instituciones de Derecho Canónico*, 3. ed., Madrid: Imprenta Saez, 1948.

Nardi, Luigi, *Dei Parrochi, Opera de Antichità Sacra e Disciplina Ecclesiastica*, 2 vols., Pesaro, 1829, 1830.

O'Connell, William E., *De Intima Natura Assistentiae Matrimonialis*, Romae: Catholic Book Agency, 1940.

Ojetti, Benedictus, *Synopsis Rerum Moralium et Iuris Pontificii*, 3. ed., 4 vols., Romae, 1909-1914.

Ottaviani, Alaphridus, *Compendium Iuris Publici Ecclesiastici*, 4. ed., Romae: Typis Polyglottis Vaticanis, 1954.

Panormitanus (Nicholaus de Tudeschis), *Commentaria in Quinque Libros Decretalium*, 5 vols. in 7, Venetiis, 1588.

Passerini, Petrus, *Commentarium in Sextum Librum Decretalium*, 2 vols., Venetiis, 1698.

———, *De Hominum Statibus et Officiis*, 3 vols., Lucae, 1732.

Petra, Vincentius, *Commentaria ad Constitutiones Apostolicas*, 5 vols., Venetiis, 1729.

Phillips, Georges, *Du Droit Ecclésiastique dans ses Principes Généraux*, 2. ed., 3 vols., Paris, 1855.

Pichler, Vitus, *Jus Canonicum secundum Quinque Decretalium Titulos Explicatum*, 2 vols., Ravennae, 1741.

Pignatelli, Jacobus, *Consultationes Canonicae*, 11 vols. in 5, Coloniae Allobrogum, 1700.

Pirhing, Ernricus, *Jus Canonicum in V Libros Decretalium Distributum*, 5 vols. in 4, Dilingae, 1722.

Pontas, Joannes, *Dictionarium Casuum Conscientiae*, 3 vols., Venetiis, 1773.

Prierias, Sylvester (Mazolinus Sabaudus), *Summa Summarum*, Venetiis, 1601.

Prümmer, Dominicus, *Manuale Iuris Canonici in usum scholarum*, 5. ed., Friburgi Brisgoviae, 1927.

Rainer, Eligius G., *The Suspension of Clerics*, The Catholic University of America Canon Law Studies, n. 111, Washington, D.C.: The Catholic University of America, 1937.

Raus, Joannes, B., *Institutiones Canonicae*, 2. ed., Lugduni-Parisiis: Typis Emmanuelis Vitte, 1931.

Raymond of Peñafort, St., *Summa*, Veronae, 1744.

Rechiusi, Franciscus, *Tractatus de Re Parochiali*, Romae, 1773.

Regatillo, Eduardus, *Institutiones Iuris Canonici*, 4. ed., 2 vols., Santander: Sal Terrae, 1951.

Reiffenstuel, Anacletus, *Jus Canonicum Universum*, 5 vols. in 7, Parisiis, 1864-1870.

———, *Theologia Moralis*, 7. ed., 2 vols., Mutinae, 1745.

Repetitionum in Universas fere Iuris Canonici partes materiasque sane frequentiores Volumina Sex, 6 vols., Venetiis, 1587; Vol. VII, *Index Repetitionum*, Venetiis, 1587.

Romani, Sylvius, *Institutiones Juris Canonici*, Vol. I, *Jus Constitutionale*, Romae: E Schola Typographica "Pio X," 1941.

Rufinus, *Die Summa Decretorum des Magister Rufinus*, ed. Heinrich Singer, Paderborn, 1902.

Sabelli, Marcus, *Summa Diversorum Tractatuum*, 4 vols., Venetiis, 1692.

Sanchez, Thomas, *De Sancto Matrimonii Sacramento Disputationum Libri Tres*, 3 vols. in 1, Venetiis, 1726.

———, *Opus Morale in Praecepta Decalogi*, 2 vols., Lugduni, 1661-1669.

Sandeus, Felinus, *Repertorium seu Index Locupletissimus in Felini Sandei Commentarios ad quinque Libros Decretalium*, Venetiis, 1570.

Sanguinetti, Sebastianus, *Iuris Ecclesiastici Privati Institutiones*, Romae, 1884.

Santi, Franciscus, *Praelectiones Juris Canonici*, 2. ed., 5 vols. in 2, Ratisbonae, Neo Eboraci et Cincinnatii, 1892.

Savaré, Tharcisius, *De Errore Communi circa Assistentiam ad Matrimonium*, Romae: Universitas Gregoriana, 1937.

Schäfer, Timotheus, *Die Kirchennämter nach dem Codex Iuris Canonici*, II Teil, *Pfarrer und Pfarrvikare nach dem Codex Iuris Canonici*, Münster, 1922.

Schmalzgrueber, Franciscus, *Ius Ecclesiasticum Universum*, 5 vols. in 12, Romae, 1843-1845.

Schmier, Franciscus, *Jurisprudentia Canonico-Civilis*, 2 vols., Venetiis, 1754.

Schröcker, Sebastian, *Die Verwaltung des Ortskirchenvermögens nach kirchlichem und staatlichem Recht*, Paderborn: Ferdinand Schöningh, 1935.

Schulz, Fritz, *Classical Roman Law*, Oxford: Clarendon Press, 1951.

Sipos, Stephanus, *Enchiridion iuris canonici, ad usum scholarum et privatorum*, 6. ed., recognovit Ladislaus Gálos, Romae: Orbis Catholicus-Herder, 1954.

Smith, Sebastian B., *Elements of Ecclesiastical Law*, 3 vols., Vol. I, 6. ed., New York, Cincinnati, Chicago, 1887.

Soglia, Joannes, *Institutiones Juris Publici et Privati Ecclesiastici*, 12. ed., 2 vols. in 1, Boscoduci, 1857.

Solieri, Franciscus, *Institutiones Iuris Ecclesiastici*, 2. ed., Romae, 1921.

Sotillo, Laurentius R., *Compendium Iuris Publici Ecclesiastici*, 2. ed., Santander: Editorial Sal Terrae, 1951.

Spada, Joannes, *Consilia*, 3 vols., Parmae, 1720.

Suarez, Franciscus, *De Censuris*, Lugduni, 1608.

Tarquini, Camillus, *Iuris Ecclesiastici Publici Institutiones*, 4. ed., Romae, 1875.

Thomas Aquinas, St., *Opera Omnia*, 34 vols., ed. L. Vivès, Parisiis, 1871-1880, Vol. VIII, 1873, Vol. XI, 1874, *Commentum in Quattuor Libros Sententiarum*.

Tirado, Victor a I. M., *De Iurisdictionis Acceptione in Iure Ecclesiastico*, Romae: Officium Libri Catholici, 1940.

Toschi, Dominicus (Tuschus), *Practicae Conclusiones Iuris in Omni Foro Frequentiores*, 3. ed., 8 vols., Lugduni, 1634; Vol. IX, *Additiones*, Lugduni, 1670.

Toso, Albertus, *Ad Codicem Iuris Canonici... Commentaria Minora*, 5 vols. in 2, Taurini-Romae, 1920-1927.

Triebs, Franz, *Praktisches Handbuch des geltenden kanonischen Eherechts*, Breslau, 1933.

Van de Kerckhove, Martin, *La Notion de Juridiction*, Assisi: Collegio S. Lorenzo da Brindisi, 1937.

Van Espen, Zegerus B., *Jus Ecclesiasticum Universum,* 10 vols. in 5, Venetiis, 1769.

Van Hove, Alphonsus, *Commentarium Lovaniense in Codicem Iuris Canonici,* Vol. I, *Prolegomena,* 2. ed., Mechliniae-Romae: H. Dessain, 1945.

Vecchiotti, Septimius M., *Institutiones Canonicae,* 19. ed., 3 vols., Augustae-Taurinorum, 1886.

Verano, Felix G., *Juris Canonici Universi Commentarius Paratitlaris,* 3 vols., Monachii, 1703-1705.

Vermeersch, A.-Creusen, J., *Epitome Iuris Canonici cum Commentariis ad Scholas et ad Usum Privatum,* 3 vols., Vol. I, 7. ed., 1949; Vol. II, 6. ed., 1940; Vol. III, 6. ed., 1946, Mechliniae-Romae: H. Dessain.

Vlaming, Th. M., *Praelectiones Iuris Matrimonii,* 3. ed., 2 vols., Bussum in Hollandia, 1919-1921.

Vromant, Georgius, *De Bonis Ecclesiae Temporalibus,* 3. ed., Bruxelles: Éditions de Scheut, 1953.

Wernz, Franciscus X., *Ius Decretalium,* 6 vols., Prati, Vol. II, *Ius de Personis,* 3. ed., 1915; Vol. IV, *Ius Matrimoniale,* 2. ed., 1911.

Wernz, F. X.-Vidal, P., *Ius Canonicum ad Codicis Normam Exactum,* 7 vols. in 8, Vol. II, 3. ed., Romae: Apud Aedes Universitatis Gregorianae, 1943.

Woeber, Edward M., *The Interpellations,* The Catholic University of America Canon Law Studies, n. 172, Washington, D.C.: The Catholic University of America Press, 1942.

Zabarella, Franciscus, *Commentarii in Clementinarum Volumen,* Venetiis, 1504.

Zallinger zum Thurn, Jakobus A., *Institutiones Juris Naturalis et Ecclesiastici Publici,* 5 vols. in 3, Romae, 1823.

Unpublished Works

Acerra, Angelo, *The Extent and Character of Parochial Jurisdiction,* Typewritten licentiate dissertation, Washington, D.C.: The Catholic University of America, 1953.

Huhmann, John, *The Pastor's Power of Dispensing,* Typewritten doctoral dissertation, Romae: Pontificium Athenaeum Angelicum, 1956.

Articles

Alonso, Sabino, "Los Párrochos en el Concilio de Trento y en el Código de Derecho Canónico, *Revista Española de Derecho Canónico,* II (1947), 947-979.

Bender, Ludovicus, "Forum Externum et Forum Internum," *Ephemerides Iuris Canonici,* X (1954), 9-27.

Cabreros de Anta, Marcelino, "Concepto de Potestad Ordinaria y Delegada," *Revista Española de Derecho Canónico,* VIII (1953), 703-744.

Capobianco, Pacificus, "De Notione Fori Interni in Iure Canonico," *Apollinaris,* IX (1936), 364-374.

Crisci, Generosus, "De Delegatione a Iure in Iure Canonico Vigenti," *Apollinaris,* X (1937), 513-535.

Da Forchia, Camillus, "La Cura d'Anime come Istituto Giuridico," *Ius Seraphicum,* II (1956), 109-124, 267-309.

D'Angelo, Sosius, "Annotatiunculae in Modos quibus Leges Canonicae Cessant 'ab extrinseco,'" *Apollinaris,* I (1928), 238-262.

De Meester, Alphonsus, "De Rectoribus Ecclesiarum," *Collationes Brugenses,* XLIII (1947), 56-59.

———, "Notio Iurisdictionis Ordinariae et Delegatae," *Collationes Brugenses,* XXI, (1921), 238-243.

———, "Notio Parochi," *Collationes Brugenses,* XXII (1922), 477-480.

Depoorter, A., "De Potestate Indirecta Ecclesiae in Rebus Temporalibus," *Collationes Brugenses,* XLVIII (1952), 414-419.

———, "De Potestate Parochorum in Foro Externo," *Collationes Brugenses,* XLII, (1947), 56-59.

Fuertes, J. B., "De Potestate Dominativa in Religionibus non Exemptis," *Commentarium pro Religiosis et Missionariis,* XXXII (1953), 198-209.

Gennaro, Andreas, "Distinzione dei Fori Giurisdizionali," *Perfice Munus,* X (1935), 505, 506.

Hilling, Nicolaus, "Begriff und Umfang der *potestas iurisdictionis ordinaria* und *delegata* nach geltendem Kirchenrecht," *Archiv für katholisches Kirchenrecht,* CIV (1924), 181-204.

———, "Die Bedeutung der *iurisdictio voluntaria* und *involuntaria* im römischen Recht und im kanonischen Recht des Mittelalters und der Neuzeit," *Archiv für katholisches Kirchenrecht,* CV (1925), 449-473.

Huot, Dorius, "Bonorum Temporalium apud Religiones Administratio Ordinaria et Extraordinaria," *Commentarium pro Religiosis et Missionariis,* XXXIII (1954), 60-76, 312-328; XXXIV 1955), 55-64, 175-192, 266-273, 365-373.

Johnson, Joseph, "De Distinctione inter Potestatem Iudicialem et Potestatem Administrativam in Iure Canonico," *Apollinaris,* IX (1936), 258-269.

Larraona, Arcadius, "De Potestate Dominativa Publica in Iure Canonico," *Acta Congressus Iuridici Internationalis,* IV, 145-180.

———, "De Potestate Paroeciali relate ad Religiosos," *Commentarium pro Religiosis,* VIII (1927), 36-41.

McReavy, Lawrence, "The Administration of Parochial Property," *The Clergy Review*, XXIX (1948), 1-11.

Monin, Arthur, "La Notion de la Juridiction 'Volontaire'—en Droit Canonique," *Ephemerides Theologicae Lovanienses*, VIII (1931), 630-637.

Nebreda, Eulogius, "Quaestiones Selectae de Iure Administrativo Ecclesiastico," *Commentarium pro Religiosis*, VII (1926), 191-198.

Oesterle, Gerardus, "De Relatione inter Forum Externum et Internum," *Apollinaris*, XIX (1946), 67-87.

Ojetti, Benedictus, "Praelatus in Codice Iuris Canonici quisnam sit," *Periodica de Re Morali, Canonica, Liturgica*, XVII (1928), 229*-231*.

Regatillo, Eduardus, "Consultas," *Sal Terrae*, XXIV (1935), 922, 923; XXXVII (1949), 302, 303.

Salaverri, Joaquín, "La Triple Potestad de la Iglesia," *Miscelanea Comillas*, XIV (1950), 7-84.

Saucedo, P.R., "Exercitium Jurisdictionis et Superiores Laici ex Ordine Hospitalario S. Joannis de Deo," *Commentarium pro Religiosis*, XIII (1932), 51-61, 106-114, 224-231, 291-302.

Schüller, Andreas, "Die Pfarrvikarie in der Diözese Trier," *Archiv für katholisches Kirchenrecht*, LXXXIX (1909), 34-53.

Sigur, Alexander, "Lay Cooperation in the Administration of Church Property," *The Jurist*, XIII (1953), 171-200.

Sipos, Stephanus, "Quaestiones Selectae," *Jus Pontificium*, XVI (1936), 66-68; XIX (1939), 96-99.

Stocchiero, Joseph, "De Jurisdictione Vicariorum Paroecialium," *Jus Pontificium*, XI (1931), 144-150, 221-231.

Van de Kerckhove, Martin, "De Notione Iurisdictionis apud Decretistas et Priores Decretalistas (1140-1250)," *Jus Pontificium*, XVIII (1938), 10-14.

———, "De Notione Iurisdictionis in Iure Romano," *Jus Pontificium*, XVI (1936), 49-65.

Wycislo, Aloysius, "Apostolic Constitution on Migration," *The Homiletic and Pastoral Review*, LIII (1953), 318-326.

Periodicals

Apollinaris, Romae, 1928—

Archiv für katholisches Kirchenrecht, Innsbruck, 1857-1861; Mainz, 1862—

Clergy Review, The, London, 1931—

Collationes Brugenses, Brugis, 1896—

Commentarium pro Religiosis, Romae, 1920-1934; *Commentarium pro Religiosis et Missionariis*, Romae, 1935—

Ephemerides Iuris Canonici, Romae, 1945—

Ephemerides Theologicae Lovanienses, Lovanii, 1924—

Homiletic and Pastoral Review, The, New York, 1900—
Ius Seraphicum, Romae, 1955—
Jurist, The, Washington, D.C., 1940—
Jus Pontificium, Romae, 1921-1940.
Miscelanea Comillas, Santander, 1942—
Perfice Munus, Torino, 1926—
Periodica de Religiosis et Missionariis, Brugis, 1905-1919; *Periodica de Re Canonica et Morali, utilia praesertim Religiosis et Missionariis,* Brugis, 1920-1927; *Periodica de Re Morali, Canonica, Liturgica,* Brugis, 1927-1936, Romae, 1937—
Revista Española de Derecho Canónico, Salamanca, 1946—
Sal Terrae, Santander, 1912—

BIOGRAPHICAL NOTE

Bernard Francis Deutsch was born July 15, 1925, in Saint Louis, Missouri. After graduating from the St. Liborius Parochial School of that city, he entered the archdiocesan minor seminary, at that time the Cathedral Latin School. He completed his classical and philosopical studies at the Saint Louis Preparatory Seminary, after which he entered Kenrick Theological Seminary, where he was ordained on May 3, 1951. After serving for several years as assistant pastor at St. Peter's Parish of Jefferson City, Missouri, he was admitted to the School of Canon Law of the Catholic University of America, where he received the degree of Baccalaureate in Canon Law in June, 1955, and the degree of Licentiate in Canon Law in June, 1956.

INDICES

Index of Names

Index of Subjects

INDEX OF CANONS

CANON LAW STUDIES*

375. Kelleher, Rev. Francis T., A.B., J.C.L., Judicial expenses.
376. Bantigue, Rev. Pedro N., J.C.L., The Provincial Council of Manila of 1771. (Its text followed by a commentary on *Actio* II, *De Episcopis*)
377. Burns, Rev. Dennis J., J.C.L., Matrimonial indissolubility: contrary conditions.
378. Deutsch, Rev. Bernard F., J.C.L., Jurisdiction of pastors in the external forum.
379. Dunnivan, Rev. John P., A.B., J.C.L., Prejudicial attempts in pending litigation.
380. Ernst, Rev. Albert C., A.B., J.C.L., Free admission to church for sacred rites.
381. Frattin, Mr. Peter Louis, J.C.L., The matrimonial impediment of impotence: occlusion of the spermatic ducts and vaginismus.
382. Henry, Rev. Charles W., O.S.B., A.B., S.T.L., J.C.L., Canonical relations between bishops and abbots at the beginning of the tenth century.
383. Hoffman, Rev. Lawrence J., A.B., J.C.L., Clergy conference: Canon 131.
384. Markham, Rev. James, A.B., S.T.L., J.C.L., The Sacred Congregation of Seminaries and Universities of Studies.
385. McGrath, Rev. John J., A.B., LL.B., J.C.L., A comparative study of crime and its imputability in ecclesiastical criminal law and in American criminal law.
386. McGuire, Rev. James D., O.R.S.A., J.C.L., The postulancy.
387. Munday, Rev. James E., J.C.L., Ecclesiastical Property in Australia and New Zealand.
388. Murphy, Rev. Joseph P., A.B., J.C.L., The laws of the State of New York affecting church property.
389. Pickard, Rev. William M., J.C.L., Judicial experts: a source of evidence in ecclesiastical trials.
390. Ruddy, Rev. James, J.C.L., The Apostolic Constitution *Christus Dominus*: text, translation and commentary, with short annotations on the Motu Proprio *Sacram Communionem.*
391. Vanyo, Rev. Leo. V., A.B., J.C.L., Requisites of intention in the reception of the sacraments.

www.ingramcontent.com/pod-product-compliance
Lightning Source LLC
LaVergne TN
LVHW050244080826
844660LV00012B/593